KT-244-738

# Practical Homemaking Crafts

Edited by Eve Harlow

250 ml

# Contents

First published 1978 by
Sundial Books Limited
59 Grosvenor Street
London W1

ISBN 0 904230 54 6
Printed in Great Britain
by Jarrold & Sons Ltd.

# Curtains and blinds

Nowadays we do not put up curtains just for privacy. We put them up for insulation, to soften the look of a room, and to add to the general decoration of the home. It is important therefore to consider what exactly you want your curtains to do before you start measuring up.

Is the room on the dark side? If so, remember to allow enough track each side of the window so that when drawn back they fall right to the side of the window so that you do not lose any light.

Have you got a bay window? Do you want to make one pair of curtains to pull right back to each end, or do you want curtains in each of the angles?

## Equipment

You will need a large flat surface – preferably not the floor. A paste-table or a large kitchen table will do. It is easiest if you can avoid having the material hanging over the edge of the surface both at the top and at the side.

Invest in a steel retracting tape measure as these are much more accurate than a dressmaker's tape measure. Sharp pins are essential. Sharp scissors, thread and a thimble are all the tools you need. A six inch metal rule, sold at most haberdashery counters is useful, but not essential. A sewing machine will make the work quicker, but all curtains can be sewn by hand.

*Left* Curtains can be positioned unconventionally for windows of unusual shape. Here the pole is just below the window arch to emphasise its dome shape.

*Below* The pattern on this matching wallpaper and fabric looks effective with light filtering through, so the curtains are not lined. Headed curtain tapes are not always needed with curtain poles; a simple casing can be stitched across the top of the curtains leaving a heading frill deep enough to touch the lower edge of the cornice. Tie backs are positioned high on the window frame so that the curtains are held well away from the windows, and sheer half curtains provide privacy.

## Curtain fabrics

Curtain fabrics are by no means cheap, but since you are going to make your own curtains (saving on making charges), and since they will look good for years, it is worth paying for a slightly better quality of fabric. It goes without saying that a better fabric will last longer and wear better.

You may have decided to start furnishing your room by choosing the curtains first and working round them. Or you may be making new curtains to fit in with the carpet and seating colours. If you are starting from scratch remember that some manufacturers make materials in different weights – a patterned material in a weight suitable for curtains and a heavy quality suitable for loose covers and upholstery.

**Cotton** is strong, longlasting, easy to launder, but has disadvantages: it may shrink, and not all colours are fast when exposed to sunlight. Cotton may also rot with dust and dirt. Under the general heading of cotton you will find gingham, towelling (suitable for bathrooms as they absorb moisture), repp (which shrinks badly and fades), glazed cotton, cretonne, cotton brocade and velvet.

**Rayon** fabrics need more careful handling when washed, and tend to fray badly, thereby needing extra care when making up. On the other hand they will take repeated washing and wear well.

**Nylon** fabrics are prone to rotting by sunlight although advances are being made to overcome this.

**Terylene** has more to offer than nylon in that it is not affected by sunlight, and while it looks airy and delicate, it is in fact very strong. Prices are usually reasonable too. Unfortunately, it needs frequent washing as dust will discolour the fabric.

**Silk** is one of the most beautiful fabrics and it will always fall in lovely folds. Sadly, it is very expensive and suffers badly in sunlight.

**Hessian** is relatively inexpensive and can be found in a marvellous range of colours. But the coarser varieties can fall out of shape rather quickly.

Most curtain materials come in widths varying from 122 cm to 135 cm. Linings are usually 122 cm.

**Lining** Apart from the ordinary standard linings in ecru (beige, and usually the cheapest), white and colours, you can get milium and blackout linings. Milium (twice the price of ordinary lining) is coated with aluminium and thereby acts as insulation, keeping the heat inside the room and the cold out. Blackout lining does exactly what its name implies, with the advantage that it insulates as well. It has a texture similar to chamois leather, but is easy to handle. The disadvantage is the price – about four times the price of lining. However, if you live in a busy road, or suffer from insomnia it is worth every penny.

### Curtain tapes

Manufacturers of curtain tapes have done their very best to make our life easier, by producing tapes in a wide range of sizes and effects.

1. Standard Rufflette tape: generally used for gathers when curtain heading will be covered by a pelmet or valance. It is available in a wide range of colours and has pockets for hooks. This tape is also made in a lightweight quality for use in gathering net curtains.
2. 'Regis' tape is 7.5 cm deep with pockets one side of tape only. Pockets should normally be placed the side furthest away from top of curtain except when curtains are to be hung from a decorative pole, when pockets should come at the top.
3. Deep pleating tape is available for making 'French headed' curtains. This tape has three gathering cords which automatically draw up the curtain into pleats and spaces, saving one the mathematical calculation required to make pleats by hand.

The machine stitching required to hold tape in place does rather spoil the finished effect.

*Right* This four-poster has both curtains and valance. The same sewing techniques are used as for making window curtains. Bed curtains are usually hung from canopy rails, and either a simple casing or tape and hooks are used. These bed curtains are lined with a contrasting fabric• and strips of this fabric have been appliquéed for contrasting borders.

## Estimating material

Put up the rail you have chosen. If you have chosen a pole, the measurement should be taken from the bottom of the ring – poles are meant to be seen and curtains must hang below them. Measure the depth from the top of the rail to hem level. If you want long curtains measure to 12 mm above the floor. If you want short curtains measure to 24 mm below the window sill. Short net curtains are measured to 12 mm above sill level, and usually go within the window frame. These lengths are known as the finished length. To this measurement add 15 cm for the bottom hem and 4 cm for the top hem. The length of the finished curtain plus the hem allowances is known as the drop.

Choose your fabric and calculate as follows:

*Sheers* allow 3 times the actual rail measurement.
*Pencil pleats* allow $2\frac{1}{2}$ times the width plus 15 cm for the side hems and 5 cm for each width join you have to make.
*French headed curtains* these are also known as pinch-pleated curtains. Allow twice the width of the rail plus 15 cm for side hems, 5 cm for any joins, plus 25 cm.

A frequent mistake is to skimp on fabric. People see a remnant in a sale and think 'that would do for the new curtains I want'. Never buy material in this way unless you have the measurements with you, or the so-called bargain turns into a white elephant. Sales assistants in fabric shops are usually expert in working out pattern repeats so do not hesitate to ask – 'I have a window with a total drop including hems of X, and I reckon I need three widths: can I do it with this remnant?'

Do remember that when you choose a patterned fabric the pattern will have to be matched at any joins you may have, and the pattern will have to run in a straight line across both curtains. Many fabrics have a border each side and a pattern in the middle. When joining one or more widths together you will have to discard one border, which means that each second and subsequent width will be narrower than the first (1). For example with 122 cm wide fabric which has a 15 cm border, then a pattern, then a 15 cm border, on the second width you will discard the first 15 cm so your material will only be 107 cm wide, as will every subsequent width.

Diagrams 1–3: the difficulties of working with patterned fabrics.

*Right* (1): how to join fabric with a printed border.

*Below* (2): the correct and incorrect positioning of a motif on the hemline.

*Below right* (3): aligning widths of patterned fabric.

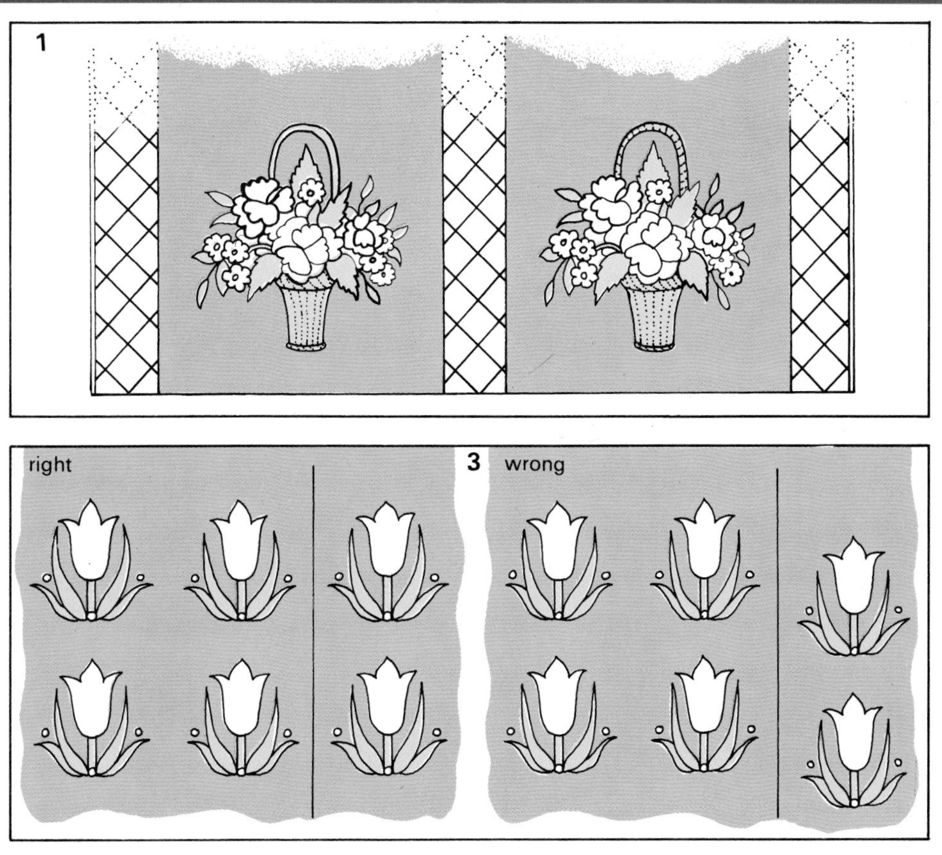


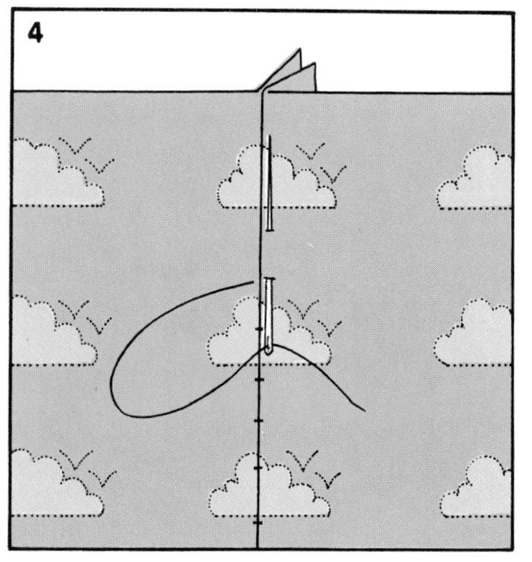


*Above* Diagram 4: ladderstitching, a method of tacking worked from the right side of the material for ease in pattern matching.

*Left* French pleats suit large-motif patterned fabrics.

### Lining

Practically all curtains (with the exception of towelling curtains) benefit from being lined. The lining protects the main material from sunlight and it catches the dirt. It also helps the material to fall into richer looking folds. It is possible to replace the lining on old curtains and make them look like new for a fraction of the cost.

You will need the same width as for the main material but for the length allow 10 cm more than the finished length.

Many materials benefit from being interlined. Interlined curtains fall in much softer, richer looking folds and they are good insulation. You will need the same width as of the main curtain fabric, plus 15 cm for the bottom hem. It is easier to make curtains *with* interlining than without as the fabric handles better.

### Stiffening tape

If you plan to French head your curtains by hand (always worth the extra trouble as it gives your curtains a professional look) you will need 13 cm wide sanforized (pre-shrunk) stiffening tape. This can be bought fusible (so that it sticks to the material when ironed into place) or plain. The plain gives the best long-term results.

## Cutting out

Before you start cutting, level off the end of the material by cutting on the thread. There is an easy way to do this. Most fabrics have a slightly more pronounced crossways thread than lengthways. Place your fabric on a smooth flat surface. Take a pencil with a sharp point, and letting the threads hold the point in place, draw a line across the width of the fabric. Provided you do not put too much pressure on the pencil, rather let it be guided by the thread, you will find you have made a perfect straight line.

Measure off the first length including hem allowances, plus the turnings at the top. If your material is patterned do consider how the pattern will look before you cut. If you have chosen a floral pattern, will the finished hem line come half way up a pattern repeat? (2). Remember that it will be better to put half a pattern up at the top where the curtain gathers will be tightest and less obvious, than at the bottom.

If your fabric is plain, cut out the required number of lengths and widths. If necessary cut one width in half lengthways (if your curtains are to be $1\frac{1}{2}$ widths each). Join the widths.

Press open all seams and snip the selvedge threads every 10 cm to prevent dragging when the curtains have been washed. Provided you snip diagonally the material will not fray.

### Cutting out patterned fabric

If you are working with patterned fabric, cut out one length and place the cut piece side by side with the uncut material so as to make sure that the pattern will match (3). Some printed materials have the design running slightly out of true with the straight grain of fabric. If the pattern is large and obvious you will have to cut 'with the pattern' rather than with the grain, but if it is a small pattern you can keep to the grain. Cut the required number of widths.

If you are joining a patterned material place the first width on a flat surface. Press in 2–5 cm down the selvedge of the next width. Place this over the edge of the first width so that the pattern matches exactly. Pin in place. Join by hand using fairly long stitches and taking your needle first under the flat unfolded piece, then slipping it through the folded material exactly where it came out from your first stitch. This is called ladder stitch (4). You will find that once you have completed the length you can open up the material and machine the widths together along your tacking threads for a perfect pattern match.

## Unlined curtains

Place your fabric flat on your working surface and press up the bottom hem allowance. Open it out and press the raw edge into this hem line. Press in 15 mm at each side seam (5). To mitre the corners, place a pin on the side fold the same height above the finished hem line as the depth of the first fold. Place a second pin on the hem fold at a distance in from the side fold twice the width of the finished side hem (6). (In this case the second side fold is to be 30 mm so you will need to measure in 60 mm from the side fold.) Fold your material so that you make a straight line from pin to pin across the corner of the curtain (7). Remove the pins then turn up the bottom hem allowance and turn in side hems 30 mm to make double hems (8). The corners will be mitred.

Slip stitch both side hems and the bottom hem in place.

With your material placed flat, measure off from the bottom hem the correct finished length of your curtains. Press surplus at the top to wrong side. Pin and tack your chosen curtain heading tape in place, turning under the raw edges of the tape 1 cm at each end (9). Machine in place. Draw up the cords so that the curtain measures half the length of your track plus 7–5 cm for the overlap if you have one (10). Do not cut off the surplus cord as you will need to let the curtains out for ease of ironing in the future, but wind them round a cord tidy. If you are unable to buy a cord tidy make a small pocket out of lining material and stitch in place near the top of the curtain, on the wrong side so you can keep the cords neatly out of sight. Cords should always be pulled up from the outside edge of each curtain. Insert hooks into tape pockets (11).

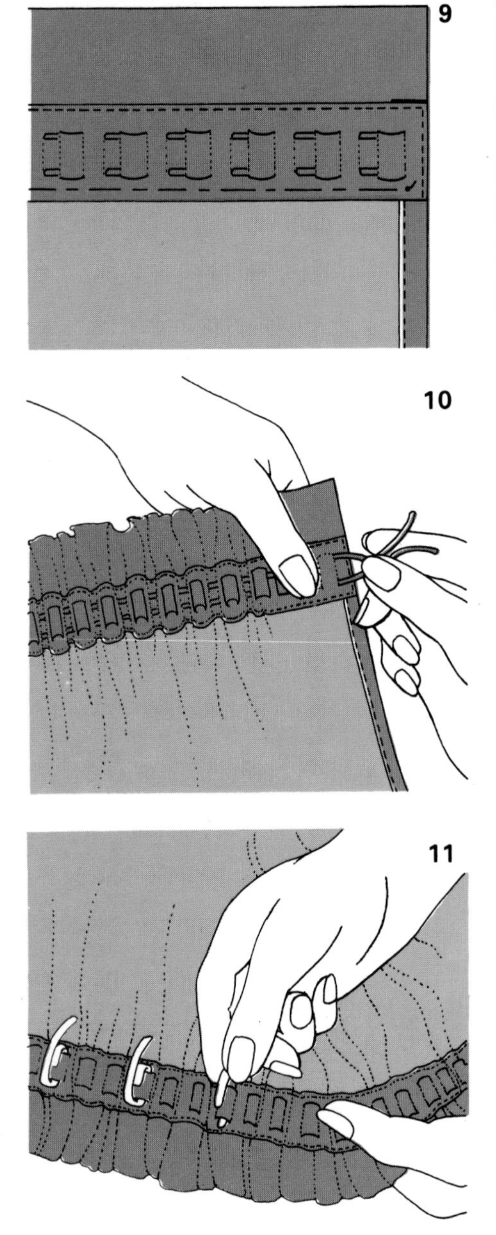

6

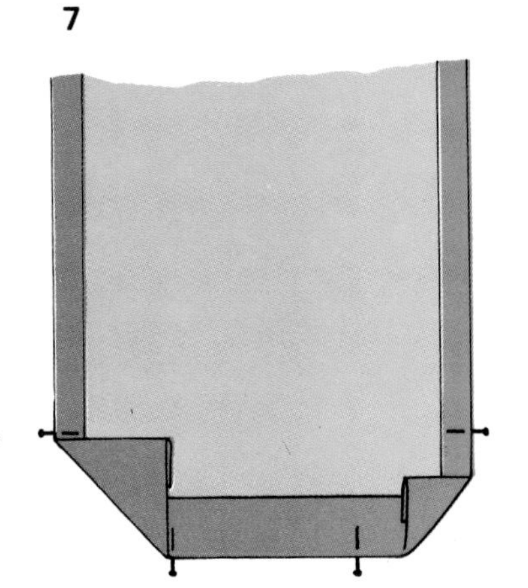


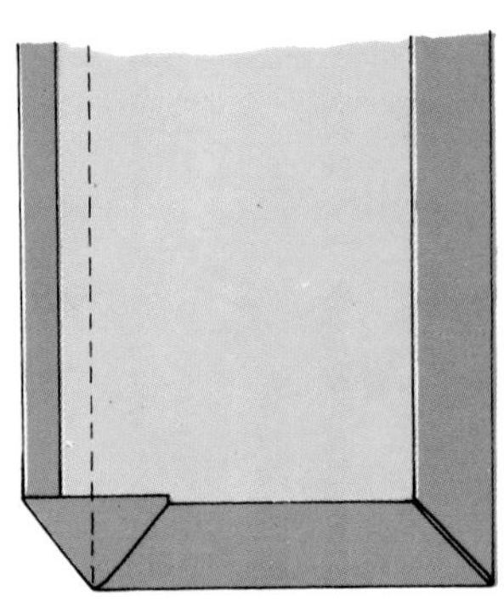

## Lined curtains

As for unlined curtains, cut out material and place it flat on the working surface. Measure off the bottom hem. With lined curtains you will only have a single fold 7.5 cm wide at the sides so to mitre the corners do not make the first side hem fold. Instead place the second pin on the hem fold 15 cm (i.e. twice 7.5 cm) in from the side edge. Slip stitch the bottom hem. The side hems should be held in place with herringbone stitch (12).

Cut out the required number of widths of lining to the finished length of curtain plus 10 cm. Join the widths together. Turn up the bottom edge 5 cm and press; turn up a further 5 cm. This hem can be machined, or hand-hemmed.

Place the curtain material wrong side up on your working surface. Place the lining with wrong side down on top and with the lining 5 cm above the hem of the curtain material. Turn under the side of the lining 5 cm on the first side and slip stitch in place. Smooth the lining over the main material, place a row of pins 30 cm in from first side. Fold back the lining and lock stitch lining to material along the line of pins from the top of the curtain to within 15 cm of the hem. Your stitches can be 5 cm apart, and you should only pick up one thread of both lining and main material at a time (13), so that no stitches are visible from the right side of the curtains. Be careful not to pull the thread too tight or your curtains will pucker upwards. Continue to lock stitch at 30 cm intervals until the opposite side is reached. Turn under lining so that it is 5 cm from the side hem of the main material, press and slip stitch in place.

Measure off carefully the required length of the curtain. Press raw edges of lining and material to wrong side. Attach chosen heading tape, turning under the raw edges 1 cm. Pull out the cord from the turned under edges. Knot the cords at one end, but leave them free at the opposite end. Machine tape in place taking care not to catch the cords. Pull up cords to half the length of track plus overlap.

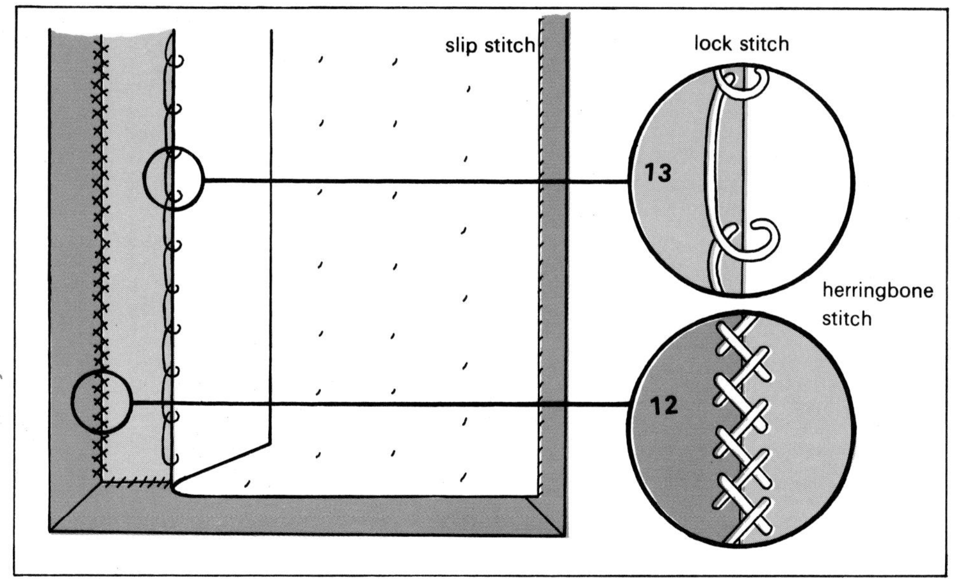


*Far left* Diagrams 5–8: how to mitre corners when the side and base hems are of unequal depth.

*Above left* Diagrams 9–11: applying curtain tape.

*Left* The reverse side of lined curtains, detailing herringbone stitch (12) and lock stitch (13).

*Above* You can make roller blinds to match your curtains (see page 24).

## Net curtains

These are the only type of curtains which should be hung on expanding curtain wires with screw eyes at each end. They look best gathered with Rufflette tape and with rings threaded through the pockets of the tape. The expanding wire is threaded through the rings.

This type of curtain needs fabric at least twice the width of your track, preferably three times.

Sew together the required number of widths using a flat and fell machine seam (14). To do this, put one selvedge 2 cm below the other edge with right sides together and machine. Turn the longer edge over the shorter, completely enclosing it and press down. Machine through three thicknesses.

Make double 1 cm hems at the sides and double 5 cm hems at the bottom. Turn down the top hem at required length. Turn under raw edge 1 cm and machine. Machine a second row 2 cm away from first seam. This forms the casing through which you can thread your expanded wire.

If you are using gathering tape apply as for unlined curtains.

## Interlined curtains

Cut out curtain material and lining. Cut the same amount of widths of interlining the finished length of the curtain plus 15 cm. Sew all widths together. Place your interlining right side up on working surface. Place curtain material right side up on top, keeping hem edges parallel. Smooth into place. Turn back curtain material at 30 cm intervals and lock stitch to interlining as for lined curtains. Turn curtain over so that interlining is uppermost. Turn in the side hems 7.5 cm and make a double 7.5 cm hem at the bottom. Interlined curtains do not usually have mitred corners, instead the edge of the bottom hem is turned in so that it can be stitched down out of sight from the right side of the curtain. Hemstitch the bottom hem in place and herringbone stitch the side hems to the interlining, taking care not to go through to the right side of the curtains. Attach the lining in the same way as for lined curtains.

Measure the required length of the curtain and cut off any surplus interlining. Ideally the edge of the interlining should sit in the fold of the material at the top, but it can be up to 1 cm shorter than the finished length of the curtain. Attach curtain tape.

*Right* Luxurious interlined curtains – an edge of the white lining shows as a decorative trim.

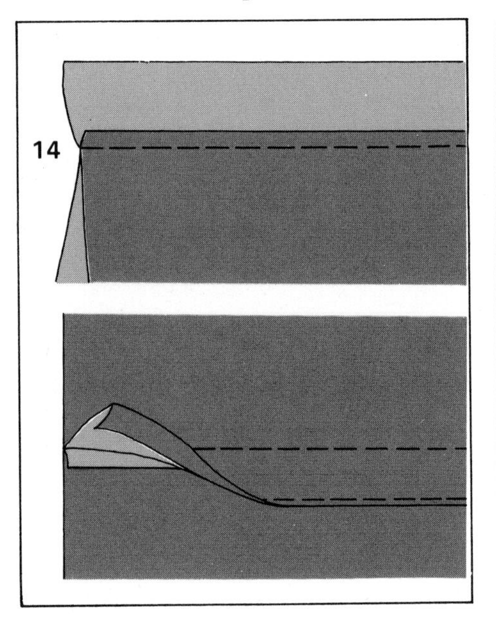


*Above* A flat and fell seam for joining widths of fabric.

*Right* A combination of sheer half curtains and sheer window length curtains, with a roller blind for night-time privacy.

## French pleats

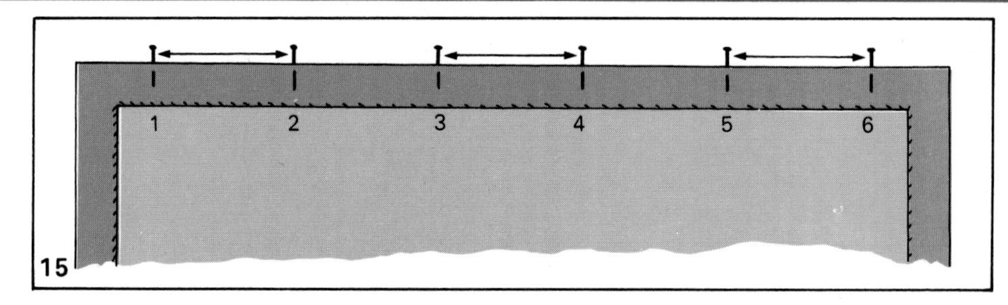


Measure the width of your track, divide by two and add 10 cm for your overlap. From this measurement deduct 15 cm (7.5 cm for each side). Divide the remainder by 10 cm to get the number of spaces you will require. You will need one more pleat than you have spaces, and you should have the same amount of fabric in a pleat as you have in a space. If you have too much material the extra should be evenly distributed in the pleats. If you have fractionally too little this should be evenly deducted from the pleats. The spaces must always remain constant.

To hand head your curtain, fold the main material over to the wrong side at the required length. Fold under the lining 2.5 cm shorter and hemstitch in place. Pin out your pleats (15). Fold material so that pin 1 lies on top of pin 2, wrong sides of material together (16). Machine from there to a point 10 cm from top of curtain. Place pins 3 and 4 together and machine. Continue until all pleats are joined. Turn curtain right side uppermost. Hold fold in hand and push down towards machine line to form three equal pleats. When you have got them even, catch them together by sewing through all thicknesses 9 cm from the top.

These curtains will need to have the hooks sewn on by hand, or you can use pin-on hooks. The advantage of the pin-on hooks is that you can push them in at just the right point so as to get your curtains exactly the right length.

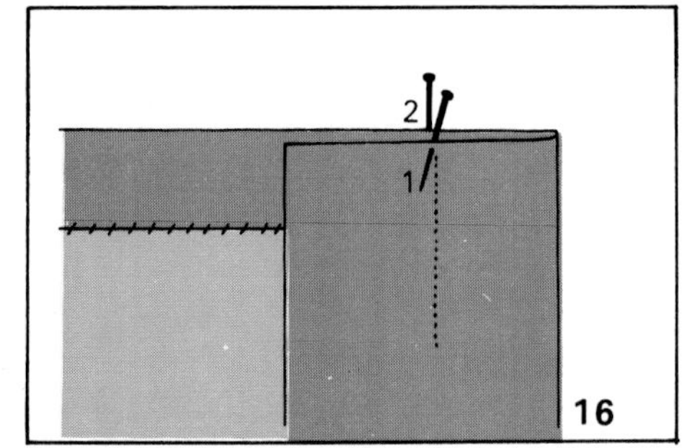


*Above* (15 and 16): hand-heading French pleats.

*Below left* Detail of a French-pleated heading.

## Café curtains

This type of curtain comes into its own when you want privacy but do not want net or full length curtains. With two-tier café curtains the upper half of the café curtains can be pulled back during the day letting in the daylight and the lower half remain drawn. The headings on café curtains are usually different from ordinary curtains as they are hung on rods, instead of from tracks.

Measure the length as for ordinary curtains but for the top hem allow 10 cm to make a casing for the rod. If you use a very thick rod, you may have to allow more for the casing.

Make the side and bottom hems as for unlined curtains. Turn over the top 10 cm to the wrong side and press. Turn under the raw edge 1 cm, press, tack and machine in place. Machine a second row 4 cm away from first row. This double row of machining constitutes your casing for the pole (17).

Alternatively you can make a scalloped heading to your café curtains. To do this allow enough material for a double top hem plus 5 cm. Take a piece of stiff paper the width of your finished curtain, and fold into equal parts until you have a section about 15 cm across. Draw your scallop on this and when satisfied that it is correct cut out through all thicknesses (18). Turn over the top hem allowance on your curtains right sides together and pin in place. Pin and tack your paper pattern to the curtain top. Machine round the exact outline of your scallops. Cut away the inside, clipping curves and leaving 5 mm turnings (19). Turn top right side out. Slip stitch the raw edges and the ends of the scallops. Sew rings to the top of the straps and suspend the curtains from these (20).

*Below* These café curtains have curtain rings sewn onto the hem fold.

*Right* Heading café curtains.

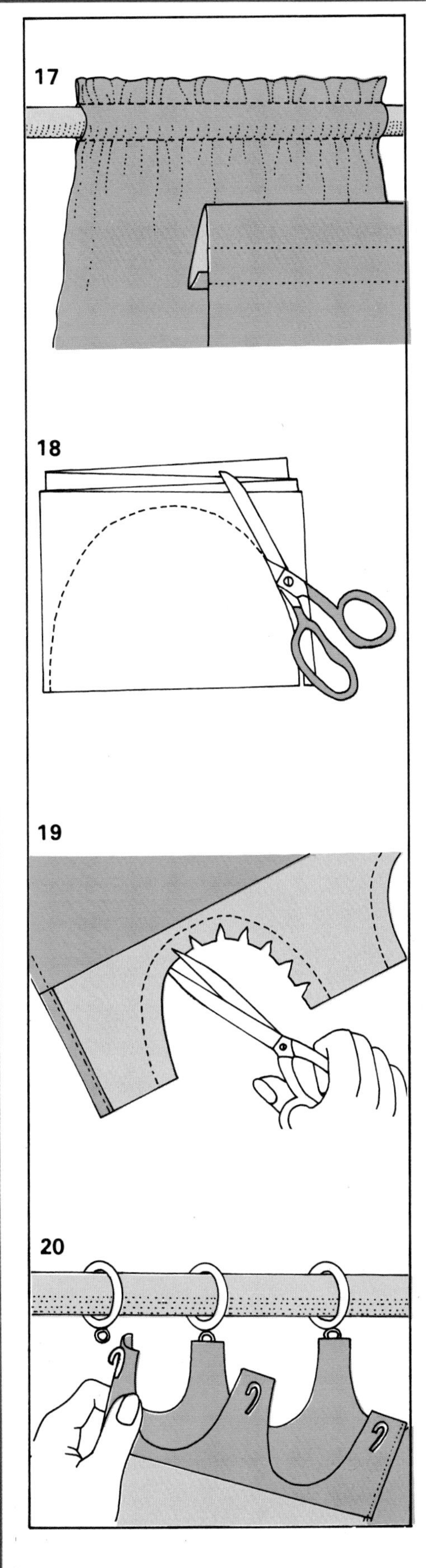

# Pelmets and valances

Pelmets are made from the same fabric as the curtains, or a plain contrasting fabric, mounted onto something stiff to give it body and they have a decorative shape to add interest to your curtains. Valances are pelmets which are made by pleating or gathering the material, but which are not mounted onto a stiffening agent.

Although pelmets are not always fashionable there are many windows and rooms which do not lend themselves to the 7.5 cm wide decorative gathering tapes so widely available. Short curtains often look better with a small pelmet or valance.

As a general rule allow 4 cm per 30 cm drop of curtain (a pair of curtains having a 120 cm drop would have a pelmet or valance 16 cm deep). If the pelmet was a shaped one it would be 16 cm deep at the deepest point. Shallow pelmets give added height to a room; deep pelmets bring the ceiling height down. Long curtains should have a pelmet one-sixth the depth of the curtains.

The best way to make a shaped pelmet is to get some stiff brown wrapping paper and pencil out the required outline. When you are quite satisfied that the shape is right, cut out the paper pattern and place in position at the top of your window. If it looks right, it does not matter whether it is a little too short or too long by the above proportions. Valances are generally fixed to a valance rail which is part of the curtain track. Pelmets are usually fixed to a piece of wood placed immediately above the curtain track and projecting by at least 10 cm from the wall.

## Gathered valance

Decide how deep you want your valance and allow 1½ times the width of the window not forgetting the 'returns' (where the valance goes back to the wall). Allow 2.5 cm hems top and bottom and 1 cm at each end. Cut out the lining to correspond.

Machine together the widths as necessary, matching the pattern throughout. Turn in 2.5 cm hems all round. Machine together the necessary strips of lining and place on top of the main material wrong sides together, and with the right side of the lining uppermost. Hemstitch together all round 1 cm from the edge.

At the top edge machine a length of

*Below* A soft French-pleated valance.

*Right* A well designed pelmet can improve the shape of a window. If the pelmet is to hang from ceiling height, the pelmet board is screwed to the ceiling itself.

Rufflette cord the entire length of the pelmet 2.5 cm down from the top, turning in the raw edges 1 cm at each end. Draw up the cords so that the pelmet is the right width and place on the valance rail.

## Pleated valance

Allow the same hems top and bottom and at the sides, but allow 2½ times the width of the window. Pleated valances are vastly improved by interlining even if the actual curtains are not interlined. Join together all necessary widths of material, lining and interlining. Place interlining on wrong side of main material, turn in to wrong side the 2.5 cm turnings and sew together with a running stitch, taking care not to go through to the right side of the valance. Place lining on top and slip stitch in place as for a gathered valance.

Make your pleats as for hand stitched French pleats (see page 18). With wrong side facing you, position length of Rufflette tape on back 2.5 cm down from top of valance. Slip stitch this in place, top and bottom. Position your hooks.

An attractive alternative to this pleated valance is to cut the bottom hem in a curve. Cut your material and sew together the various widths. Before you attach the lining or interlining work out your pleating. Draw a curve, the deepest point being at the centre of the space between two pleats, the shallowest at the exact centre of the pleat. The lining on this valance will be very visible so use a plain contrast (or pick up another colour used in the room). Make up as for plain pleated valance but the bottom hem of the lining should be exactly at the bottom of the valance. Hemstitch the two hems together.

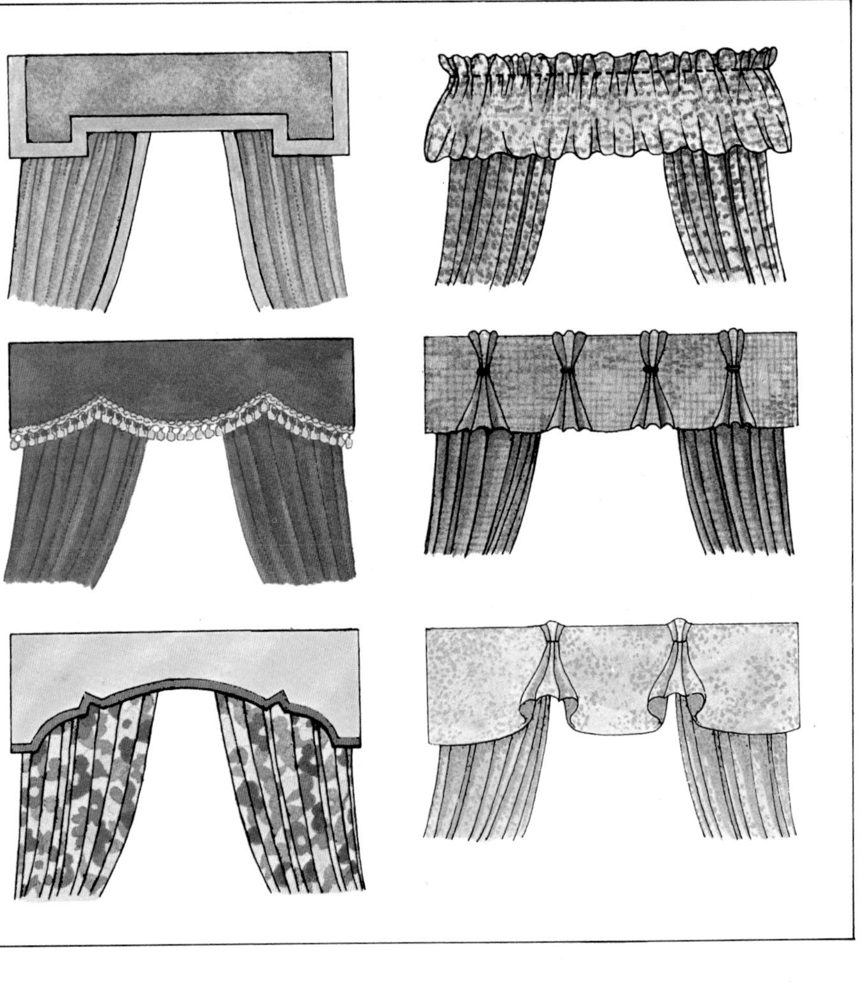

*Above left* Top and centre: pelmets with contrasting braid and trimmings. Below: plain pelmets often suit patterned curtains.

*Above right* Top: gathered matching valance. Centre and below: French-pleated valances with varied spacing.

## Pelmets

These should be designed to complement the architectural features of a room. A long narrow window can take a fairly elaborate style of pelmet, whereas a wide shallow window needs a much plainer shape. For best results cut out a paper pattern and position it in place to see how it looks. Adapt this paper pattern until it is satisfactory. Use this to estimate the quantity of material required, remembering to take the pattern on your material into account. Some patterns lend themselves to being cut into specific shapes.

**Materials** Buckram – a heavy form of canvas which has been stiffened to hold the shape of the pelmet.

Fabric to allow 2.5 cm turnings all round (taking into account the pattern repeat if any).

A similar amount of lining and interlining.

Braid to finish off the bottom edge if desired.

Do not forget the return on your pelmet board. If you are putting up the pelmet board make it 5 cm longer each side than your curtain track and deep enough so that it projects at least 7 cm in front of the front of your track. If you allow less the curtain will get jammed up by the pelmet.

**Making up** Place your paper pattern onto the buckram and draw round it. Buckram should never be joined, but should be one continuous strip. It is however sold in 30 cm widths so this is not as extravagant as it seems. Cut out the shape. Join the necessary widths of interlining and press onto the buckram with a steam iron. Most buckrams are adhesive. Trim interlining 5 mm longer and wider than the buckram. Place interlined side of buckram to wrong side of main material. Bring over the raw edge of the material and slip stitch to the buckram at the back. This is done by taking the needle first through the fabric, then through the buckram. It will be necessary to clip the turnings on curved shapes and to mitre the corners.

Place the lining on top, wrong side of lining to wrong side of buckram. Turn under all edges 5 mm narrower all round than the finished shape of the buckram and slip stitch in place.

Place a length of Rufflette tape the entire length of the pelmet and slip stitch in place, fixing it very firmly at each end.

**Trimmings** If you are applying braid or fringe this should be attached before the lining is sewn in, and it should be sewn through the buckram, using prick stitch (see page 47).

# Trimmings

## Braid

If you feel your curtains are going to be too plain you can add a braid down one side and across the bottom, down both sides and across the bottom, or simply at both sides. There are a wide variety of braids and trimmings available. Usually they are hand-stitched to the main material about 5 mm in all round and any corners are mitred (21). A matching braid can be used on your pelmet or valance.

## Binding

Alternatively you can bind your curtains. To do this you need a suitable length of contrast material which you cut out on the cross in strips wide enough to give you the required depth allowing for 1 cm turnings both sides. If you want 1 cm binding you will need 5 cm strips.

To cut your material on the cross, place your material on a flat surface. Take one corner diagonally across so that the straight cut edge runs parallel to the lengthways grain. Press the fold flat and cut. Join the necessary amount of strips together as for piping (see page 33). Press in a 1 cm seam the entire length. Pin this to the right side of curtain at the correct distance from the edge. Slip stitch in place, through all thicknesses. Turn curtain wrong side uppermost. Using the stitches as a guide, turn under the 1 cm hem allowance and slip stitch in place. Mitre the corners.

## Frill

To give your curtains a very feminine look you can add a frill all round. The frill should be double. For an 8 cm frill you would need 16 cm plus 1 cm for turnings. The actual length should be $1\frac{1}{2}$ times the finished length. Cut and machine together the necessary lengths of material. With the raw edges together and right sides facing, machine the entire length 5 mm in from raw edge. Turn right side out. Turn raw edges at each end and slip stitch together. Run a gathering thread 5 mm in from one edge and pull up to fit curtain. Hem to curtain approximately 2.5 cm in from edge (22). Remove gathering thread.

## Tie backs

Curtains can be made to look more formal by adding tie backs. These can be made in a variety of shapes, and can be piped or bound to match the curtains.

*Above* Sheer curtains trimmed with bobble braid.
*Below* Diagram 21: how to make a neat mitre.
*Right* Diagram 22: how to hem a doubled frill to the curtain hem.

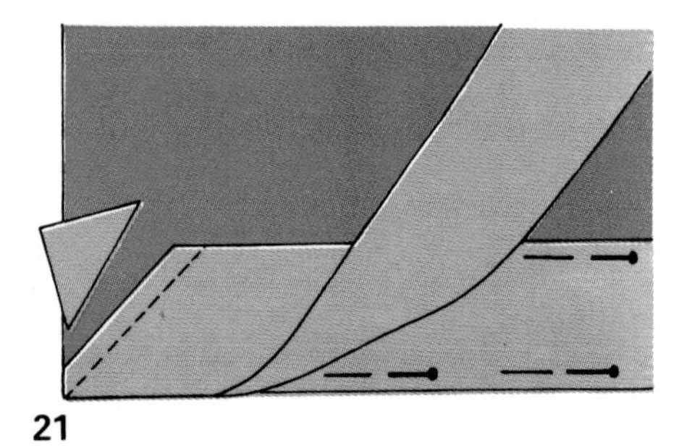
21

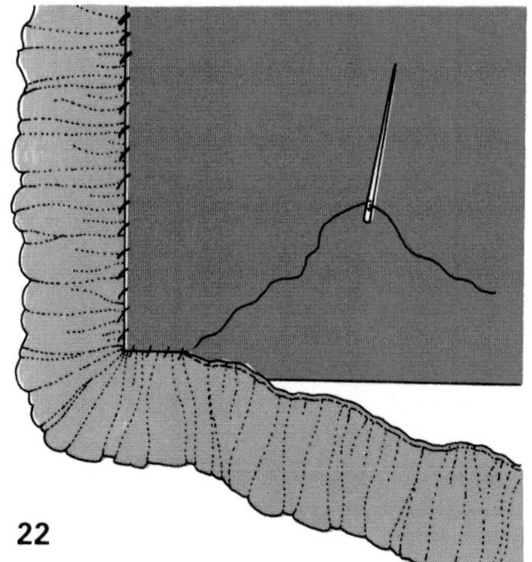
22

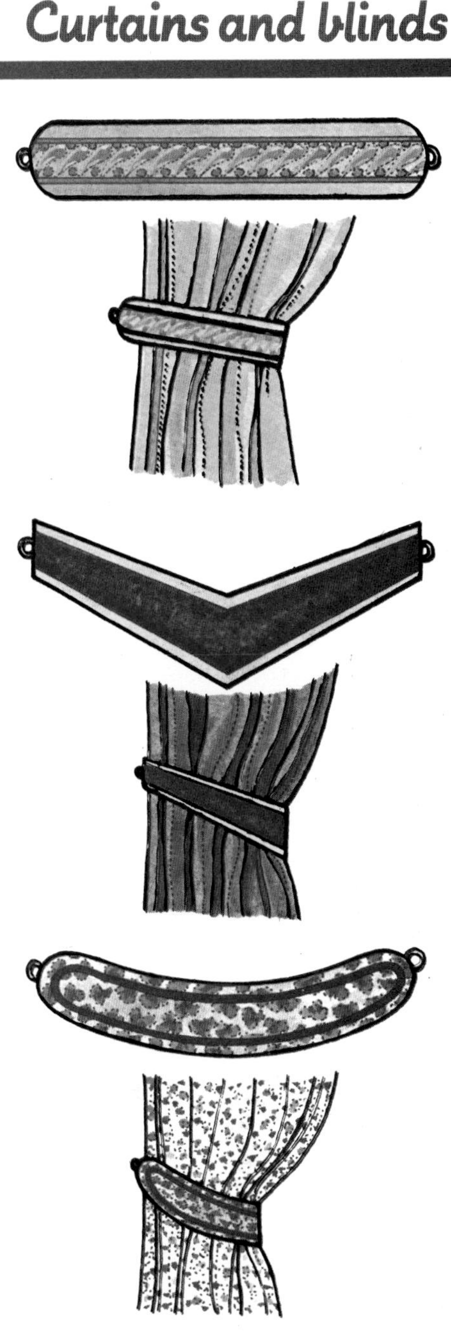

*Above* Decorative tie backs.
*Left* Bias trimming and matching tie back.

They are usually made out of the curtain material or in a colour to complement the curtains themselves.

Decide on the shape you want and cut out a template in paper. As a rough guide a 70 cm long tie back nicely draws back a curtain 1½ widths (180 cm) wide. How much the curtain should be drawn back is a very individual choice so pin your paper round the curtain and see what you prefer. Lengthen or shorten accordingly. If you pull them back too tightly, the curtains will crease.

For each pair of curtains you will need:

2 pieces of buckram the size of your paper template and enough material plus 2.5 cm all round for your seams to cover the buckram. If you are making a shaped tie back, place the template on a piece of newspaper and measure from 2.5 cm above the highest point to 2.5 cm below the lowest point.

The same amount of lining and interlining as of main material.

Two rings per tie back.

Trace the outline of your paper pattern onto the buckram and cut round. Place pattern on main material, making sure pattern is central and allowing 2.5 cm all round, cut out. Cut out lining and interlining to match.

Place interlining onto buckram and press with steam iron so as to bond together. Trim interlining to 2 mm from edge. Place interlined side of buckram on wrong side of material. Fold over raw edges of material and slip catch to buckram using fairly small stitches and drawing the material fairly tight. Place wrong side of lining to wrong side of buckram and slip stitch all round, 2 mm in from the edge. Using strong thread attach a ring to each point of each tie back.

If you want to pipe the tie backs, the piping should be attached with small running stitches to the main material after it has been attached to the buckram. The lining should then be sewn tight up to the cord covering the machine stitching on the piping.

## Roller blinds

Commercially made blinds are produced in a wide range of colours and patterns but you may want to make your own and you will be able to use material which matches curtains at other windows in the room. Blinds are a very simple way of giving you privacy, and in some cases are more suitable than curtains.

Most good hardware shops sell blind kits, and armed with these and a length of material you can make a blind in a matter of hours.

The first step is to establish where you will place your blind so that you can measure up. If it is to hang within the window reveal you will need to know the height and width from reveal to reveal. If it is to hang outside the window frame allow 10 cm each side and at the top and bottom.

**Roller blind kits** Kits are sold in various sizes graduating by 30 cm. Unless your measurement is the exact size of one of the kits, buy the next size up and cut it back.

Each kit contains a wooden roller fitted at one end with a spring, a round metal cap which fits over the other end once you have cut it to the right size, two wall brackets, one with a hole into which you slot the spring end and one slotted, a wooden batten to weight your blind, a length of cord and a pull, screws and tacks. You have to buy screws separately for fixing the brackets to the wall.

**Fabric** The fabric you choose should be closely woven and not too thick so as to avoid creasing and loss of shape. Linen, canvas, or glazed cottons are all suitable. PVC coated fabrics, available in a wide range of colours and patterns, are ideal for kitchens or bathrooms; they are easily wiped down and are not affected by steam.

You will need a piece of fabric the length of your window plus 15 cm for hems. If your window is wider than the fabric you will need two widths.

### Making up roller blinds

Place the brackets in position and if necessary, cut your roller to fit.

If you are using more than one width of material you must cut the second width in half lengthways and join the selvedges of the cut piece to the selvedges of the complete piece. This way, you will have one complete width in the middle of your blind and a part of a width at each edge. When joining widths for a blind use a flat and fell stitch (see page 16).

The width of the fabric should be the same as the wooden part of the roller plus 4 cm. Turn in the side edges 1 cm and then turn in a further 2.5 cm. Machine these two side hems either with a straight stitch or using a decorative stitch if your machine has one. Turn up the bottom hem 1 cm, then again a further 2 cm and machine stitch it, leaving ends open. Cut your batten 1 cm shorter than the width of the blind.

*Right* Diagrams 1–3: making a roller blind.

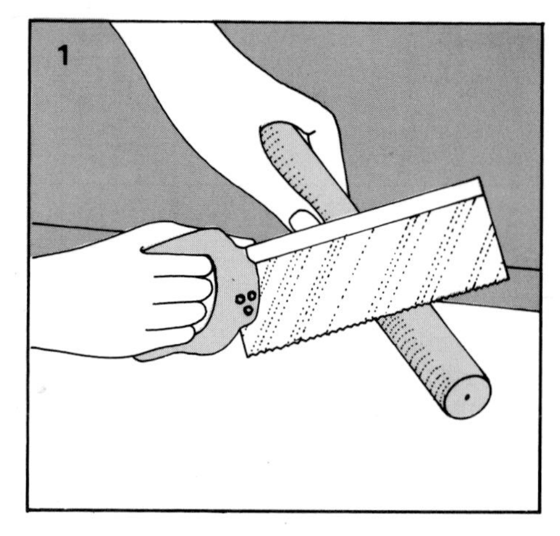

*Left* A shaped hem on a roller blind. The finished hem can be bound with bias-cut binding, or with a narrow braid.

*Below* A plain blind is decorated with fabric-paints (see page 144).

*Far left* Roller blinds are convenient for work areas such as kitchens.

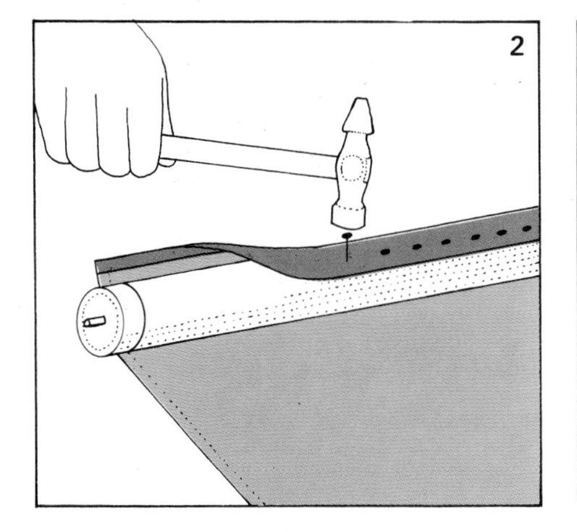


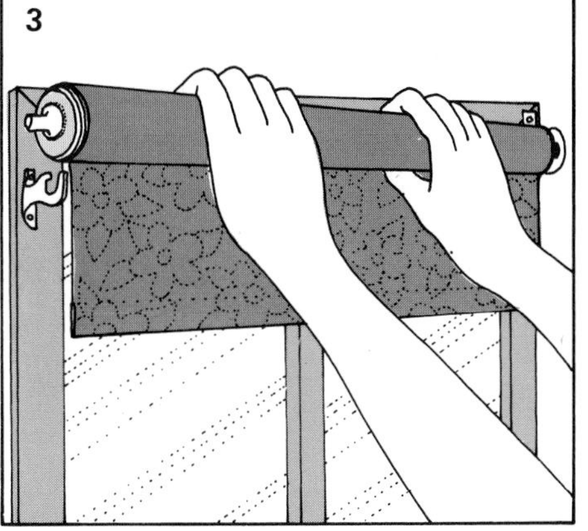


Place it in the slot and sew up both sides so as to completely enclose it.

Place the blind on a flat surface, right side up. Press a 1 cm hem at the top, right side of fabric to right side. With the spring side of the roller on the left, place roller to top of the blind and tack. The roller has a straight line marked on it for guidance.

Take your cord and, with a knot one end, thread it through the widest end of the acorn. Thread cord through cord holder from the domed side and make another knot. Screw cord holder to middle of batten. Put acorn's cap on once you have established right length of cord.

To make your blind a little different you may wish to have a scalloped or shaped hem, to go below the batten. Alternatively you may wish to discard the batten and buy a wooden or brass pole with decorative ends. These are available from curtain departments in most department stores.

**Shaped hems** Cut a piece of paper the width of your batten and 15 cm deep and fold in half to find the èxact centre. Draw the design you want on the paper and, still folded in half, cut out round your outline.

Cut a piece of fabric 15 cm deep and 2 cm wider than your blind. Light fabrics, and glazed cottons benefit from interfacing, which should be ironed onto this fabric.

Pin facing fabric, stiffened side up, to bottom edge of hem on the right side of the blind. Pin your pattern very carefully onto double fabric and cut out. Machine-stitch facing to blind 5 mm in from cut edge. Clip any curves or angles and turn facing to wrong side of blind. Turn in the side edges of the facing and slip stitch to blind.

Turn under top 5 mm of facing and machine to blind. Make another row of machine stitches 2.5 cm below so as to form the casing for your batten.

**To make a decorative casing** Cut several strips of material 10 cm long and 7 cm wide. Take two strips, and with right sides together machine down long sides 5 mm in from raw edge. Turn right side out and press. Repeat until you have enough. Fold all these strips in half and pin the raw edges to the bottom right side of the blind. Place a straight piece of facing fabric on top, right side of facing fabric to right side of blind and stitch through all thicknesses. Turn facing to wrong side of blind, turn under raw edge and machine to blind. You can now place your decorative rail through the slots.

## Roman blinds

Roman blinds are more unusual than blinds, and are a good substitute for windows and doors where you feel that curtains would take up too much room at the sides. The difference between Roman blinds and roller blinds is that instead of rolling up, they 'concertina' up into soft folds, having rings sewn to the wrong side through which strings are threaded, the string being firmly knotted to the bottom ring When drawn up they form a decorative addition to any room.

### Materials

**Fabric and lining** The same types of fabric can be used as for roller blinds. Roman blinds must be lined. If you are putting the blind inside the window reveal, measure the height plus 15 cm top and bottom hems, and the width plus 7 cm each side for the side hems. You will need the same quantity of lining. For blinds outside the reveal, measure from 7 cm outside the reveal and a suitable height above and below your window.

**Wooden battens** One batten 5 cm by 2.5 cm and to the width of your finished blind and a second batten 2 cm wide to slot through the bottom hem to weight your blind. This is called the stretcher batten.

**Tacks**

**Tape** Enough 1 cm wide tape to sew strips every 30 cm from top to bottom. A piece of tape 3 cm wide the length of your batten plus 5 cm.

**Brass rings** Enough to sew one brass ring every 15 cm down each of the tapes.

**Nylon cord** Double the amount of your tape plus some to go across the top of the blind.

**Screw eyes** The same quantity of 1 cm screw eyes as you have strips of tape

**A cleat hook and screws** to anchor the cords when the blind is drawn up.

### Making up

Cut the fabric to the required length and join any necessary widths, matching the pattern. Press seams open. Join together any necessary widths of lining. Place material on flat working surface and lining on top, wrong sides together. Smooth into place carefully as you will be working the two together as one fabric.

At each side turn inwards 1 cm hems and press. Turn over a further 5 cm. Press, tack and machine in place.

Turn up 1 cm on the bottom hem. Turn up a further 10 cm. Press.

Position your tapes, the first one 35 cm in from the edge. Tuck the raw edge 1 cm under the bottom hem. Tack all the way up to the top. Next place a tape 35 cm in from the far side, in the same way. Measure the distance between the two tapes. You will need to put tapes spaced approximately 30 cm apart, with equal distance between each tape. Once all the tapes are positioned, machine stitch the tapes on both sides of each tape close to the edge. Now machine your hem down with a row of stitches close to top edge of hem. Make a second row of stitching 2.5 cm down from the first. This will hold your stretcher batten.

Mark the position of the rings on the tapes (15 cm apart), starting just above the stretcher batten slot. Place a further row of rings on the side machine lines. Sew firmly in place.

Turn over top edge 2.5 cm. Place your 3 cm tape level with the top edge of the blind, with the ends tucked under 2.5 cm. Make a row of machine stitching on the bottom edge of the tape. Machine a second row 1 cm above this (2 cm from the top of the blind). By hand catch the tape and the blind at the very top every 10 cm. This will stop the blind tilting forward at the top when it is tacked to your batten.

Your batten should be screwed into position and painted to match the walls or reveals. Tack the blind to the batten, placing a tack every 7 cm.

Place a screw eye in the bottom of the batten to line up exactly with each of your tapes carrying the rings. Position your cleat hook on the side most convenient for drawing up the blind.

Thread your nylon cord through the row of rings on the far side to the cleat hook, and carry it through all the screw eyes on the batten, and let it hang down loosely beside the blind. It is easiest to work with the complete length of cord and not cut it off until you have tied a knot in the first ring, and the end is hanging down loose to the right length. Repeat until you have cords running through all rows of rings. Check that the cords are taut but not pulling and tie them together in a knot.

Draw up the blind by pulling on the cords. Tie another knot at the position of the cleat hook, and hook cords over. Smooth the pleats of the blind into position evenly and leave for a day so that the folds will form automatically when the blind is drawn up.

Slot the stretcher batten into position. (It should be fractionally shorter than the slot so that the ends can be sewn up, completely encasing the batten.)

If your blind is hanging outside the window frame a decorative pole can be used and the finials will stop the pole from slipping out.

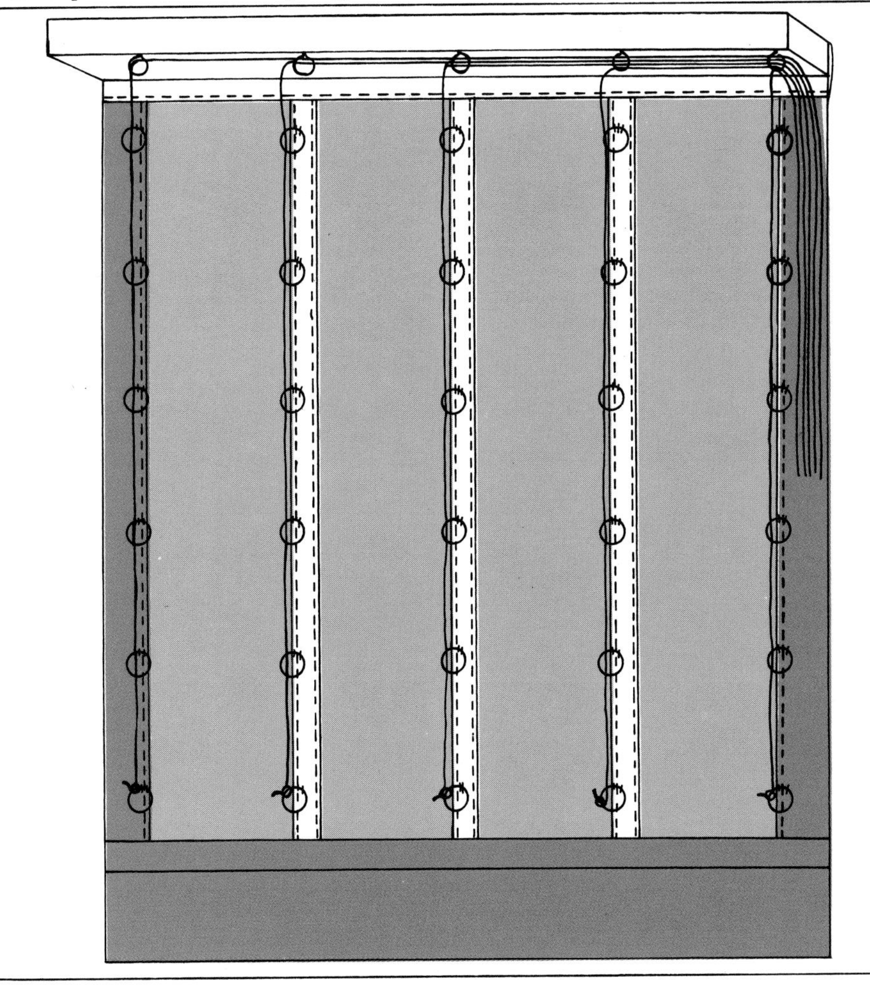

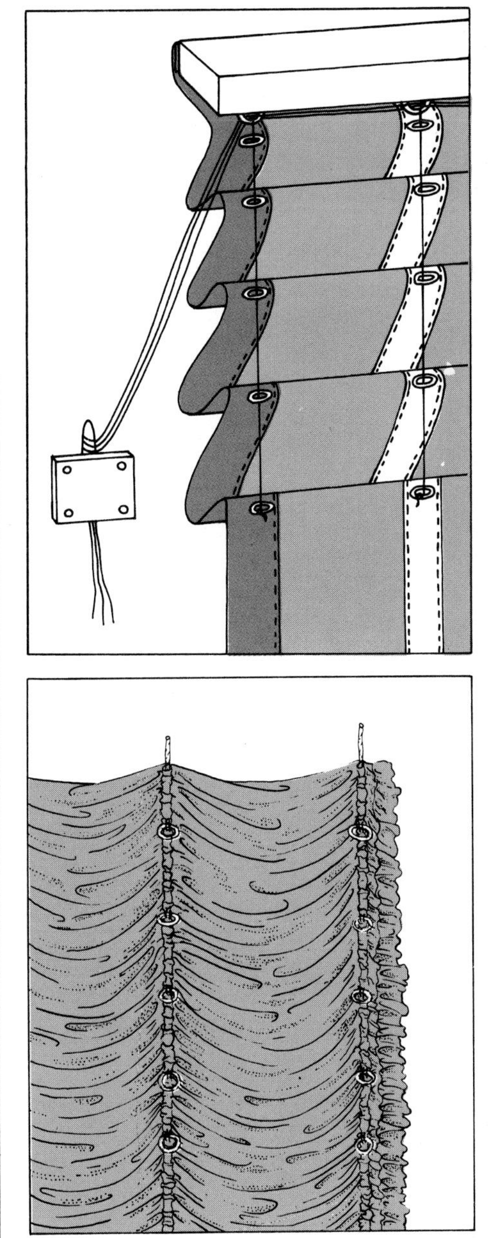

*Left* Wrong side of a Roman blind.
*Top* Roman blind pulled up.
*Above* Festoon blind.
*Far left* Roman blind pulled up.

# Festoon blinds

This is a very decorative and feminine blind particularly suitable for a bedroom. It is more extravagant than a Roman or roller blind requiring fabric approximately twice the width of the finished blind. Like Roman blinds they hang from a batten and are drawn up with cords, but a festoon blind has additional cords sewn into the fabric at regular intervals to draw it up into horizontal gathers (see page 27).

Fairly thin, lightweight fabrics are the best for festoons; silk or its imitations are perfect. Lining festoons is entirely optional.

## Materials

**Wooden batten** One batten to the finished width of the blind.
**Nylon cord** Enough to gather the blind at regular 38–46 cm intervals, plus enough to draw up the blind at the same intervals.
**Brass rings** Enough to sew on at 15 cm intervals behind the cord before the blind is drawn up.
**Four lead weights**
**Tape** A piece the length of the batten plus 2 cm for turnings.
**Fabric** Decide on the position of your batten and screw to wall or reveal. Measure the length of your batten. Deduct 15 cm from this measurement and divide the remainder into equal parts of between 38 cm and 46 cm. For each equal part add on 12 cm to allow for the horizontal gathers. Add 17 cm for side hems. The length should be $1\frac{1}{2}$ times the finished length. Any joins should be placed where the cords lie.

You will also need material for the frill at the bottom of the blind. Allow 10 cm per drop and $1\frac{1}{2}$ times the width of the blind before it is gathered up.

## Making up

Cut out the fabric into the right lengths and make any joins. Unless there is a wide selvedge make 5 mm seams. If there are wide selvedges cut off the surplus. Make a double 5 mm hem round all four sides of the material.

If you want to line the blind the lining should be joined together at this stage and the material placed on top of the lining with wrong sides together. Turn in double 2 mm hems round all four sides of the material and thereafter work lining and material as one. Place material on flat surface right side up and place a row of pins 7 cm in from the edge down the length of the blind. Do the same on the other side. Place rows of pins at equal distances between 51 cm and 59 cm. You should now have several rows of pins lying parallel between the top and the bottom of the blind.

Fold material wrong sides together along first row of pins and with a piece of cord inserted the entire length of the material and 2 cm longer each end, tack in place. Repeat till every row of pins has a cord behind it. Machine all cords in place taking care not to catch the cord at any point with the stitching. At the bottom of the blind attach the cord firmly to the material with several back stitches. Join the necessary widths of material to make the lower frill. Make a double 5 mm hem all round and machine. Run a row of gathering stitches 1 cm down from top of frill, and a second row 5 mm below that. Draw up gathering stitches so that frill is exact width of blind. Distribute gathers evenly and tack to the right side of blind, between two rows of gathering stitches. Tack it 2 cm up from the bottom of the blind. Machine in place and remove gathering stitches.

Take a piece of tape the length of your batten plus 2 cm for turnings. Turn under 1 cm of tape and pin to wrong side of blind at the top, as far as first cord. Repeat on opposite side. Place pins at equal distances in the tape between 38 cm and 46 cm (according to your original calculation). Place one cord over each pin. Each portion of the material will be about 11 cm longer than the corresponding portion of tape. This fullness is absorbed into two tucks to each side of each cord.

*Above and left* Festoon blinds only differ from Roman blinds by having horizontal gathers (see diagrams on page 27). They can have tight gathers (left) or loose gathers (above) according to how tightly the gathering cord is pulled.

Tack the blind to the tape and machine 1 cm down from the top. At the very top of the blind catch material to tape every 7 cm to stop top of blind dipping.

Sew on brass rings to wrong side of blind at the back of each cord starting just above the frill and placing them at 15 cm intervals, to just below the top of the blind.

Draw up the cords from the top of the blind so that it is the right length, distributing gathers evenly. Cut off surplus cord and back stitch enclosed end of cord firmly in place.

Make little bags out of material or lining to enclose two weights each and sew them to the blind at each end just behind where the frill is attached. Without these the blind would pull into the centre when not drawn up.

Screw in screw eyes to batten to correspond with cords. Using tacks through tape on wrong side of blind only, tack blind to batten. Thread up your blind in exactly the same manner as for Roman blinds.

# Loose covers

A well made armchair will easily last 50 years, but unfortunately the upholstery will start to look grubby and worn long before that. Making a loose cover for a favourite armchair will give it a new lease of life; a loose cover on a new chair will protect it from the wear and tear of a young family.

The chief skill for making a loose cover is common sense and you will probably get a better result than someone who comes to your home, cuts out the cover and then goes home to sew it together. You can place each piece individually and if you have any doubts about a particular seam, you can always try the cover on the chair to check.

## Materials and equipment

**Fabric** Do not skimp on material – either quantity or quality. If the tuck-ins are too short the chair cover will never stay in place. The wonderful remnant you bought will not turn out to be a bargain if it does not allow you to have a back to your cover.

You are going to spend quite a few hours on making your cover and you probably want it to last quite a few years (and even more launderings) so buy the best fabric you can afford. A cotton and linen mixture is still the best. It is easy to work with and has a certain amount of 'give' so that it can be eased round shapes, rather than having to make tucks. Fabrics with a certain amount of elasticity will be easier to launder. Brocades and cretonnes make up well, as do heavy quality repps, but the latter need to be pre-shrunk.

Consider the use your chair has before buying your material. A small occasional chair can probably have a cover made in a lighter fabric than the chair which everyone in the family makes a bee-line for. You will also need some lining for the skirt. A lined skirt looks very professional and much neater altogether. It also adds a bit of weight to the skirt, making it hang better.

**Piping cord** There is a myth that piping is horribly difficult. The fact is that it is more difficult to make a neat cover without piping than with it. The piping provides a nice straight line to work up to.

Piping can be used as a decorative feature. If the chair material is patterned consider doing your piping in a plain colour material picking up one of the colours in the pattern. Or pipe your cover if it is a plain material with a darker shade of the same colour: dark brown piping on a beige cover, for instance, looks very smart.

**Scissors** You will also need a pair of large, sharp scissors.

**Tape measure** A fabric tape measure is easier than a steel one for measuring curved arms and backs.

**Thread** No. 36 sewing thread.

**Fastenings** Hooks and bars for closing the back opening; a zip for the cushion if your chair has one.

**Sewing machine** You will not be able to make a very satisfactory cover without a sewing machine, and you will need a zip foot for making the piping. The type where the foot can be placed on either side of the needle is best.

**Labels** A packet of small self-adhesive labels is also useful. As you cut out each piece of material, write on a label which part it is, and stick it to the fabric.

A traditional armchair covered with a modern patterned fabric.

# Piping

Fold the piece of material you have allowed for piping so that the straight cut edge lies parallel with the lengthways grain of fabric (1). Press the fold and cut along this line. Using this bias as your guide, cut even strips 4 cm wide. If you try and make chalk lines, or pencil lines, the material will 'walk' giving you very uneven lines – so to help you cut straight place pins at the correct distance. For an average easy chair with one cushion you will need about 14 metres of piping. For each extra cushion, measure around the top and bottom where piping goes.

## To join the strips

Place two strips at right angles, right sides together. Sew together leaving 5 mm seam allowance (2). Cut off the projecting points and press the seam open. Ideally, all joins should run in the same direction.

## Making piping

Place the piping cord in the centre of the wrong side of the bias strip. Fold the material over and tack fairly close to the cord (3). Machine the entire length but do not sew too close to the actual cord as you want this line of machine stitches to be enclosed by the next line when you are fitting the piping into the cover.

## Making a continuous strip

Tack the piping in place round the item, until the two ends of piping are within 5 cm of meeting. Untack the bias strip 3 cm on each end, releasing the cord. Making sure that the join slants in the same direction as any others in the piping, fold back the turnings so that the folded edges just meet where they will be joined (4). Tack and machine the folded edges together, trim off any excess material to 5 mm and press open. Lay the cords down flat and cut through both where they meet. Wrap casing round cord and stitch down.

# Skirts and valances

## 1. Straight skirt with corner pleat

Measure the distance between each corner and add 4 cm seam allowance for each of the side hems. Measure the depth of the finished skirt and add 4 cm for the bottom hem and 2 cm for your top seam allowance. Cut out the required number of pieces and join any widths as necessary.

A straight skirt to a sofa would require more than one width at the front and the back. Always have a complete width in the middle and a half (or part) width to either side. The seams in this case should be matched up to those on the front facing, the seat and the back.

*Below* Armchair with piping in a toning colour and a straight skirt.

*Right* Diagrams 1–4: making piping. Diagram 5: lazy gathering.

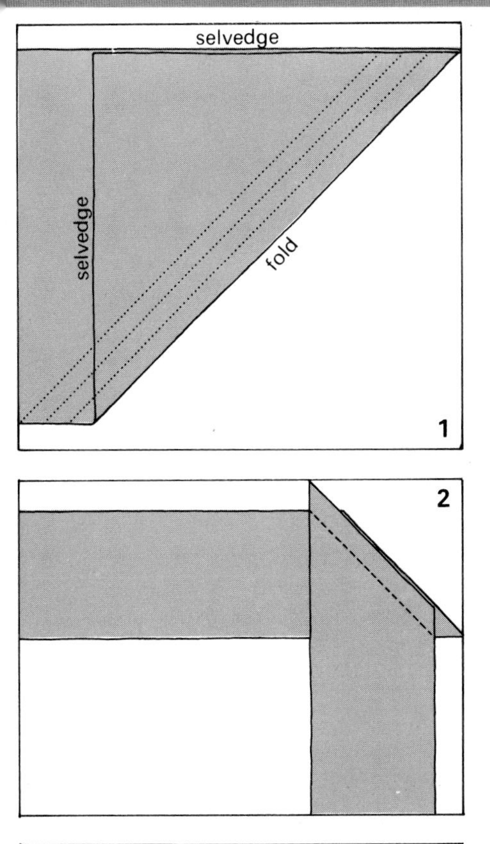


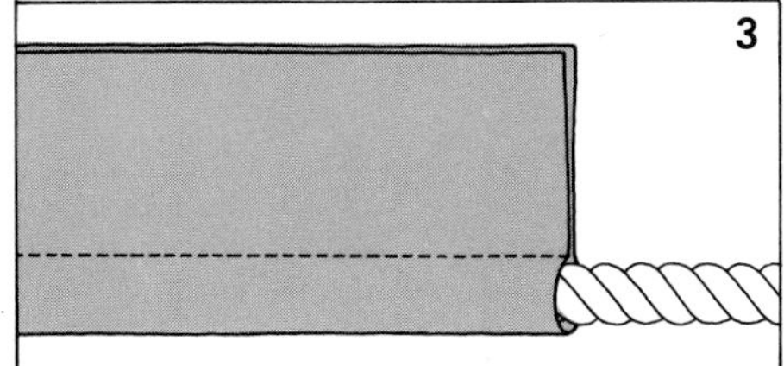


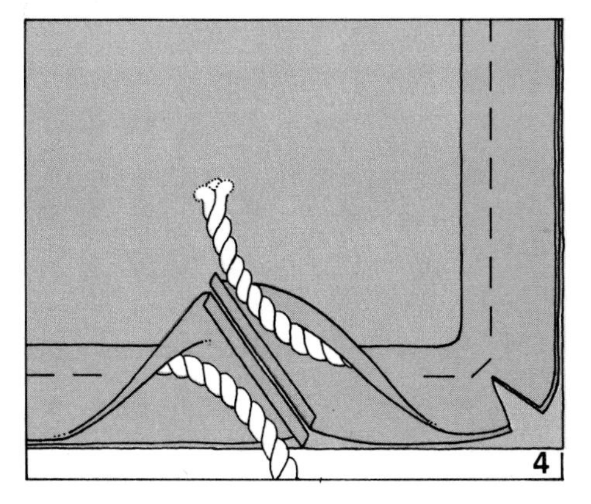


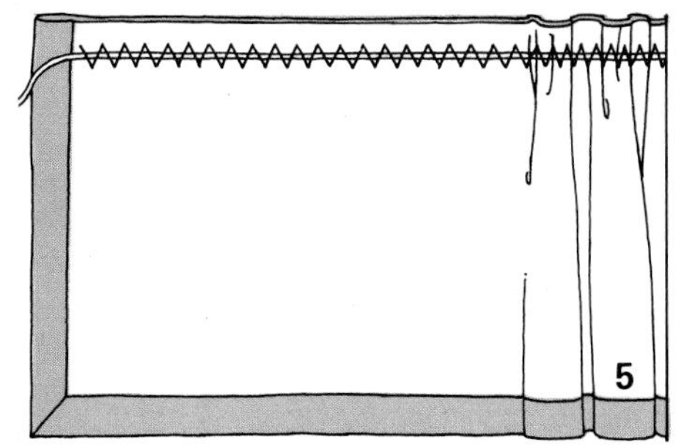


Place fabric right side down and press open any joins. Turn in the side hems 2 cm, and the bottom hem 4 cm. Mitre the corners. Herringbone stitch hems in place.

Cut 4 pieces of lining 2 cm wider and 1 cm longer than your hemmed skirt pieces. Place lining wrong side down on wrong side of skirt with raw top edges level and turn in lining towards skirt so that lining is 1 cm narrower and shorter than main material. Slip stitch in place. Measure and mark off your seam allowance at the top. Machine the lining to main skirt material along this line. Press all raw edges to wrong side so that machine line lies just on the wrong side of the skirt pieces. Attach skirt to cover as described in the instructions for making up the cover.

You will have 4 gaping corners. Out of the wastage cut off from main skirt, cut 4 pieces 20 cm wide and the same depth including hem and seam allowances as the main pieces. Press in side and bottom hems and hemstitch. Cut out the lining and line as for main pieces. Mark off and machine the top seam allowance.

Take the cover and pin and tack one small piece across each corner, with the right side of the small piece to the lining side of main piece. Turn right side towards you to check that you have positioned it correctly. Machine in place.

When making a skirt for a chair or sofa with a placket, the corner piece for the corner opening should go across to the edge of the placket. When the cover has been fastened the back will overlap beautifully, needing no hooks and bars on skirt.

## 2. Pleated skirt

This is more extravagant on material (and a nightmare to iron) but is a very attractive finish to a chair. When measuring for spaced pleats allow twice as much as the perimeter of the piping where it is to be attached. For close pleats, treble the amount.

Cut the necessary widths of material, allowing 2 cm at the top and 4 cm for side and bottom hems. Join the widths together matching the pattern if necessary, and press seams open. Turn in the side and bottom hems to wrong side, mitre the corners and herringbone stitch in place.

Cut your lining 2 cm wider and 1 cm longer than your material. With wrong side of lining to wrong side of material, turn under hems of lining to 1 cm shorter and narrower than material. Slip stitch in place.

Measure and mark off (across the entire width) the right depth of the skirt.

Mark out the position of the pleats by placing a pin 5 cm in from the right-hand side. Place a second pin 10 cm further along. Continue to place pins at 5 cm and 10 cm alternately, across all the material.

Go back to the first pin and fold the material so that the first pin meets the second, the third pin meets the fourth, and so on, folding them on alternate sides. Tack and press well.

Machine along measured off line at top of skirt, and turn raw edges into wrong side of skirt. Pin, tack and machine to cover.

## 3. Gathered frill

This finish is very suitable for a bedroom chair where you may want a more feminine look. Allow $1\frac{1}{2}$ times the perimeter of the piping where it is to be joined. Allow 2 cm for your top seam allowance and 4 cm for side and bottom hems.

Join the widths, matching the pattern as necessary. Turn in seam allowance on side and bottom hems. Mitre the corners and herringbone stitch all hems. Cut the lining 1 cm wider and longer than hemmed material.

With wrong sides together turn in hem of lining so that it is 1 cm shorter and narrower than material. Hemstitch in place.

Mark off depth of frill. Run a row of gathering stitches just above your stitching line and a second row just below. Draw up the gathers to fit the cover and pin in place. Tack in place, taking your tacking stitches between the two rows of gathering stitches.

*Note* When gathering thick furnishing fabrics you may find that the thread snaps before you have finished gathering. If your machine can do a zig-zag stitch, there is a lazy way of gathering. Set your machine for a fairly long, wide zig-zag. Take a length of strong thread (the sort used for sewing on buttons is ideal) and place it under the foot of the machine. Feed material through machine keeping strong thread straight. The needle will skip to each side. You can now gather up the material very quickly and easily (5).

When making a gathered skirt, divide the joined up widths of the material into four sections, and mark off each quarter. Measure the cover where the skirt will be joined and mark that off in quarters.

Now pin skirt to cover, matching the pins, and gather up. This is an easy way to ensure that the gathers are evenly distributed.

# Chair without arms

## Measuring up

First check the width at the widest point of the outside back and the inside back. Even with seam allowances it is sometimes possible to make both pieces out of one width of fabric. Measure the length of the outside back, and add 2 cm top and bottom for seams. Measure the inside back of the chair from the point at the top where it meets the back to the seat, and add 2 cm at the top and 10 cm at the seat for the tuck-in.

Measure round the seat edge, from one back leg, round the front, to the other back leg, to see whether you need more than one width of material for side band. Now measure from seat edge to lower edge of chair and add 2 cm seam allowance top and bottom, and double this figure if you need more than one width.

Decide on the type of skirt you want, and work out the number of widths you will need accordingly. Many of these small chairs have longer legs at the front than at the back. The skirt must be exactly the same depth the whole way round, so although the skirt may join the side band at its bottom edge in the front, it may be as much as 5 cm up at the back (6).

You will need piping cord for the seams where it is to be applied, lining for the skirt, and some Velcro for the back opening. To decide on the size of the opening, measure from the widest part of the back of the chair to the point where the skirt will be attached, plus 4 cm.

## Cutting out

Place your material on a flat surface, and mark your measurements on it with pins. The diagram is marked out in squares and oblongs (7). The square for the outside back is made by taking the measurement across the widest part, and the length from the highest part, to the edge of the chair, and adding 2 cm all round for your seams. The same applies to the inside back and the seat, plus tuck-ins. It is easier to cut these basic shapes first and leave the final shaping of each piece until you have it pinned on the chair.

Pin out all the measurements on the material, making sure that if the material has a pattern, the pattern is in the centre of each piece. Check all the measurements and add seam allowances.

*Above* A chair without arms with a gathered skirt.

Cut out the pieces and name them. If you do not have adhesive labels, use scraps of paper and pin them on. Do not use a system of pins as it is easy to forget what they represent. Make up piping.

## Making up

Place seat piece in position, right side up and with the inside back tuck-in allowance folded under where the material touches the back of the seat. Check position of pattern, pin material to chair to avoid slipping and cut off any material in excess of your seam allowance.

Pin the inside back in position, turning the 10 cm tuck-in allowance under the seat tuck-in and pin in position. Cut round the shape of the chair allowing for seams.

At each side of your chair it will be necessary to cut off part of the tuck-in allowance so that the seat and the inside back will lie flat when taken round the corner. Place a pin at each side where you want the curve to start, and work inwards from that point. The shaded part in diagram 8 is what is cut off.

Tack and machine the tuck-in, and neaten the edges. Clip the side angles fairly close to the machine line. Replace inside back and seat on chair.

Pin the piping round the top of the seat, matching raw edges, following the line of piping on the original upholstery. Machine the piping then clip close to

*Below* Diagram 6: chair without arms showing equal depth of skirt all round.

*Right above* Diagram 7: cutting layout.

*Right below* Diagram 8: joining inside back and seat.

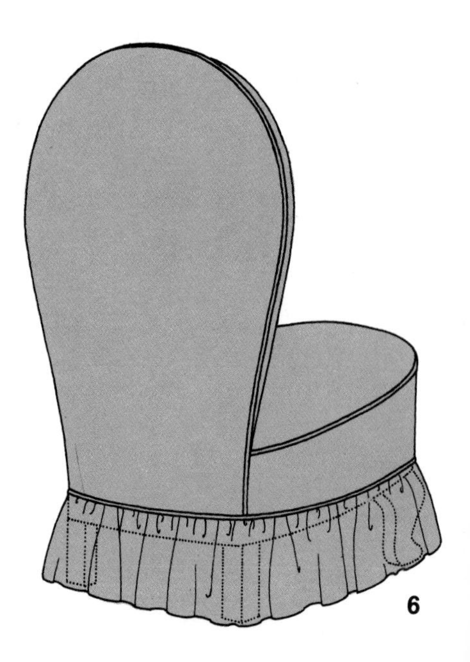

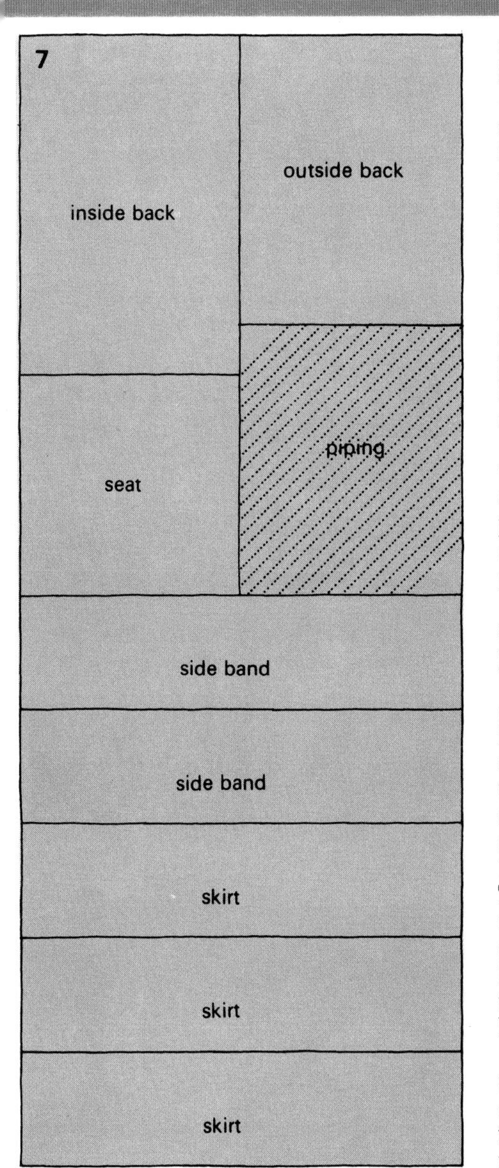


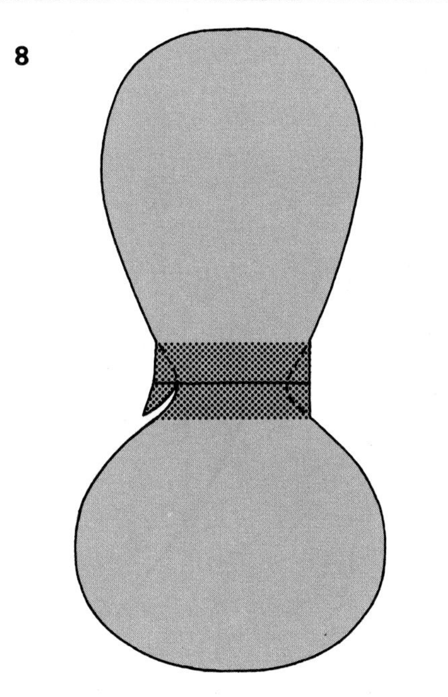


tacking or machine line to make it lie flat.

Join any widths for the side band. To do this have one complete width at the front of the chair and cut the second width in half and join one half to each selvedge of the complete piece, matching the pattern. Machine these seams, and press open.

Fold side band in half to find exact centre and mark with pin. Find the centre of the seat and put in a pin. Turn in the 2 cm seam allowance on the side band, and matching the pins at the centre of seat, pin side band to seat.

Continue to pin both pieces together, working outwards and towards the back on both sides from this centre pin. Place pins at right angles to the piping, to ensure a good fit. Check there are no puckers and that pattern is correct.

Without removing material from chair slip-tack side band to seat. Remove all pins.

Place a pin through piping to mark off where you want the cord to be cut, leaving the casing strip empty as the cord must never overlap. Measure from there to end of casing to see how much surplus cord you have. Remove the pin and place through casing and cord about 7 cm away from where you want to cut. Take hold of the cord only and pull it out of the casing (the casing will gather up) and cut off the required amount of cord. Ease the casing back and you will find that the end of it is empty, and can safely be machined over, later on.

Remove pieces from chair, open out to wrong side and machine the seam close to piping using zipper foot. Neaten the seams and trim off any surplus material. Replace on chair and smooth into place, then anchor with a few pins.

Pin piping round front, bringing it right down as far as the bottom of the side bands.

Find the centre of your outside back piece, and the centre of your inside back piece at the top. Turn under the seam allowance and pin outside back and inside back together at centre top. Pin the outside back at the bottom to the chair so that you do not pull the fabric more to one side than the other.

As you work round pinning from the top, round the curve towards the bottom you will have to take in more than 2 cm seam allowance, so that the outside back lies flat against the chair.

Pin very carefully the complete way round but when slip-tacking remember to finish half way down one side. The remainder will have Velcro fastening, and constitute the opening.

Remove cover from chair and sew in Velcro before machining the rest of the seams joining front and back pieces.

Cut the Velcro 4 cm longer than the opening. Neaten the raw edges of the chair opening. Separate the two pieces of Velcro and place the woolly one right side up over the seam allowance on the outside back piece. Tack and machine in place, the edge of the Velcro just inside the edge of the back.

Stitch the smooth strip of Velcro to inside back piece, with the edge tight up to the piping.

Close the Velcro strips exactly in position, turn cover inside out and machine through both strips together at the top. Machine twice across to stop opening splitting.

Turn cover inside out and machine round remainder of back. Cut off any surplus and neaten the raw edges. Replace cover on chair.

Starting from the back opening, pin piping in place round bottom of chair, keeping piping level. Cut off piping 1 cm longer than back. Place a pin through piping 7 cm in, withdraw cord and cut off surplus. Turn under the raw edges of the casing so that turning is level with back opening.

## Skirt

Cut out and make up the skirt according to the kind of skirt you plan to have (see page 32). Remember that with a straight skirt or a pleated one any joins in the material must be hidden in the pleats.

Pin and tack skirt to line of piping round bottom edge of chair. Check that it is level. Remove cover and machine skirt in place. Neaten edges and oversew. Sew a popper to the overlap on the skirt where it goes behind the back skirt. The cover is now complete.

## Chairs without skirt

Small chairs often have their legs set in by about 3 cm from the outside edge of the chair. If you do not want a skirt to the cover, finish off in the following way.

Place the piping to the exact edge of your chair so that when you turn under the raw edges, only the piping is visible. Tack in place and remove cover from chair.

Take a piece of ordinary Rufflette tape and tack on the right side with the edge of the tape as close to the piping cord as possible. Machine all round. Machine the lower edge of the tape to the raw edge of the cover.

Put cover back on chair and draw up cords in tape to fit tightly under chair. The tape should not be visible at all. Tie the cords firmly and tuck between cover and chair.

## An armchair or sofa

### Measuring up

This is made easier with a little chart. Put all the measurements on it, including the tuck-in allowance. Take this with you when you are buying the fabric so you can see how a particular pattern will work out.

**The inside back** Measure from the piping at the top of the chair (A) to the seat, plus 2 cm at the top, and 15 cm for the tuck-in.

**The seat** From the point where it touches the back, plus 15 cm for the tuck-in, to the front (C) plus 2 cm.

**The facing** From C to D plus 2 cm either end for seams.

**The inside arm** From the seat plus 15 cm for tuck-in, to the bottom of the curve of the outside arm (F) plus 2 cm. Most chairs have arms that slope down towards the back, so check the measurement at the front end of the arm against the back end. You will need two inside arm pieces.

**The outside arm** From F (directly underneath the arm curve) to G plus 2 cm top and bottom for seams. Two pieces will be needed. Again check the measurements at the front end of the chair and at the back, and use whichever is the longer.

**Outside back** From A to the point of the skirt, plus 2 cm top and bottom.

**The scrolls** These can be cut out of wastage on the back piece, or arms.

**The skirt** Measure for the type of skirt you want (see page 32). As a general rule a finished length of 15 cm looks best for an average armchair.

Measuring up for a sofa is exactly the same although you will of course need more width for the back, the inside back, the seat and the front facing. When joining widths for a sofa never have a join at the middle. One complete width is used in the centre of each piece, and half a width or less placed to each selvedge side of this centre panel. These seams should correspond, so that the seams from the inside back meet exactly with those of the seat and with the seams of the outside back, divided merely by the piping. The seams on the front facing and the back of the sofa should also meet those of the skirt, if you are having a plain skirt with a pleat at each corner. These little details make your cover look very professional.

### Calculation chart

| Part of cover | Number of pieces | Size including turnings | Width | Total |
|---|---|---|---|---|
| Outside Back | 1 | 50 cm | 76 cm | 50 cm |
| Inside Back | 1 | 80 cm | 99 cm | 80 cm |
| Inside Arm | 2 | 56 cm | 89 cm | 112 cm |
| Outside Arm | 2 | 30 cm | 76 cm | 60 cm |
| Seat | 1 | 78 cm | 91 cm | 78 cm |
| Facing | 1 | 15 cm | 61 cm | 15 cm |
| Scrolls | 2 | out of outside back remains | | |
| Plain Skirt | 4 | 20 cm | 122 cm | 80 cm |
| Piping | | 14 metres | | 90 cm |
| Cushion | 2 | 61 cm | 56 cm | 61 cm |
| Cushion Gusset | 2 | 12 cm | 122 cm | 24 cm |
| **Total** | | 6.5 metres | | |

The secret of making a good loose cover is to fit it at every stage. It is easiest to work with the right side of the material facing you, so that you can see exactly how the pattern runs. Whether the pattern is small, geometric or large floral, it must flow in a continuous line from the top of the inside back, down across the seat or cushion, down the front facing and the skirt. The pattern on the arms must go towards the seat from the outside arm join, *not* from the back to the front scroll.

Do not assume that your chair has identical arms, and that the slope on the inside back is the same at both sides – treat each section separately.

### Cutting out

It is easiest to lay the material out on the floor or a flat surface near the chair to be covered. With the material spread out flat you can see exactly how the pattern will be placed. Cut out each piece as a rectangle measuring from widest point to widest point and from highest point to longest point. The final cutting away of surplus material is done when the cover is pinned on the chair.

One important point when cutting out concerns the cushion. If there is a cushion, remove this from the chair for ease in working but do not forget that any pattern on your material must be centred from the top of the cushion to the top of the back and not from the beginning of your tuck-in to the top of the back. The same applies to the inside arm pieces.

Cut out the inside back, two inside arms, two outside arms, and the front facing. Cut your scrolls out of the wastage from the back. It is wise to cut out the seat last so that if you make a mistake you can substitute calico for part of the seat piece if you have a cushion.

*Right* Armchair with straight skirt and piping.

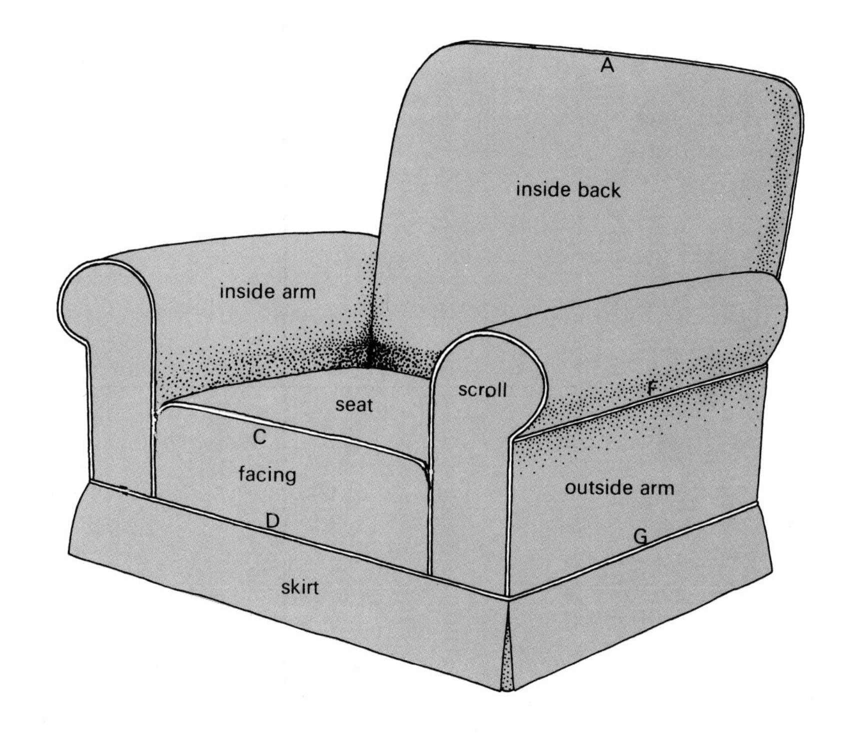

Should it be necessary to have a calico seat you should allow for a finished section 7 cm deep of main material which will be joined to the front facing. The remainder will be calico. Join material to calico by machine, neaten and oversew the edges, then treat this as one piece of fabric.

If you have miscalculated the amount of material and were planning on a pleated or gathered skirt you could rectify your mistake by having a plain skirt.

Check the amount of material you have left against your measurements for seat, skirt and piping. Cut out seat and skirt. Cut out and make up piping (see page 32).

## Making up the cover

Pin the scroll pieces in place on the chair. Carefully pin the piping in place round scrolls following the line of the piping on the upholstery, raw edge of piping to raw edge of scrolls, right sides together. Tack and machine.

Tack a piece of piping along the front edge of the seat piece so that the piping is the exact width of the seat, plus 2 cm each end. The actual piping cord in the 2 cm allowance must be cut away leaving the casing strip empty.

An easy way of doing this is to place a pin through piping cord and material about 7 cm away from where you will cut. Take hold of the cord only, pulling so that the casing gathers up as the cord is exposed. When you have exposed 2 cm of cord, cut it off. Smooth back the casing and you will find that the last 2 cm is empty and quite easy to machine over. This step must be followed every time a seam crosses a line of piping. If the cord is machined over and the cord shrinks when washed, the whole cover will be pulled by the piping. Machining over the cord may also break the needle.

Tack the front facing to the seat at the piping and machine in place. Oversew raw edges: always oversew each seam as it is completed as it is much easier to oversew at this stage than later when so many seams overlap each other.

The front facing can be joined to the seat after the inside arm pieces (9). Join the inside arm tuck-in to the seat (side) tuck-in. Repeat on other side. Join the inside back to back of seat as in diagram.

Place cover on the chair pushing the tuck-in down into place all round the seat. Smooth the inside arm pieces over the arm and pin into position on the chair. Place piping cord along edge of inside arm where outside arm joins. Tack and machine.

Re-position cover on chair, smoothing side tuck-ins to inside back piece across arm. Turn under tuck-ins of inside arm pieces over inside back ones. Pin from back edge round to front and down to seat. Place a marker pin at highest point of arm in front where it touches inside back.

With raw edges of piping and scroll material turned in, pin scroll to remainder of cover (10). Ladder stitch in place, easing any fullness at the top of the arm.

To ladder stitch, take needle through scroll making a 5 mm stitch. Take needle through outside arm material at exact point opposite where you came out of scroll, making a 5 mm stitch (11). Repeat whole way round.

If you find you have to have tucks on the arm these should be identically placed on both arms.

Remove cover and machine scrolls in place. Overstitch all raw edges.

Turn cover right side out and ladder-stitch inside back tuck-ins together. Turn cover to wrong side and machine along tacking line to marker point at the top of the arm, then taper seam out, away from tacking till at the bottom there is a 15 cm allowance, and seam meets other tuck-in seams. Trim off surplus material and overstitch raw edges. Clip seam round corners at top of arm, so it will lie flat.

Place cover back on chair and smooth into place. Position piping cord round all raw edges where back section will be joined. Pin and slip stitch back into place leaving one side open. This opening should be long enough for you to get cover on and off easily. Remove cover.

From the scraps of material take a piece 10 cm wide and as long as the back opening. Press in half lengthways. With the raw edges overlapping the piping of the opening by 1 cm, machine in place.

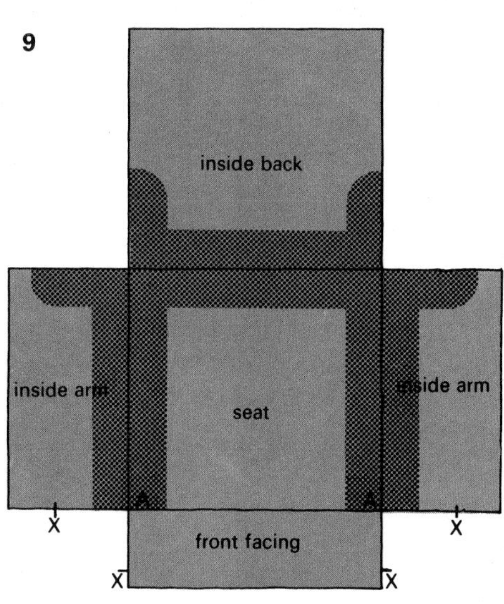


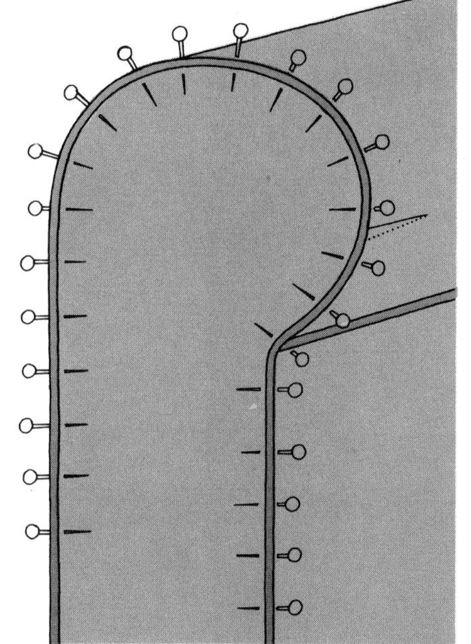


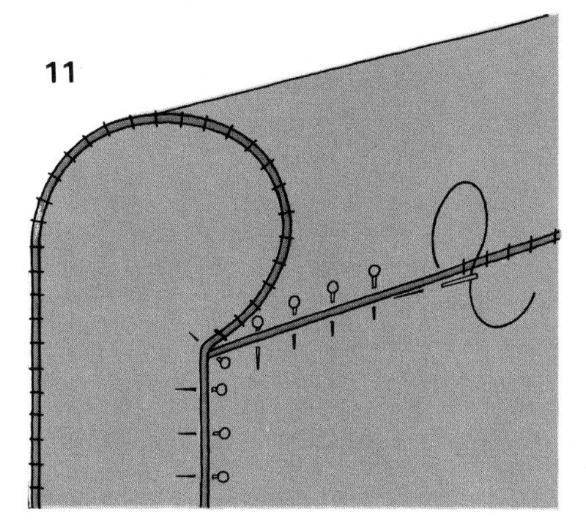


*Above* Loose covers for a sofa are made in exactly the same way as for an armchair.

*Right* Diagram 9: cutting layout; Diagrams 10 and 11: pinning and ladderstitching the scroll.

Turn this double piece of fabric away from the piping and machine through all thicknesses 1 cm away from piping cord. The 'bars' of the hooks and bars (by far the most satisfactory way of fastening your cover) will be sewn to this 'placket' at 7 cm intervals. The hooks will be sewn to the outside back.

## Skirt

Place cover on chair once more, and smooth carefully in place. Pin the piping for the skirt all round the chair (starting from the outside edge of the placket), 15 cm off the floor. A convenient method is to cut a piece of card the exact depth of the skirt, rather than fiddle around with a tape which slips and slides.

Prepare the skirt (see page 32).

Pin skirt to cover along line of piping, starting from outside edge of placket. At both ends of this line of piping, the cord should be cut off 5 mm shorter than casing, and casing turned under to face main part of cover. Slip-tack skirt in place.

Remove cover from chair and machine skirt in place. Trim seam allowance and oversew raw edges.

Sew on the hooks and bars evenly spaced, starting with the first one 5 mm above line of skirt. Replace complete cover on chair.

## Loose cover without skirt

You may not wish to have a skirt at all on your loose cover. In that case, cut the back, the front facing, and both outside arm pieces, measuring to the bottom of the chair, plus 2 cm for turnings. Make up the cover to the point at which you would attach piping for skirt.

Cut 4 pieces of material 15 cm deep and 2 cm narrower than each of the sides, back and front of the chair. Turn in a double 1 cm hem on each short side of the four pieces. Machine in place. Turn under one long edge 1 cm, then a further 2 cm. Machine hems. This forms the slot through which you thread the tape to anchor the cover down.

Pin each of these four pieces of material round the cover, exactly at the bottom of the chair. Make sure they fit, when turned under, between the castors or legs of the chair, lying flat against underside of chair. Slip-tack in place.

Remove cover from chair and machine, continuing the machine line across the single thickness of material at corners. Overstitch the raw edges of the cover carefully all round, including the corners. Press all raw edges up towards chair. Sew on hooks and bars.

Replace cover; slot tape through casing and draw up tight. Tie the tape and tuck up out of sight between cover and chair.

## Loose cover with fringe

Certain chairs look attractive with a heavy fringe round the bottom edge. In this case the chair would be finished off completely as just described for a cover with no skirt; the fringe should then be pinned on so that the bottom of the fringe lies evenly 1 cm above the floor or carpet. It would then be machined in place with a double row of machining at the top of the fringe.

## Box cushion

Boxes or ottomans can be invaluable for storage and they can be made to look very attractive with a loose cover.

Measure the length and width of the box. Add 5 mm to all four sides. Buy a piece of foam 5 cm deep and to the length and width of your measurements.

Foam nowadays is cut in standard sizes so you will probably have to cut it down to the right size. Mark off the width and the depth using a black felt tip pen. Place on a flat surface and cut with a very sharp carving knife but not one with a serrated edge.

The foam must be lined so that the top cover will sit nicely. It is also much easier to remove a lined foam pad from the cover as foam tends to 'stick'.

To line the box cushion, either use up old lining or buy new. You will need a piece for the top and for the bottom plus 1 cm seam allowance all round, and for the gusset enough widths the depth of the pad to go round plus 1 cm seam allowance top and bottom.

Cut out top and bottom, and the right number of widths for the gusset. Measure the four sides of your pad and join the widths together with 1 cm turnings, to form a 'circle' of material the exact measurement of your four sides.

Pin and tack one raw edge of the gusset to the raw edge of the top piece of lining. Machine together. Take the bottom piece of lining and tack to the other raw edge of gusset, leaving one side open for inserting the foam pad. Make sure that the corners align with the corners of the top piece. Leave one side open for inserting the foam pad. Machine.

Turn right side out and slip the pad in (you will discover why the cushion would be difficult to get in and out of its cover without a lining) and slip stitch the open sides together.

### Making the cover

For top and bottom, measure the width and length of your cushion plus 2 cm seam allowance on all sides. For the gusset, measure the width round the four sides and divide by the width of the fabric you are using to find how many widths you will need. The gusset pieces should be the depth of the cushion plus 2 cm seam allowance top and bottom, with the exception of one long side which should be 5 cm deeper, to allow for the zip opening. Measure for your zip down one long side. Remember to allow enough material for your piping. 46 cm should be adequate but if you allow less you will have too many joins.

Cut out the pieces for the cover, remembering the seam allowances all round, and mark the required finished size on wrong side of material.

Cut out and make your piping.

Pin piping to top of cover, right sides together and raw edges parallel. Snip piping at corners so as to be able to pivot the cover on the machine. Join the two ends of piping where they meet.

Repeat with piping on bottom of cover.

### Putting in the zip

Cut the wider gusset strip in half down its entire length. Machine these two pieces together with a 2 cm seam, oversew the raw edges and press open. Place zip in centre of seam. Tack and machine in place. Unpick seam over zip.

Measure the width of the four sides of

*Above* Sofa with box cushions and without skirt. The side bands tuck under the sofa and are pulled up tightly by tape slotted through a casing.

*Right* An ottoman with a box cushion. The ottoman has been covered separately and it has tightly fitting side bands, made in exactly the same way as for the sofa above.

the cushion and join together the gusset strips to make one continuous strip to go round exactly. If you have to cut off some of the strip containing the zip, cut off the same amount each end so that the zip is still placed centrally.

Pin and tack gusset to top and bottom pieces of cushion cover, all the way round, making sure that corners at the top are directly over corners on the bottom and open zip a little so you can turn the cover right side out. Clip the edges of the gusset at the corners for ease of working.

Machine top and bottom. Neaten all raw edges and oversew. Turn right side out and fit.

## Adding a skirt to your box cushion

Ottoman boxes can either have a cushion attached to the cover of the box or a separate skirt. If you make a skirt round the cushion you will not be able to reverse the cushion (turn it upside down when the top has become a bit soiled) so you can make the underside out of ordinary lining.

To the measurements you made for the original box cushion cover add the amount needed for the skirt depending on whether you are having gathers, pleats or a straight drop (see page 32).

Cut out the top and bottom piece for your cushion pad. Sew the piping round the top, and attach the gusset complete with zip, to top piece only.

Tack a piece of piping the whole way round the bottom edge of your gusset. With right side of gusset to right side of skirt, pin together. Tack and turn right side out to check on the fit.

Take the bottom piece of cushion cover and press in the seam allowance on all four sides. Pin this to the underside of the piping that holds skirt in place. Place your pins at right angles to the piping cord and fairly close together.

Open the zip, and turn cover inside out so that skirt is enclosed in the cushion cover, exposing the raw edges of the pinned seam. Tack carefully in position. Machine close to piping. Trim off excess material and oversew.

Turn right side out, press skirt, and insert foam pad.

To stop the cover moving on the top of the box you can sew small squares of Velcro to the bottom of the cushion at the corners. If the box was originally padded or upholstered you can sew the corresponding half of the Velcro to the padded surface. If the box is whitewood or made of non-valuable wood, stick on the corresponding piece of Velcro with suitable glue.

# Cushions

Cushions add both comfort and decoration to a room. They can be scattered on furniture, used as seat pads or used by themselves as floor seating. They can be any size or shape and made in virtually any type of material, including carpet offcuts, fur, leather or suede, lace, canvas work, patchwork, quilting, knitting, crochet and macramé. Decorations such as embroidery or appliqué can look very original and attractive. You do not need much fabric to make a cushion cover so you can buy remnants or use offcuts from other projects. If the offcut is not large enough you can add a border of another fabric or make each side of the cover from different fabrics. Cushion covers may have plain edges or you can incorporate a frill or piping, or add a fringe or cord to the edges when the cover is finished. Conventional shapes for cushions are squares, rectangles and circles. Other attractive shapes are hexagons, hearts, triangles and bolsters. Conventional cushion shapes can usually be bought as filled pads which you simply insert into your cover.

## Cushion pads

Use ticking for feather fillings to prevent them from working through, and foam sheeting for foam chippings. For other fillings use cheap fabric such as calico, casement or curtain linings.

With the exception of foam sheeting, make the casing for the pad to the same size and in the same way (but excluding any edge finish) as the main cover. Turn the cover right side out and poke out the corners with the point of a knitting needle. Insert the stuffing, poking into the corners well so that the cushion is neither flabby nor hard. Fold under the edges of the opening and machine-stitch or oversew together.

For a casing made from foam sheeting, cut out the foam as for fabric. Using small scissors, bevel (trim at an angle) the side faces of the sheeting. Apply adhesive to these edges, omitting about 7.5 cm in the same position on each piece for an opening. Place the edges together and secure with clothes pegs until dry. Fill the cover with foam chippings, apply adhesive along the edges of the opening and stick together.

### Fillings

**Feathers** are the most luxurious type of filling for pads – they are easily available in ready-made pads but more difficult to obtain for making your own. However, you can re-use feathers from old pillows.

**Foam** – made from rubber or polyether – is easily obtainable either in ready-made pads or for making your own. You can buy foam in block form or as chippings. If you use chippings it is best to make the casing for the pad from foam sheeting for a smooth finish.

**Wadding** – either kapok or synthetic is easily obtainable. Synthetic wadding is the only type of cushion padding which may be washed (never dry clean it because it retains dangerous fumes).

Cushions can be any shape or size and can be decorated with almost anything. The cushions below are fabric painted (see page 144), trimmed with cord, and embroidered.

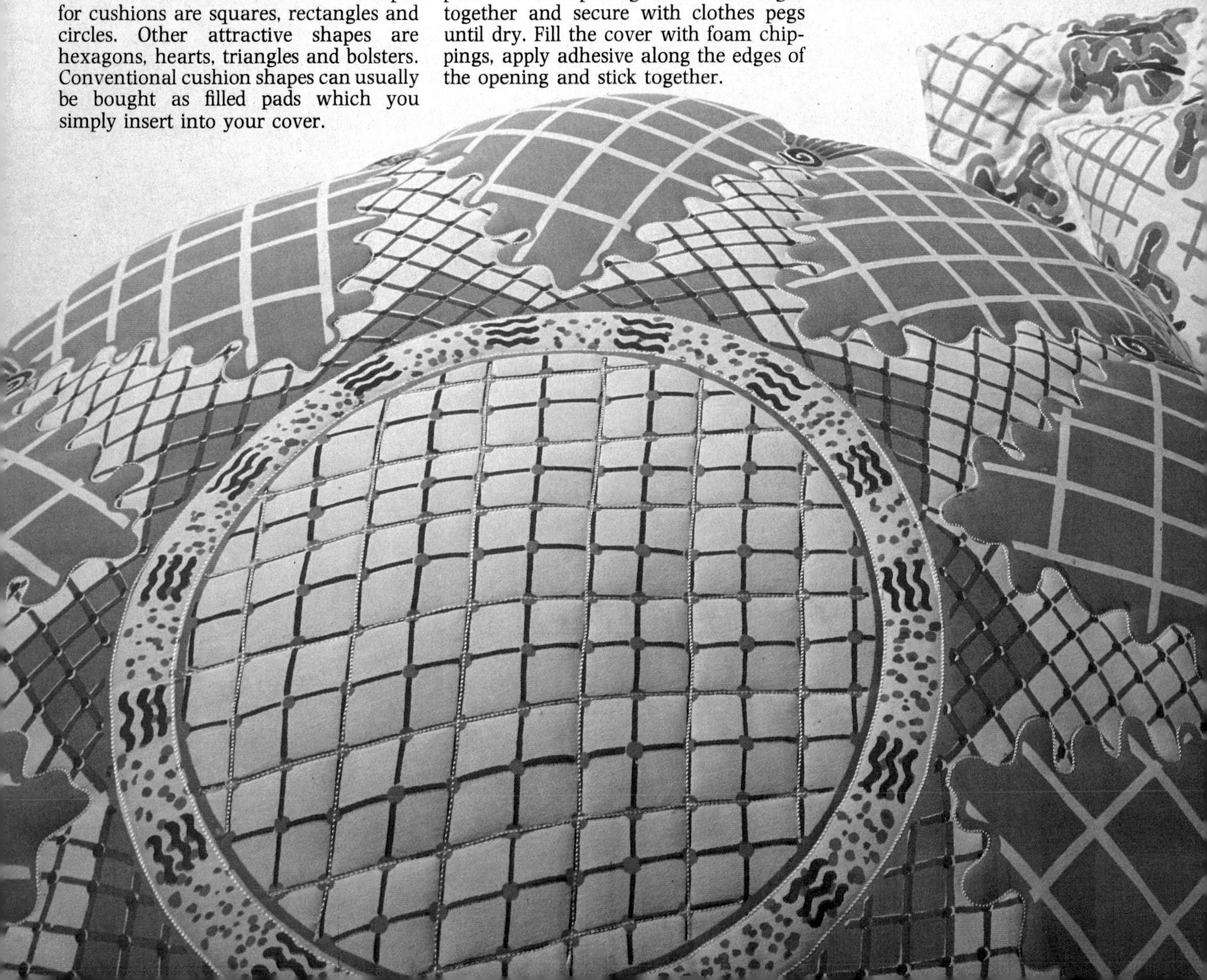

## Making the cover

Even if you are making a simple square or rectangular cushion it is worth making a paper pattern first so that you can estimate the quantity of fabric required and cut out and position any prominent design accurately. If straight lines and right angles are involved it is easier to draw the pattern on graph or dressmaker's paper; otherwise trace or draw on greaseproof, parcel or shelf lining paper. Avoid intricate curves as these will be difficult to sew.

In all cases after you have drawn the shape of the cushion draw another line 1.5 cm outside the first one, to allow for seam turnings. Cut out the pattern on the outside line.

### Circles

If you have a round plate, cake tin or tray of suitable size, use this as a template to draw a circle on paper. Alternatively, you can draw a circle by using a pencil, string and a drawing pin. Cut out a square of paper with sides equal to the required diameter of the circle. Fold in four. Working on a suitable surface to hold a drawing pin, place the pin at the corner which was the original centre of the square (point A on diagram 1). Tie the string round the pin and round the pencil, so the length between them is half the diameter length (i.e. the radius). Holding the pencil upright, draw a quarter circle from B to C (1). Draw a second line 1.5 cm outside this to allow for seam turnings. Cut round the second line and open out the paper to give the full circle.

### Hexagons

Make a circle on paper using the drawing pin method as described above. Place the drawing pin anywhere on the edge, and keeping the same distance between pin and pencil as you used for the radius, make a mark on the circle edge. Move the pin to this line and draw another line on the edge. Continue in this way all round and then draw straight lines between the marks to form the hexagon (2). Cut out along these lines.

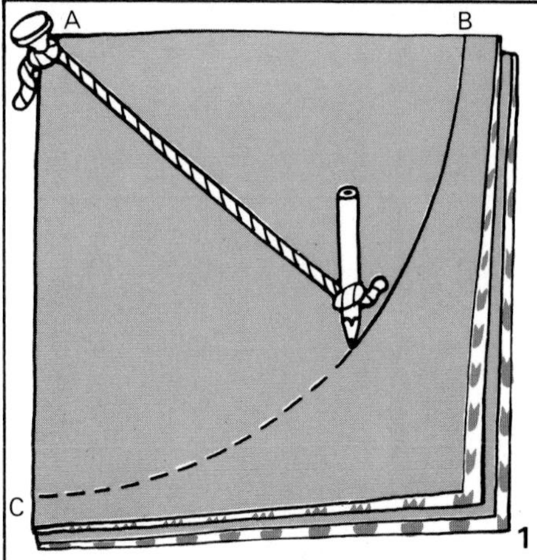


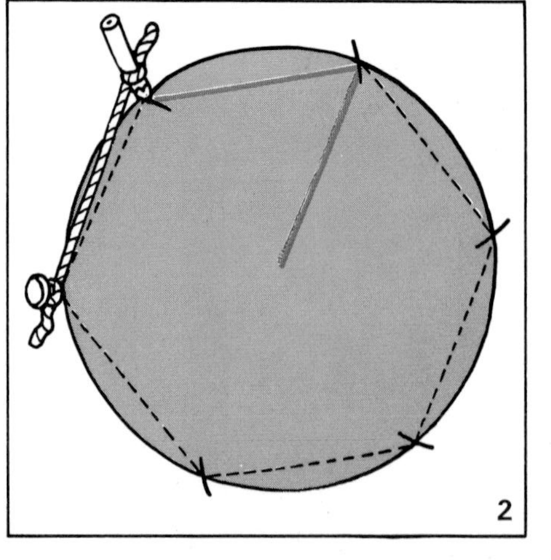


*Above right* Scatter cushions, appliquéed and embroidered with motifs from the loose cover fabric.
*Right* (1) and (2): drawing a circle and hexagon. (3): estimating fabric for an unusual shape – the tail will be made from offcuts. (4): stitching a square cushion.

*Above* Rich embroidery panels bordered with bands of striped cotton fabric. Cushions such as these are usually backed with plain fabric.

## Estimating fabric

Mark the centre of the pattern with a line across it vertically and horizontally. Measure the overall length and width of the pattern on these lines or on lines parallel to them if longer (3). Allow two pieces of fabric to these measurements for back and front. If you have trouble in calculating this, cut a piece of paper to the same width as the fabric you will be buying. Lay the pattern on it and draw round the edge. Reposition the pattern away from the first outline and measure the length of paper used up to give the amount of fabric you need. If you want to use fabric which has a pattern or motif which should be centred or matched at seams, remember to allow for this when positioning the pieces. If you intend to add piping or a matching frill, mark in the pieces for these too (see page 50).

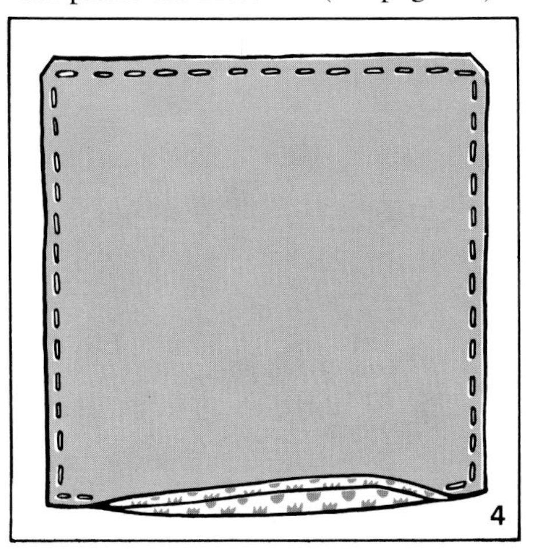


## Cutting out

If you are making both sides of the cushion cover from the same fabric and it does not need centring or matching at seams, you can cut them together. Fold the fabric in half parallel to the selvedge. Pin the pattern to the fabric with the centre vertical line parallel to the selvedge and cut round the edge. Unpin the pattern.

If you are making the sides of the cushion from different fabrics or wish to position the fabric design accurately, it is wisest to cut the two pieces separately. Pin and cut out the pattern on a single thickness of fabric with the centre vertical line parallel to the selvedge and mark on the pattern the position of the design to be matched on the other piece. Pin the paper on the second piece of fabric, using the mark to match the design and cut it out.

## Making up

Place the pieces of fabric with right sides together. Mark off the position of the opening you will need for inserting and removing the pad. Pin and tack the remaining section 1.5 cm from the edges. Remove the pins. Starting at one corner of the opening, machine-stitch along the line of tacking (4). Trim any corners diagonally and clip into the seam turnings along curves. Turn the cover right side out and finish the opening.

## Cushions from unusual fabrics

### Carpet

This is not easy to sew by machine and is best hand-stitched. If the edges of the carpet are not already bound, smear adhesive along the backing to prevent fraying. Place wrong sides together and oversew or blanket-stitch the edges with linen thread and a carpet needle. Alternatively insert eyelets along the edges and lace the sides of the cushion together.

### Leather

Most leathers and suedes can be machine-stitched provided you use a spear-pointed needle and synthetic sewing thread. Place any pins holding the pieces together on the seam turnings so that they do not leave noticeable holes on the cover.

### Knitting, crochet and macramé

These are easiest to make if hand-stitched using matching yarn. Finish the openings by slip stitching.

### Fur

Shave the pile away from its backing along the seam turnings. Machine-stitch using a piping foot and a spear-pointed needle if it is real fur.

## Cushion fastenings

Always make the opening long enough for the cushion to be inserted into the cover easily.

You can fasten the opening in a number of ways, including hooks and eyes, press studs, ties, Velcro, slip stitching or with a zip fastener or a button.

### Button and loop

You must decide to do this type of opening before cutting out the cushion cover. Cut the front of the cover from the pattern in the usual way. For the back, fold the pattern in half on the vertical centre line. Fold the fabric in half lengthways and place the pattern on it so that the fold of the pattern is 2.5 cm from the fabric fold (5). Cut round the sides. Cut along the fabric fold turning under both these edges to the wrong side for 1.5 cm and stitch. Lay the front of the cover on

5

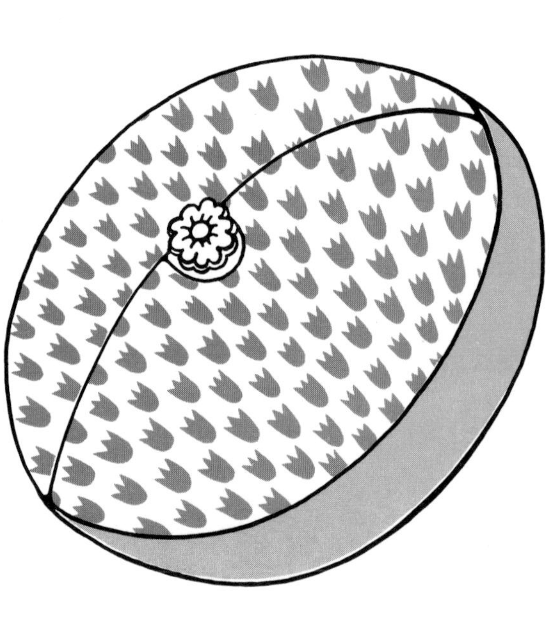

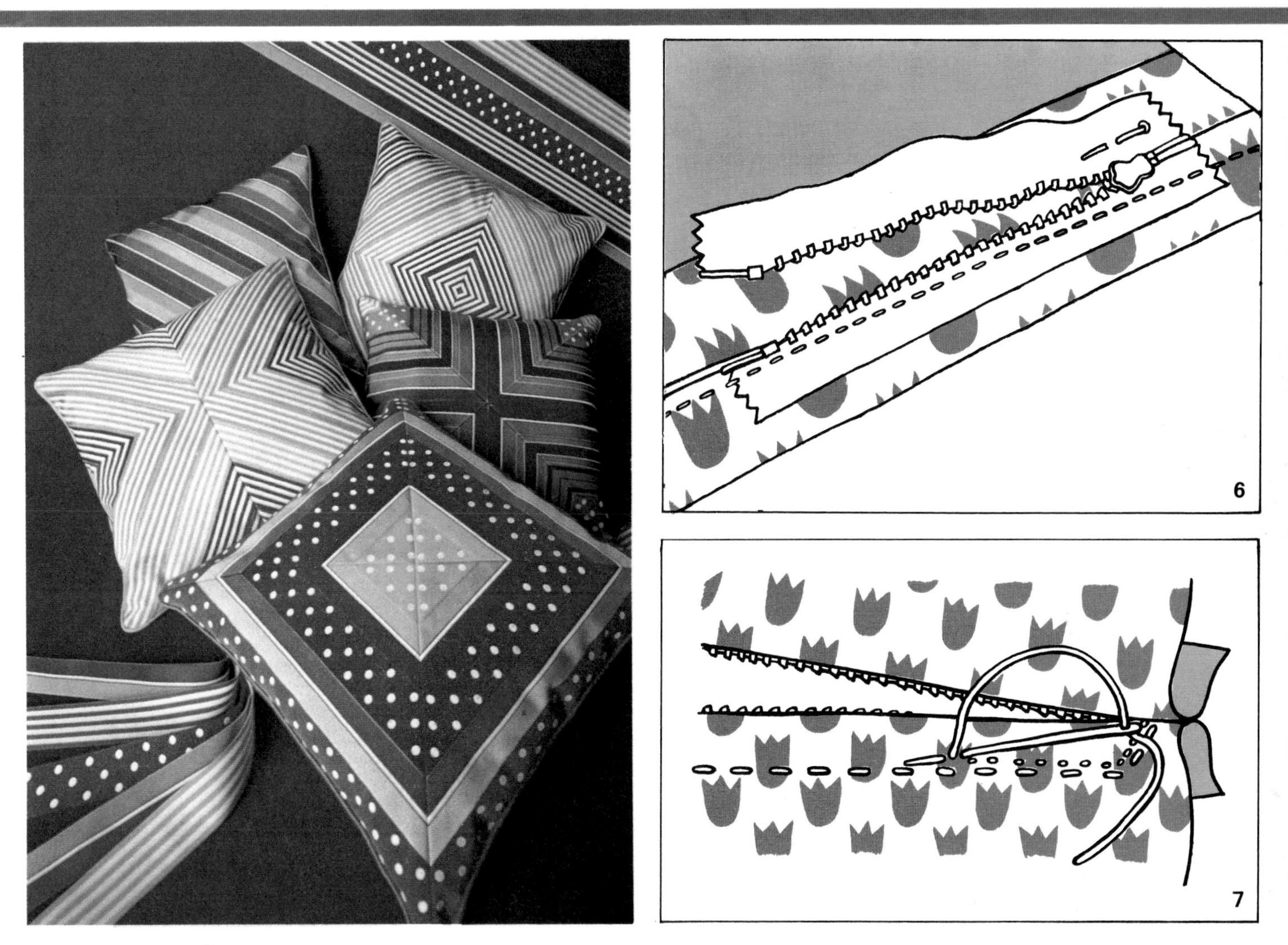

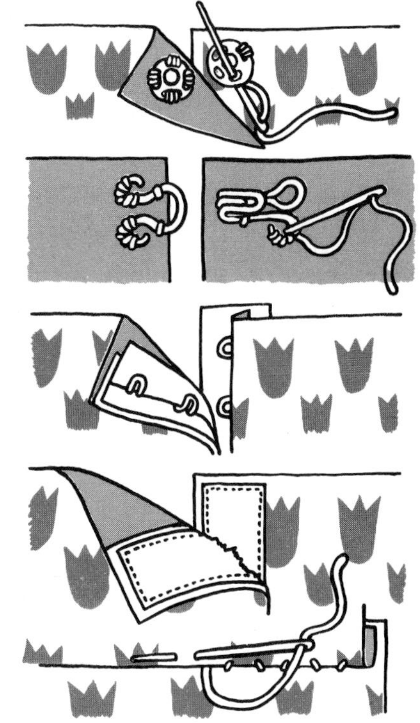

*Far left above* Old neckties are appliquéed to a plain fabric semi-circular cushion.
*Far left below* Button and loop cushion with inset details of cutting out fabric and attaching loop.
*Above left* Striped and spotted fabrics cut into geometric shapes.
*Above right* Inserting a zip by machine (6), and by prick-stitch (7).
*Left* Fastenings: press-stud, hook and eye, hook and eye tape, Velcro, slip stitching.

a flat surface with the right side uppermost. Place one half of the back on it so that the right sides are together and the raw edges are level. With right sides together, place on the other half of the back so that the stitched folds overlap. Pin, tack and machine-stitch round the edges of the cushion cover. Turn right side out. Fasten the opening with two press studs or with a button and loop.

## Zip fasteners

Buy a zip in a suitable weight (dress-weight for most fabrics, heavy-weight for heavy fabrics) and matching colour, to the length of the opening. It does not matter whether you insert it before or after making up the cushion cover.

The following method may be hand-stitched or machine-stitched if you fit a piping foot to the machine.

Fold under the seam turning on each side of the opening. Press the folds lightly then open the zip and place it face down along one of the folded sides of the opening (not the piped edge) so that the inner edge of the teeth aligns with the fold line. Keeping the seam turning flat, back-stitch or machine-stitch the zip tape to it close to the teeth (6).

Close the zip for about 5 cm. Place the fold of the free edge of the opening over the zip so that it touches the opposite fold of fabric. Pin and tack the tape parallel to the fold at a distance of 5 mm from it. Machine-stitch, or if you prefer to sew by hand, prick-stitch (7), along the line of tacking, starting and finishing the stitches at the fold. Fasten off securely. If the edge is piped, work the stitching along the gulley between the piping and fabric. See also pages 50–51, inserting a zip with piping.

# Decorative edges

## Frilled edge

You can buy ready-made frills such as broderie anglaise or you can make them from fabric strips to match or contrast with your cushion cover. A suitable depth for the frill is 2.5 cm–4 cm plus 3 cm for the hem and seam turning. For the length of the frill, measure the perimeter of the cushion and allow 1½ times the length for thick fabric and twice the length for fine fabric.

If using a fine fabric you can eliminate the hem by using the fabric double. Cut the frill to twice the required depth plus 1.5 cm seam turnings along each edge.

**Making the frill** If you need more than one piece of fabric to make the length of the frill, join the pieces with plain seams. Oversew the edges together and press to one side. Join the ends of the strip to form a continuous length (8).

If you are making the frill from single thickness, make a hem along the outer edge taking a first turning of 5 mm and a second turning of 10 mm; hand-sew or machine-stitch in place.

If you are making the frill from doubled fabric, fold the strip in half lengthways with wrong sides together.

Run gathering stitches along the strip 1.5 cm and 1 cm from the top edge, working through both thicknesses on doubled-fabric frills. With right sides together and raw edges level, place the frill onto one section of the cushion cover, drawing up the gathering so that the frill fits. Arrange the gathers evenly, placing slightly more fullness at the corners and ease the frill round (9). Tack 1.5 cm from the edge. Remove the gathering threads and machine-stitch the frill along the side of the opening only.

Keeping the frill pointing inwards, place the second section of the cover on top with right sides together. Stitch round, excluding the opening. Turn the cushion right side out and finish off the opening.

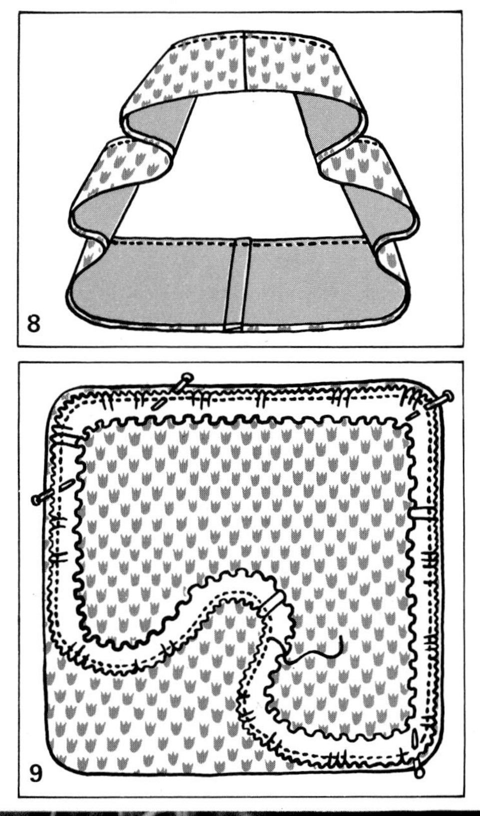


*Left* Cluster of cushions made from fabric remnants.
*Right* (8) and (9): making a frill.
*Below* Cushions with decorative edges.

## Corded edges

You will need a length of cord to the perimeter of the edges on which it is to be applied plus 2.5 cm allowance for joins. If the cord is not pre-shrunk, allow extra and wash before using.

Place the cord round the edge of the finished cushion so that it covers the seamline and the ends of the cord fall on one side, not at a corner.

Starting and ending 2.5 cm from the ends of the cord, sew it to the cushion passing the thread through the cord and taking tiny stitches along the seamline of the cushion (10).

To join the ends of the cord, unravel the strands for 2.5 cm. Trim 2.5 cm from two strands of one end and the same amount from one strand of the other end (11). Twist the remaining ends together neatly (12) and oversew to hold in position. Stitch this section of cord to the cover as before.

## Piped edges

Piping is made by covering cotton cord of 5–10 mm diameter in fabric which is then inserted between the sections of the cushion cover when they are stitched together.

You will need an amount of piping cord equal to the perimeter of the edges on which it is to be applied plus 2.5 cm allowance for seams and joins. If the piping cord you buy is not pre-shrunk, allow extra and wash before using.

To make the piping you need a bias strip the length of the perimeter of the cushion and the width of the circumference of the cord plus 3 cm. To cut the bias strips, start with fabric where one edge is parallel to the selvedge and the adjoining edge is at right-angles to it. Fold the fabric diagonally so that the edges are level (13) and crease the fold lightly with your fingers. Unfold the fabric and draw along the fold line lightly in pencil or in tailor's chalk.

Draw lines parallel to the first one, leaving the required width of the bias strip between them (14), until you have the correct length of piping when the pieces are cut and joined together.

Before joining the strips check that the short edges are on the straight grain. With right sides together, place the ends of the strips together (15). Machine-stitch 5 mm from the raw edges. Press the seam open and trim off the protruding corners (16).

With the right sides of the fabric together, place one edge of the strip level with the edge of one section of the cushion cover. Cut into the edge of the strip for 1.5 cm at corners so that it turns smoothly (17). Pin and tack the strip to one section of the cover 1.5 cm from the raw edges. To join the ends of the strip, fold back the ends diagonally so that they butt together. Finger-press the folds, then open out and place with right sides together so that the fold lines meet. Stitch along the fold lines and trim off the protruding corners.

Lay the piping cord along the centre of the wrong side of the strip and butt the ends together. Fold the strip over it so that the raw edges are level. Clip into the corners as before. Tack through all layers close to the edge of the cord (18).

Place the second section of the cover on the first with right sides together; pin and tack close to the edge of the piping all round except for the opening.

Stitch round the tacked sides, keeping the needle close to the edge of the piping. Trim the seam turnings 5 mm from the stitching. At the opening, stitch the piping to one section of the cover only. Remove all the tacking, turn the cover right side out and finish the opening.

**Inserting a zip** Place the open zip face down on the seam turning so that the inner edge of its teeth aligns with the stitched line of the piping (19). Tack and stitch along this line. Press the turning inside the cover. Close the zip for about 5 cm. Fold under the turning on the free edge of the opening and place the fold over the zip so that it touches the piping. Pin, tack and stitch the tape to the fold close to the zip teeth (20).

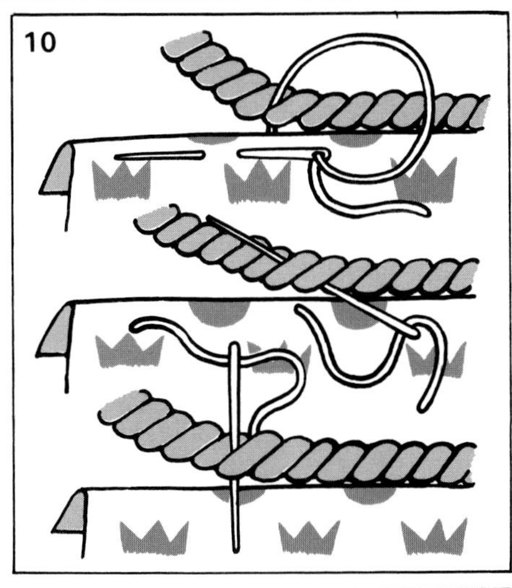


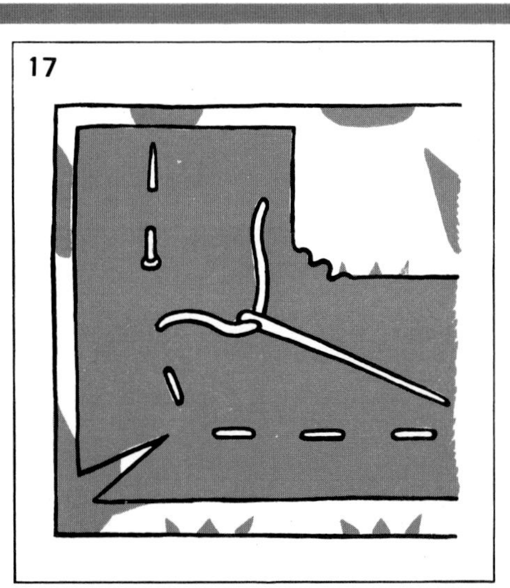

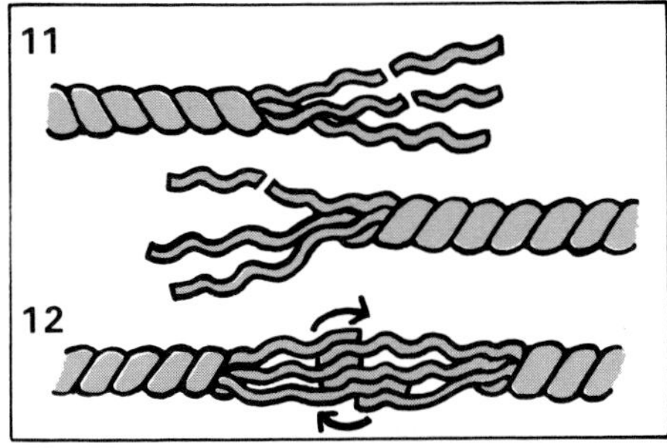


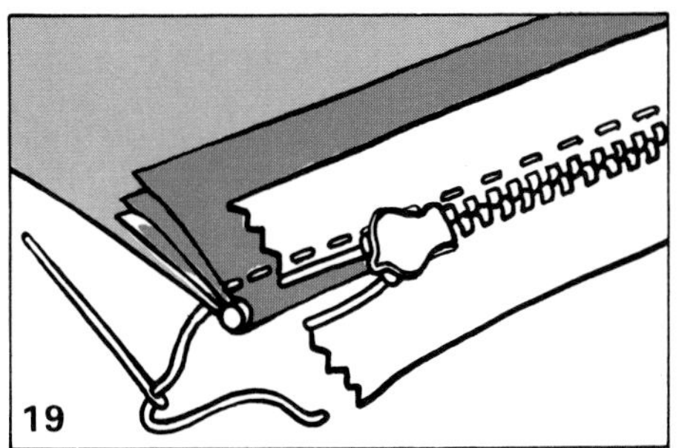

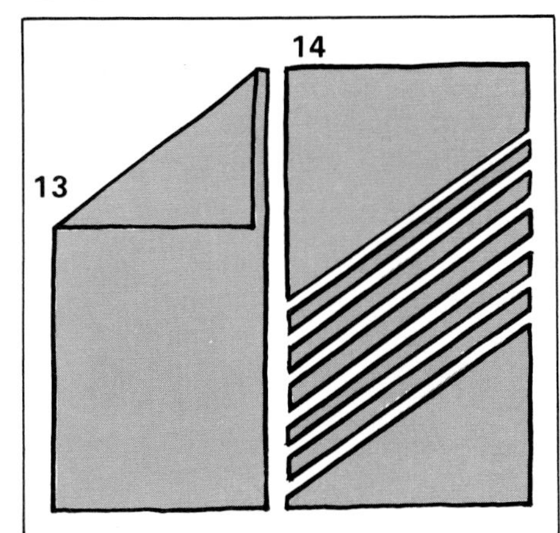


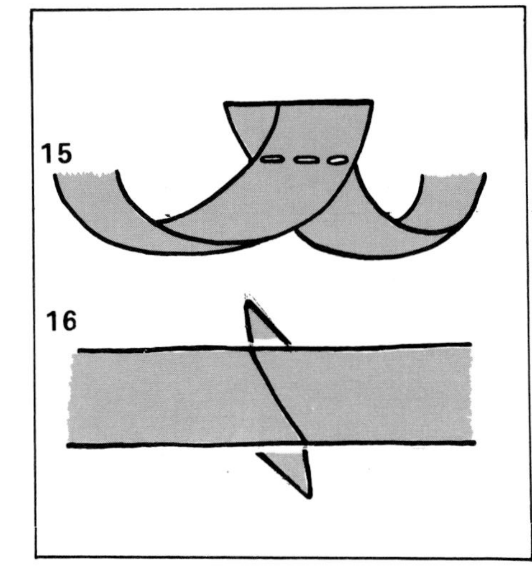


*Far left* Cushions with corded edges.
*Above left* (10, 11, 12): applying cord.
*Below left* (13, 14, 15, 16): making bias strips.

*Above* (17, 18): inserting piping at corners.
(19, 20): inserting a zip with piping.
*Below* Floor cushions are made as larger versions of square cushions.

## Bolsters

Bolsters look best if piping is inserted round the edges of the ends or if cord is attached to the seamline of these edges after making up.

### Estimating fabric

For the circles at each end of the bolster allow two pieces of fabric to the required diameter plus 3 cm.

For the main section allow one rectangle of fabric, with width equal to the circumference of the bolster ends plus 3 cm (sides A–B) and the length of the bolster plus 3 cm (sides C–D).

### Making up bolsters with plain ends

Work a line of stay stitching 1.5 cm from the A–B edges of the main section. Clip into these edges to the line of stitching at 1.5 cm intervals.

With right sides together pin one of the clipped edges to one of the circles – the clips should open out as you do so (21). Pin, tack and stitch the edges C–D together for 2.5 cm at one end where they meet, parallel to the raw edge (this may not necessarily be 1.5 cm – it depends on the accuracy of your calculations). Press the seams open and neaten their edges.

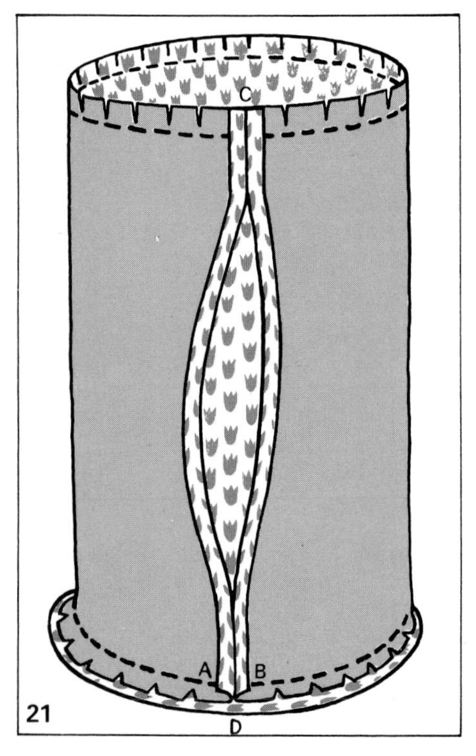


*Above* Diagram 21: making up the bolster. A–B represents the circumference.

Fit the other clipped end of the bolster to the second circle in the same way. Tack and machine-stitch round both ends with the clipped sides uppermost in your machine. Trim the edges to 5 mm of the stitching.

Turn the cover right side out and finish the opening.

## Sag bags

These can be made as giant versions of bolsters. The main difference is in the filling, which is made from polystyrene granules. Make up the casing for the cover allowing an opening just large enough to insert a cardboard tube. Tie the opening of the sack of granules round one end of the tube and insert the other end of the tube into the opening of the casing. Pour the granules down the tube until the casing is three-quarters full. Remove the tube and sew up the opening securely. Make the main cover in the usual way but with a bigger opening for inserting the filled casing.

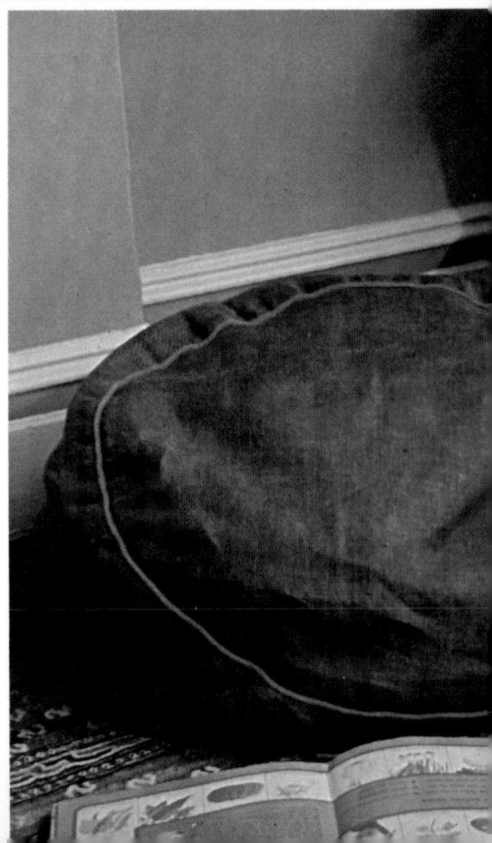

## Pillows

These are made larger than the pillow for ease in putting the pillow in and out. They are also usually cut in one piece which incorporates a pocket flap instead of an opening. French seams are used as they enclose the turnings and prevent the fraying that results from constant washing. Make pillowcases from sheeting or any washable fabric of suitable width.

### Making up

Measure the pillow. The width of the fabric should be the length of the pillow's shorter sides plus 5 cm, and its length twice the length of the longer sides plus 22 cm.

Make a hem on the wrong side along one short edge of the fabric, taking 4 mm for the first turning and 1.5 cm for the second turning. Repeat on the opposite edge but this time taking 4.5 cm for the second turning.

With wrong sides together, fold down the edge with the narrower hem for 10 cm. Bring up the opposite edge to meet the first fold. Stitch down the long sides of the case, taking 5 mm turnings. Trim the turnings. Turn the case so that the wrong side is facing out and then turn the pocket so that it is over the edge with the wider hem. Press the seamlines so they are exactly on the edges and then stitch each side again taking 1 cm turnings. Turn the cover and pocket right side out.

## Duvets

Make these in the same way as cushion covers but allowing 2.5 cm seam turnings along the edges of the opening. One of the neatest and easiest ways of closing the opening is with no-sew press studs.

To make the opening with press studs, stitch the cover and fold down the turnings of the opening to the wrong side. Fold under the raw edge for 5 mm and machine-stitch. Apply the press studs at 10 cm intervals along the opening.

*Above left* Frilled duvet and frilled pillowcases. Frilled pillowcases must be made in two sections plus the pocket because of the frill. The frill must be incorporated all round one of the sections and the pocket added before stitching both sections together (right sides together) along the remaining 3 sides. French seams are not used because of the frill.

*Left* Sag bags made with the bolster technique.

# Upholstery

Modern upholstery falls into two categories – that which uses traditional materials for the padding such as horsehair, and that which uses foam rubber, thereby eliminating the need for many of the traditional techniques needed with horsehair which have made upholstery a skilled craft.

Although most modern furniture is made with foam-rubber padding, horsehair should usually be used to re-upholster furniture originally made with it (this covers most items up to 1939). It is sometimes possible to substitute foam rubber or plasticized horsehair for real horsehair but this should not be done on anything of antique value and it should be borne in mind that although easier to apply, foam rubber generally only lasts for about five years whereas horsehair stuffing correctly done can last for more than 15 years.

If you have never done any upholstery, the best items to begin with are drop-in-seat dining chairs or, if using foam rubber, over-stuffed dining chairs. You can also re-cover this latter type of chair if it has horsehair, but if the upholstery itself needs attention it is wisest to have it expertly done.

## Equipment

As in all crafts there are special tools for upholstery. For small, one-off projects, however, you can usually substitute more common tools.

**Tacks** All materials are applied to the chair frame with tacks (never nails as these split the wood). For a complete re-upholstery job you will need 12 mm improved tacks (these have large heads) for attaching webbing and 1 cm fine tacks for attaching the other layers.

**Tack hammers** Tack hammers have small heads designed to hit the tack without also hitting the wood around it. You can usually substitute a small carpenter's hammer.

**Tack lifter or chisel** To lever out the tacks holding the old cover, you will need a mallet with a wooden head and a ripping chisel (an old blunt wood chisel can be used) or a tack lifter.

**Scissors** You will also need sharp scissors for cutting fabric.

**Tape measure**

**Webbing stretcher** To apply woven webbing so that it is really taut, you will need a webbing stretcher. This is not expensive to buy or you may be able to borrow one. You can substitute a small wooden block but the job would be more difficult. No special tool is needed to apply rubber webbing.

Two over-stuffed chairs ready for re-upholstery. If horsehair is to be used again for the chair on the left, it is best to have the chair professionally upholstered as shaping a seat from scratch is quite difficult. The chair on the right was originally stuffed with horsehair but has since been upholstered with foam.

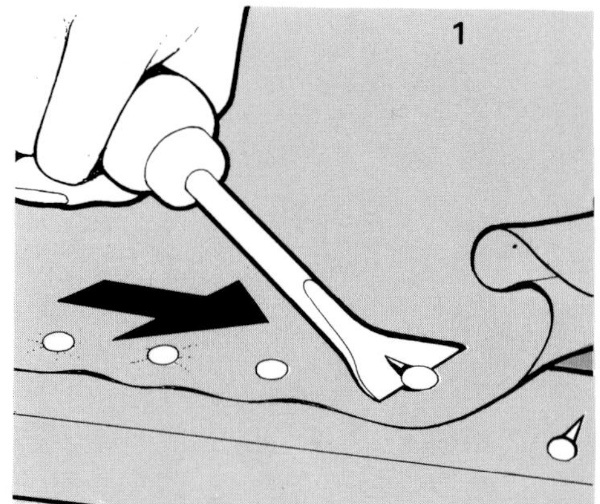


*Left* A set of drop-in dining seats, upholstered with checked fabric.

*Right* (1): using a tack lifter. (2–7): applying webbing.

*Below* Cross-section of an overstuffed chair showing the different layers. From top to bottom:

1. top cover
2. wadding
3. calico
4. horsehair
5. hessian
6. fibre
7. hessian
8. lacing cord
9. springs
10. webbing

## Materials

**Webbing** This forms the basis of all upholstery worked on an open frame. It is applied to the frame in strands which span it in both directions. If one strand is loose or broken, the rest of the upholstery sags. There are two types of upholstery webbing: the traditional type woven from jute or flax, and modern rubber webbing which is stretchy and mostly used with foam padding.

To estimate the amount of webbing required, measure across the frame between its outside edges and allow 5 cm extra for woven webbing. Allow enough strands to place them so that the space between each strand is equal to the width of the webbing and add 15 cm to the total for woven webbing.

**Hessian** For covering the webbing when using horsehair padding to prevent it from falling through. It is not necessary with foam rubber. Use proper upholstery hessian with 275 g to 90 sq cm. Allow enough to cover the frame with 2.5 cm margin all round.

**Horsehair** This is expensive and not easy to obtain in pure form although you can often buy it recycled or mixed with other animal hair. For a drop-in dining seat you need about 450 g – you may be able to re-use some of your old stuffing but it usually needs augmenting. To apply the horsehair you will need about 2 metres upholstery twine which is waxed to prevent it rotting, and a curved needle.

**Foam** Buy seating-grade foam in an appropriate thickness – usually 7.5–10 cm. Make a paper template to the seat shape plus 2.5 cm all round and then cut out the foam with a sharp knife (not a serrated one). To apply the foam to the seat you will need adhesive suitable for foam and 4 strips of calico fabric 10 cm wide to fit each side: allow an extra 2.5 cm length for the pieces to fit the side and front edges of the foam.

**Calico** Used to cover both foam and stuffing, shaping it and making a smooth foundation for the top cover. Measure the old cover and allow a piece about 7.5 cm larger all round.

**Wadding** This forms additional padding between the calico and the top cover. Allow a piece to the size of the seat.

**Top cover** Use a fabric recommended for upholstery. Easy fabrics to use are plain velvets, brocades and some satins, and you can also use canvas-work. Avoid striped patterns for a first project because they are difficult to keep straight.

Do not try to re-use the old cover because there will not be enough margin for attaching it.

Estimate the amount required for the top cover as for the calico.

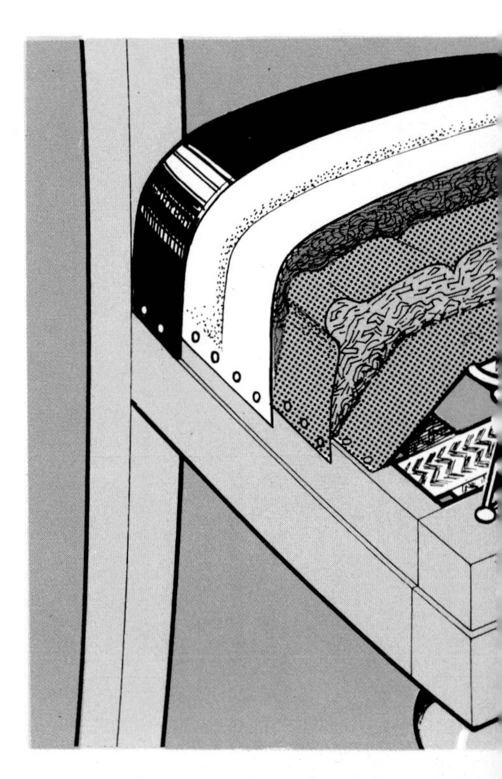

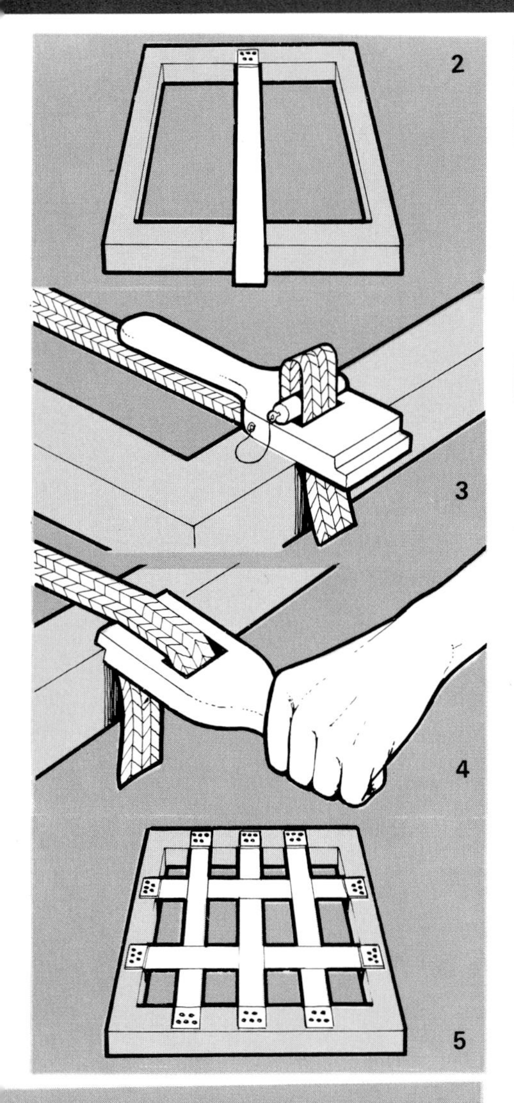


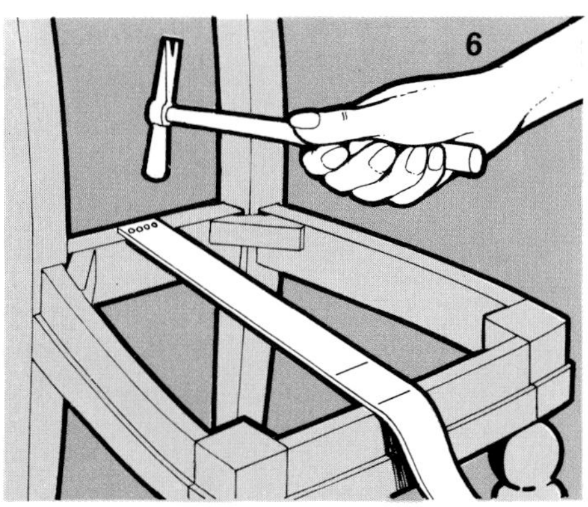

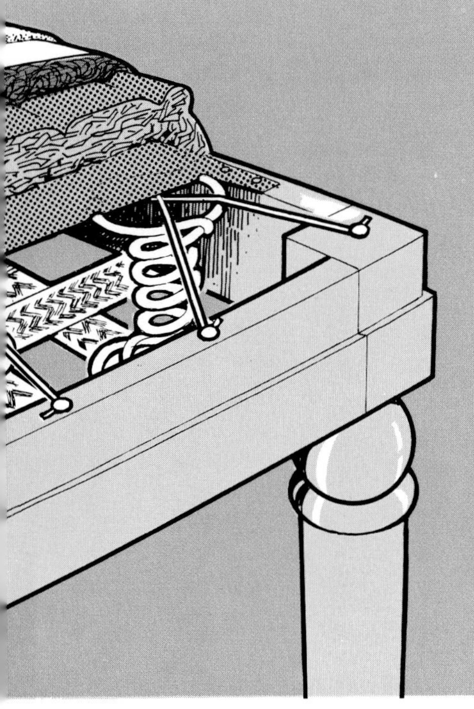

**Braid** Many over-stuffed and pin-cushion chairs are finished with braid which covers the tacks and raw edges round the top cover. Choose a similar width to the old braid in a colour to match the top cover and buy enough to fit the edges plus 5 cm for turnings. To apply the braid you will need a clear adhesive.

**Bottoming** This is black fabric, often linen, which is applied to the underside of the seat to finish it neatly. You may be able to re-use the old fabric but if you have to buy new, allow the same amount as you have taken off plus about 2.5 cm all round.

# Basic techniques

## Removing old materials

To remove the tacks holding the layers of old materials, hold the tack lifter or chisel parallel with the side of the frame you are working on and place the tip of it against a tack head (1). Tap the handle smartly with the mallet until the tack works loose and then prise it up. Remove all tacks in this way, always driving with the wood grain and not across it, or you may split the wood. Do not be tempted to save time by banging some tacks hard into the wood if they are difficult to remove because they may get in the way of new tacks.

## Applying woven webbing

Working straight from the roll to avoid waste, turn up the end for 2.5 cm. Place the webbing in position on the frame so that the fold is just more than halfway across it towards the outside edge. Insert one tack through the fold in each corner and one in the middle. Insert two more on the inside edge to make a W-shape (2). Holding the web stretcher with the handle away from you, insert the webbing in a loop through the slit from underneath. Insert the peg into the loop (3). Turn the handle towards you (4) and adjust the webbing for length so that it is taut across the frame. When correct, hold the webbing flat on the frame, using the stretcher like a lever on the side. Insert three tacks in a straight row through the single thickness along the centre of the frame. Cut off the excess webbing leaving 2.5 cm overlap. Fold this back level with the tacks and insert two more to form another W-shape. Repeat for the remaining strands, interweaving crosswise strands before attaching. On frames where the back of the seat is narrower than the front, splay the webbing out at the front so that the strands are equally spaced along the front edge (5).

## Attaching rubber webbing

Place the webbing in position on the frame so that the cut end is halfway across the wood. Apply with four tacks placed so that their heads are completely flat on the webbing (6). Rubber webbing must be stretched by $\frac{1}{10}$ th. To do this, make a mark on the frame halfway across the opposite edge. Lay the webbing across the frame without stretching and mark it to match. Measure back from the mark to the tacks and divide by 10. Measure this amount back from the first mark and make a second mark. Stretch the webbing until this mark corresponds to that on the wood and tack down (7). Cut off the excess webbing outside the tacks. Repeat for each strand, interweaving crosswise strands.

## Temporary tacking

Whenever attaching materials to the frame it is wisest to temporary tack them first. This means hitting the shank of the tack only halfway down into the frame – it will hold the materials in position securely but is easy to remove if you have to make adjustments later on. The tacks can easily be banged home when you are quite satisfied with their position.

## Drop-in seat

### Materials

Woven webbing
Hessian
Stuffing
Calico
Wadding
Top cover
Tacks
Bottoming

### Tools

Webbing stretcher
Tack hammer
Mallet and ripping chisel or tack lifter
Scissors

### Removing old materials

Remove the seat from the chair. Remove the bottoming and top cover. Check the webbing – if it is a different colour where a strand is moved, it is about to rot. If the padding is flabby and lumpy remove it too.

### Webbing

Attach the webbing (see page 57).

### Hessian

Cut a rectangle of hessian on the straight grain to the overall size of the seat plus 2.5 cm all round. Turn up the back edge for 2.5 cm and place it centrally on the frame, over the webbing, so that the fold is uppermost and at least 5 mm from the outer edge and an equal amount overlaps at each side. Insert a tack through the fold at the centre, stretch the hessian to each back corner and tack through double thickness. Insert more tacks between them at 2.5 cm intervals. Pull the hessian to the front edge, keeping the grain straight, and insert a tack at the centre through the single thickness only. Stretch to the front corners, keeping it straight and taut from the back edge, and insert temporary tacks. Put more temporary tacks at 4 cm intervals in between. Check that the hessian is straight and taut, adjusting as necessary, and hammer the tacks completely home. Fold up the excess and tack down, placing the tacks between those underneath (8).

Turn up one side edge of the hessian so that the fold is at least 5 mm from the outer edge of the frame and tack down as the back edge. Stretch it to the opposite edge and tack down as the front edge.

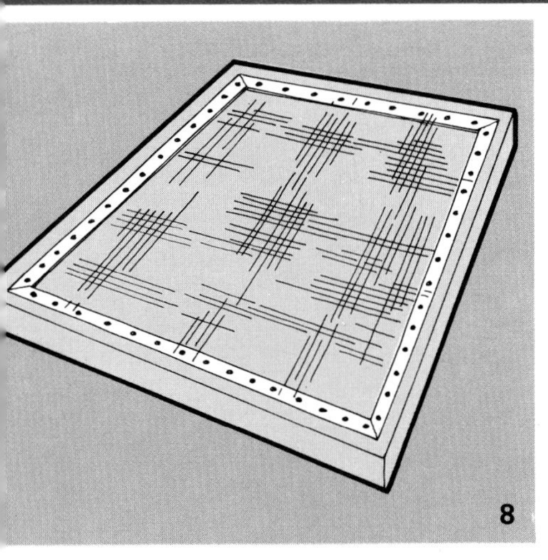


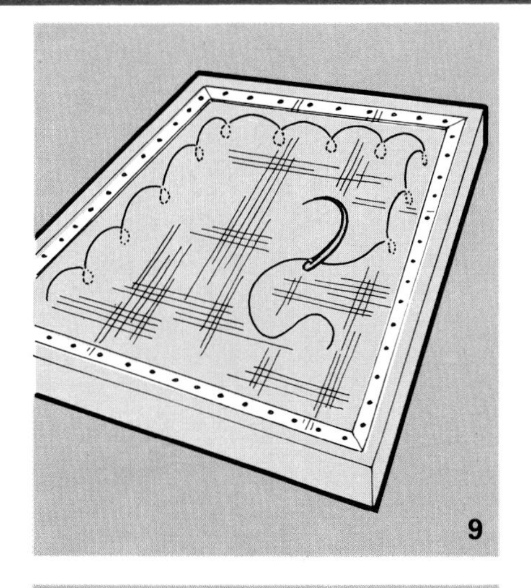


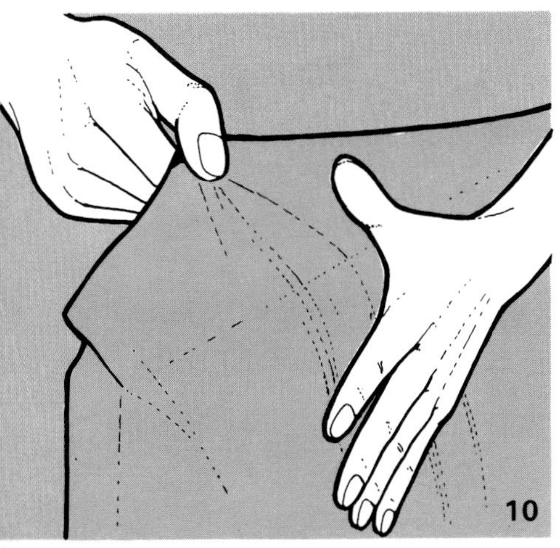


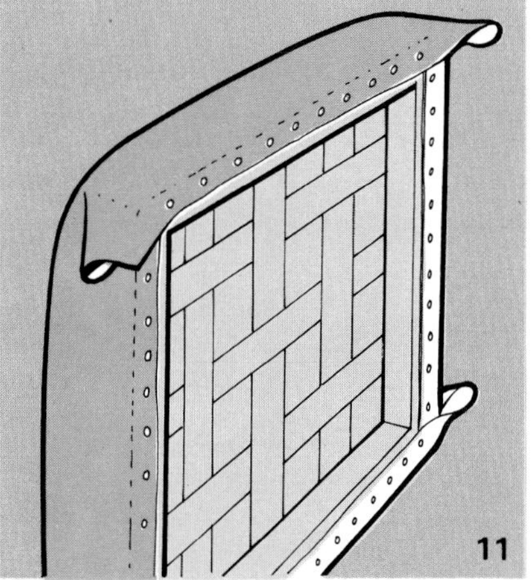


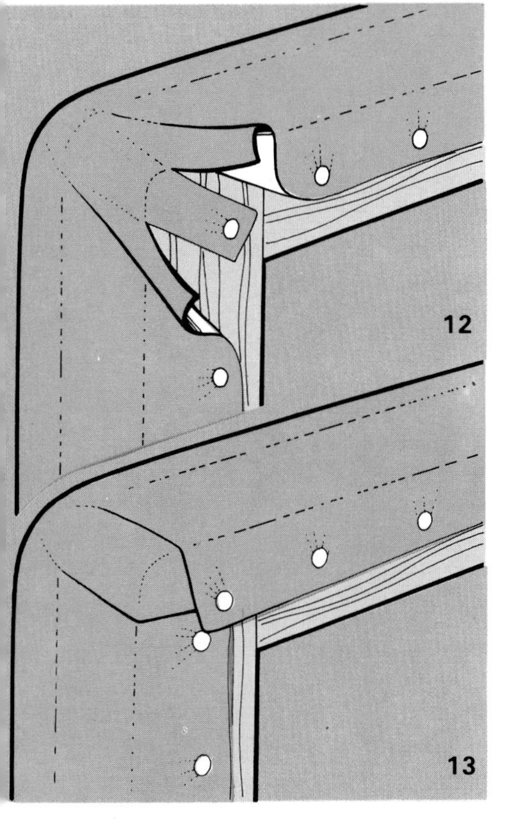


*Far left* A drop-in dining seat covered with satin-striped brocade, a strong furnishing fabric which wears well. Dressmaking fabrics are usually too loosely woven for upholstery. Stripes can be difficult for beginners to set straight.

*Above and left* Diagrams 8–13: upholstering a drop-in seat.

## Horsehair

A series of twine loops must be made into the hessian to hold the hair in place. These are called bridle ties. Thread the curved needle with 1 metre of twine. Secure it with a slip knot near one corner of the hessian base and work round, making back stitches about 2.5 cm long and leaving loops large enough to insert two fingers (9). Finish off by tying the end of the twine to the previous loop.

Tease out handfuls of hair and insert under the loops until tightly packed and extending to the edge of the frame. Insert more into the middle to make a dome. The stuffing should appear quite high and fluffy until you compress it with the palm of your hand.

## Calico lining

Lay the calico flat on your working surface and place the seat, stuffing side down, on top. Bring up the calico on the back edge of the frame and attach through single thickness to the underside with temporary tacks placed 10 mm from the edge and 2.5 cm apart to within 5 cm of the corners. Turn the seat so that it is resting on its back edge, smooth the calico over the stuffing to the front edge and then smooth it over the frame to the underside (10). Starting at the centre and working outwards to within 5 cm of the corners, apply temporary tacks so that the calico is quite taut and there is no looseness when you run your hand across it (the stuffing will flatten considerably as you complete the process). Temporary-tack one side edge in the same way as the back edge, and the other side edge as the front edge (11).

Working each corner in turn, pull the calico diagonally over the edge of the frame to the underside. Tack down once in each corner. Fold the fabric into pleats which point towards the corner and press the folds with your fingers. Lift up and cut away the excess fabric inside the pleats (12), refold and tack down (13).

Look at the shape of the stuffing critically – it should be domed and balanced on each side. Run your hands across it to check for lumps. If necessary, remove some tacks and even it out. You can often even it out at the corners and along the edges by poking a pointed instrument such as a smooth skewer or a knitting needle through the calico, hooking it round some stuffing to move it. Check that the calico is smooth and unwrinkled; if necessary adjust it by moving and re-tacking.

## The main cover

Lay the wadding, skin side down, over the calico and trim if necessary so that its edges are above those of the frame. Then apply the top cover in the same way as the calico, ensuring that any patterns are centred and straight. Trim any excess fabric to within 1.5 cm of the tacks.

## Bottoming

Turn under the edges of the bottoming so that the folds are 5 mm from the outer edge on the underside of the frame. Tack down, placing the tacks 2.5 cm apart. Replace the seat in the chair frame.

# Overstuffed seat

## Equipment

Tack hammer
Mallet and tack lifter or chisel
Scissors
Razor blade

## Materials for foam upholstery

Rubber webbing
Foam rubber shape
Adhesive
Calico
Wadding
Top cover
Braid
Bottoming
Tacks

## Materials for re-covering horsehair seats

Calico
Small amount of horsehair
Wadding
Top cover
Braid and adhesive
Tacks
Bottoming

## Removing old materials

Turn the seat upside down and remove the bottoming and top cover. Turn the seat right way up and remove the wadding. At this stage you should be able to tell by feeling whether the padding is foam or horsehair and whether it needs attention. Check the webbing carefully too. If you have hair stuffing which is quite firm but which has lost its dome shape, remove the calico lining to expose a layer of the stuffing. Tease out some of the stuffing, reshape and replace it, adding more stuffing if necessary (14). Apply new calico, wadding and top cover as described for foam upholstery.

If the padding is foam, it should probably be replaced, so strip the chair down completely.

## Webbing

Attach the webbing to the upper side of the frame (see page 57).

## Foam

If the chair has small high sections ('horns') at the front corners, saw these off level with the rest of the frame. Mark a border 5 cm wide round the edge on

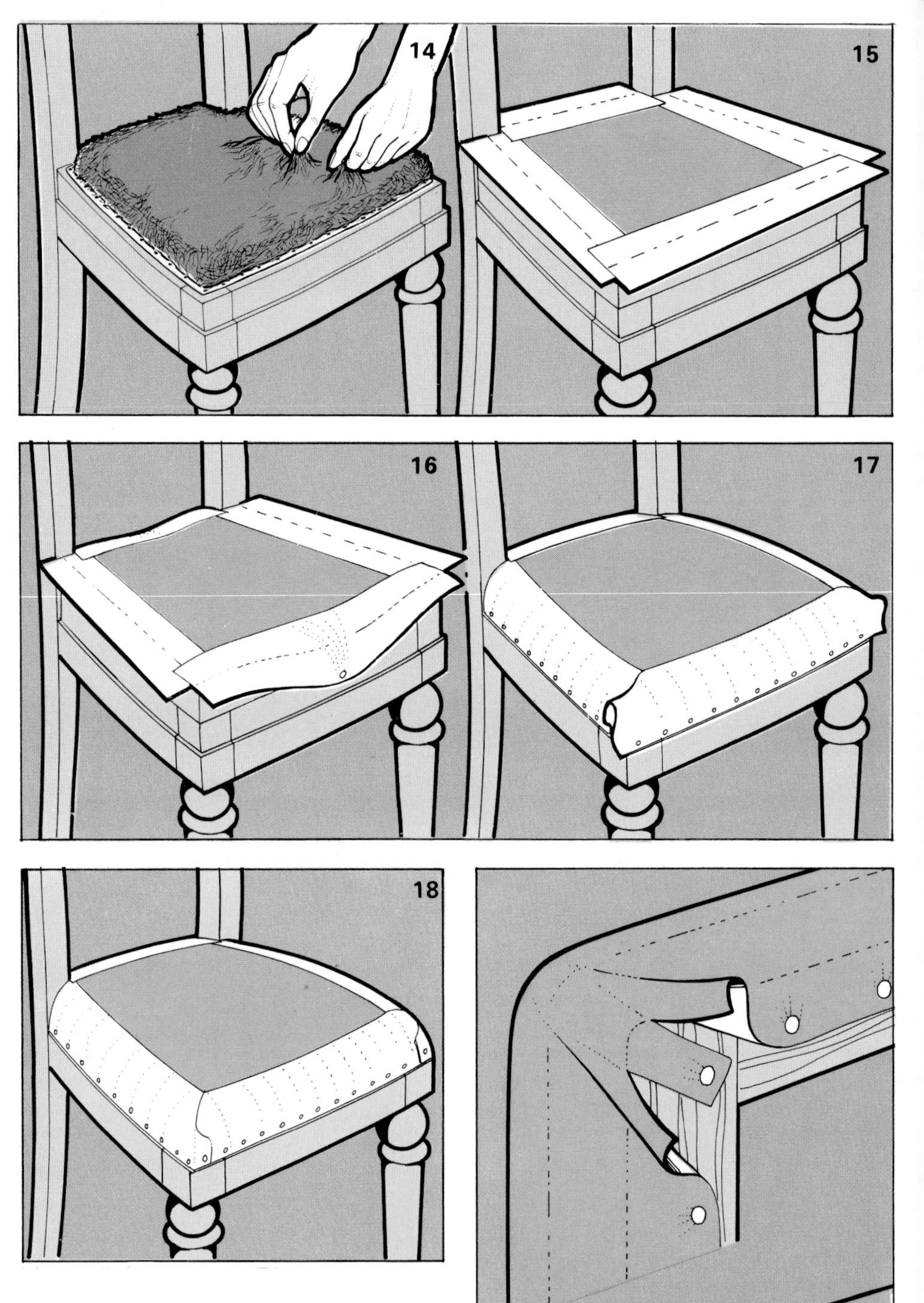


*Above* (14): teasing horsehair. (15–18): upholstering with foam. (19): working a round corner.

*Right* An overstuffed chair covered with dralon velvet, a strong fabric which can be wiped with a damp sponge for cleaning.

the side of the foam which will be placed uppermost on the seat. Apply adhesive to cover the border completely. Cut 4 calico strips 10 cm wide, to fit the back edge and 2.5 cm longer than the side and front edges of the foam. Fold the calico strips in half lengthwise and, when the adhesive is tacky apply the strips so that the lengthwise fold lines are level with the edge of the border and the ends of the strips overlap at each front corner.

Place the foam on the seat and cut it diagonally at the back corners for the depth of the upright sections of the frame. Squash the foam to each side of the uprights. Trim away the calico strip on the back edge to fit between the uprights (15).

Roll under the side of the foam on the front of the chair and pull the calico strip down so that it is flat on the side of the frame and gives a firm rounded edge to the foam. Temporary-tack it at the centre, placing tacks 15 mm from the top of the wood (16). Repeat on the back and on each side of the chair.

Return to the front and add more tacks at 2.5 cm intervals, rolling the foam under as you do so (17). You will find that the foam rises from the seat in the middle as you progress – this will be rectified when the calico lining is in place. Tack down the sides in a similar way. Pull the fabric round at the corners and tack; cut off the excess (18).

## Calico lining

Place centrally over the foam and temporary-tack to the side face of the frame at the centre back. Smooth it across the foam and temporary-tack to the side face at the centre front. Return to the back and tack the calico in position to within 5 cm of the uprights, placing the tacks at about 2.5 cm intervals and just below the line of tacks holding the calico strips.

Keeping the calico straight and taut but not strained, smooth it to the front. Then smooth it away from the centre and tack 5 cm from one corner. Repeat on the opposite corner. Fill in with more tacks placed at 2.5 cm intervals. When you run your hand across the seat, the calico should be smooth without wrinkling or puckering.

Tack down the sides in a similar way, keeping the grain straight and working from the centre towards the corners.

If the front corners are rounded, pull the fabric down diagonally and tack. Fold the excess fabric on each side in pleats to meet at the corner (19). Cut away excess fabric from inside the pleats and then tack down the pleats. This is the same method as for the drop-in seat.

If the front corners are square, pull the excess fabric down firmly at the sides and then round to the front. Tack down (20). Fold the excess which is now on the front into a pleat which lies on the corner. Cut away the excess fabric from inside the pleat and then tack down (21).

At the back uprights, fold the fabric back diagonally from the corners so that the fold touches the upright (22). Cut in from the corner of the fabric up to the fold (23). Take each triangle that this forms and pull down over the foam to the side face of the frame so that the corner is wedged between the foam and the upright. Fold each edge of the triangle into a pleat which lies in line with the upright, cut away the excess fabric from underneath and tack (24).

When you are satisfied with the fit of the calico, hammer all the tacks down.

## Wadding

Cut a piece of wadding to cover the seat and sides of the foam. Place it over the foam, skin side down and cut out squares at the back uprights and at the front so that it lies flat over the corners.

## Top cover

Lay this over the wadding and apply as the calico cover, placing the tacks on the underside of the frame or just above the show-wood, according to the style of chair. When you have completely tacked it down, trim off the excess fabric 15 mm from the tacks if on the underside, or as close to the tacks as possible if just above the show-wood.

## Applying braid

Starting at a back corner, place the end of the braid right side down and pointing towards the front corner. Tack down with one tack. Smear adhesive along the wrong side of the braid for about 15 cm, fold it so that it is right side out and stick down to cover the tacks and raw edges of the cover (25). Continue sticking it round the frame. Insert temporary tacks at intervals to prevent it from slipping while the adhesive dries. At the end, cut off the braid with 15 mm to spare, fold under and stick down.

## Bottoming

Turn the chair upside down and lay the bottoming across the frame so that it is centred. Working on the back first, fold under the raw edge so that it is 5 mm in from the outside edge of the frame. Tack down, working from the centre to within 5 cm of the legs, placing the tacks at 4 cm intervals. Pull the fabric to the front edge, keeping it straight and taut and tack down. Tack the sides.

At the legs, fold back the fabric diagonally so that the fold touches the inside of the wood. Cut in from the corner to the fold (26), turn under the triangles on each side of the leg and tack so that the folds touch the wood (27).

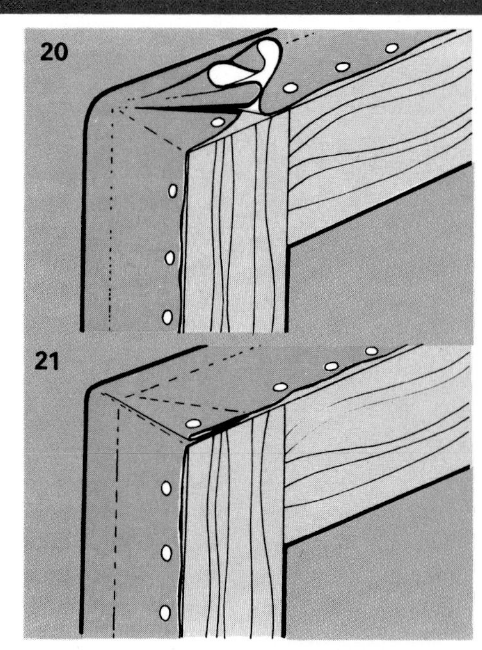


*Right* (20, 21): working a square corner.

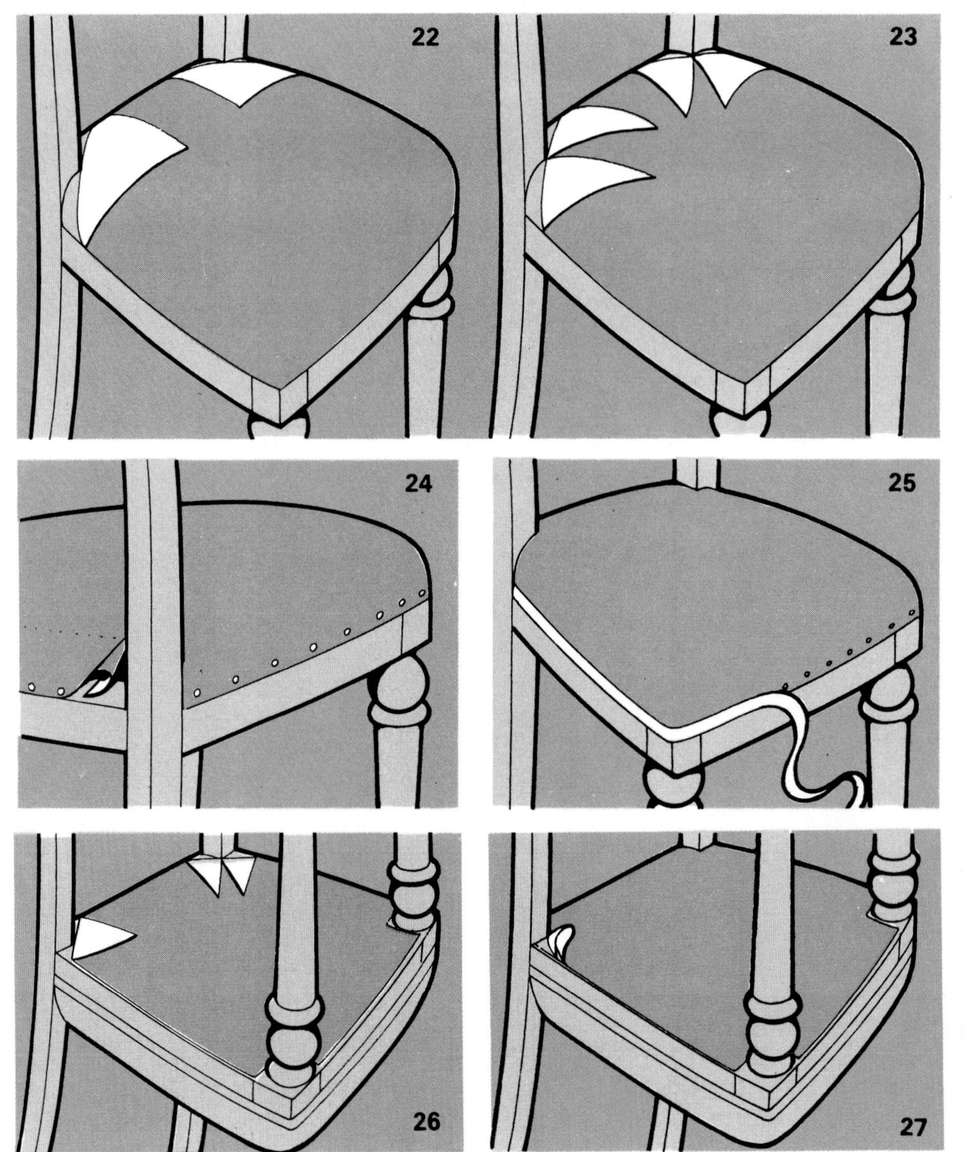


*Below* (22–24): working the back corner. (25): applying braid. (26, 27): bottoming.

# Pin cushion seat

The materials and method of upholstering these are similar to drop-in seats but because all the layers are applied to a narrow rebated ledge on the chair frame itself, great care must be taken in stripping and applying the tacks and in protecting the show-wood surrounding the ledge. To cover the tacks and raw edge of the top cover, you will need a piece of braid to fit the perimeter of the seat plus about 15 mm and some adhesive.

## Removing old materials

Do this as for a drop-in seat. Check the wood on the rebated ledge carefully and fill or repair if it is cracked or broken or if it is full of old tack holes.

## Webbing

Apply the webbing (see page 57), but do not turn back and tack the second edge until turning back the hessian edge (this saves the space of a few tacks).

## Hessian and horsehair

Apply these as described for drop-in seats.

## Calico lining

Lay the calico over the stuffing and tack the centre of the back edge to the rebate, placing the tack the width of a tack head from the outer edge of the rebate to allow for the tacks that will hold the top cover. Stretch the lining to within 5 cm of the back corners and temporary-tack. Fill in with more temporary tacks at 2.5 cm intervals. Smooth the calico over the stuffing to the front, pulling it quite taut. Temporary-tack at the centre and then 5 cm from each corner. Fill in with more tacks as before. Tack the sides in the same way, adjusting the stuffing and the tacks until the lining is quite smooth and taut. Run your hands over the stuffing to check that it is quite smooth. Stand back from the seat to check that it is even and dome-shaped. If necessary, add more stuffing through the corners, hooking it into place with a smooth skewer or knitting needle.

Pull the corners diagonally until taut and tack down, adjusting any nearby tacks if the fabric is now puckered. Hammer all the tacks home and trim off the excess calico close to them.

## Wadding

Cut the wadding to the seat shape and place skin-side down over the calico.

## Top cover

Apply as for the calico lining but place the tacks 15 mm apart so that the heads are just inside the outer edge of the rebate. If you have trouble in hammering the tacks completely down without also hitting the show-wood, use a nail punch for the final stage (i.e. temporary-tack in the usual way and then place the tip of the punch on the tack head and hammer the end of the punch to drive the tack down).

Use a craft-knife or razor blade to trim the excess fabric as close as possible to the tacks.

## Braid

To apply the braid, place the end flat on the back of the seat so that its outer edge is level with the inner edge of the show-wood. Temporary-tack the end in place. Apply adhesive for 15 cm along the underside of the braid and stick it down, keeping it straight and pressing firmly. Continue round the seat easing round or mitring corners. Remove the temporary tack, fold under the second end and stick down to cover the raw edge of the first end.

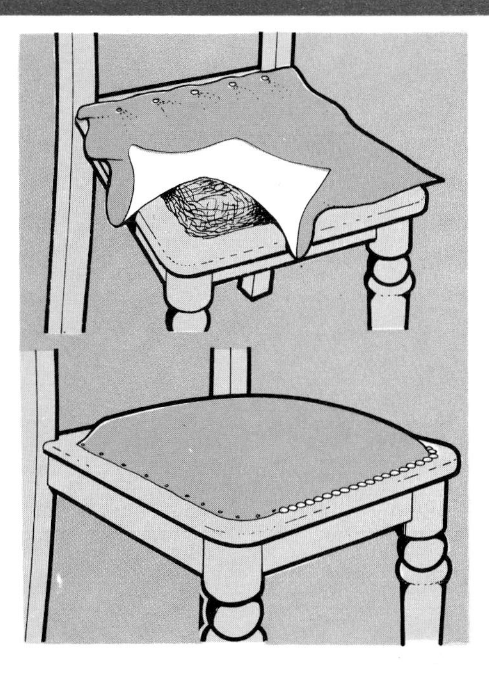

*Top* Applying calico lining to a pincushion seat.

*Above* Applying decorative tacks outside the working tacks at the edge of the top cover. This is an alternative to braid.

*Below* A pin cushion chair, trimmed with braid.

# Caning

Chairs to mend, chairs to mend – one of the old cries of London, and even right up to the 1950s you could still see plenty of travelling chair caners and rush seaters in the streets of many towns. Now they have all disappeared so people have to do their own caning and rushing. Cane and rush have the great advantage of fitting in happily with both old and modern houses and the craft has become extremely popular.

## Materials and equipment

**Cane** for chair seating is imported from South-east Asia and is the hard bark of the rattan cane. It is available in sizes from 1 to 6. For the six-step traditional pattern, two different sizes are used: no. 2 and no. 4 are the most common and suit a chair that has holes 1 cm apart from the centre of one hole to the centre of the next. If your chair has holes that are closer, use finer cane, but if the holes are farther apart, use thicker cane. Approximately 50 g cane is required for an average chair seat.

*Left* A cane chair in need of re-caning.

*Right* The same chair, stripped and re-caned.

You may use the cane either damp or quite dry. Some caners prefer one way and some another. Dry cane is brittle and is easily broken, especially at the working end, but you may cut off any cracked bits as you work. Damp cane is pliable and does not break but it is much harder to pull damp lengths of cane through the work, especially on the diagonals, which makes the caning much slower. Dampen the cane by dipping it in hot water. Never leave it to soak or it will become discoloured. It is a good idea to have a bowl of water beside you and you can dampen the cane as you work by dipping your fingers in the water and running them along the underside of the cane.

**Pegs** to hold the work tight. These may be made from short 5 cm pieces of No. 15 centre cane, small pieces of willow or even golf tees. To peg the chair at the end of the work, you will find that No. 10 or 12 centre cane is the easiest to use.

**A clearer** to clean out the holes of an old chair.

**Small hammer**
**Scissors**
**Craft-knife** or **pen-knife**

## Removing the old cane

Remove the old cane by cutting it carefully away, and then punch all the cane and any old pegs out of the holes with the clearer. It is a good idea to save the old cane for reference but always remember that the previous caner was not necessarily correct.

## The six-step traditional pattern

**Step 1**: *the first vertical or the first setting*
Place the cane in a hole next to one of the corners in the back rail. (The rails are the wooden edges of the seat in which the holes are drilled.) Leave 10–15 cm of cane underneath and peg tightly so that the cane does not slip and is able to cross to the opposite hole in the front rail with the glossy side on top. Pass the cane through the opposite hole in the front rail and peg it again. Bring the cane up through the next hole in the front, making sure that the glossy side of the cane is still uppermost and peg again. Now the cane returns to the back again and then backwards and forwards until all but the corner holes are used. Keep the tension reasonably taut.

The first peg is left in because it is securing the end of the cane and, if removed, the cane will become too slack. But the second and third pegs are travelling pegs and move along with each stroke of the work.

Lengths of cane always start and finish at a rail, never in the middle of the fabric. When the length of cane is nearly finished, peg it into a hole and leave the peg in to keep it tight. Start again with a new length of cane in the next hole and peg securely.

**Step 2**: *the first horizontal or the first weaving*
Exactly the same as the first vertical but travelling horizontally across the seat instead of up and down. This stage lies on top of the first vertical. Keep the ends of the cane well pegged and use the travelling pegs to keep the tension fairly taut. Remember to keep the glossy side of the cane uppermost.

**Step 3**: *the second vertical or second setting*
A repetition of the first vertical – this step lies on top of the first horizontal, thereby creating a 'sandwich' of a vertical strand top and bottom with a horizontal one in the middle. No actual weaving is done at this stage for a simple seat. Try to push the first vertical to the left in each hole and set the second vertical to lie to the right of the first. When you reach a hole that is pegged because it has an end of the cane underneath, remove the peg, insert the working cane, and re-peg the hole keeping the end well stretched.

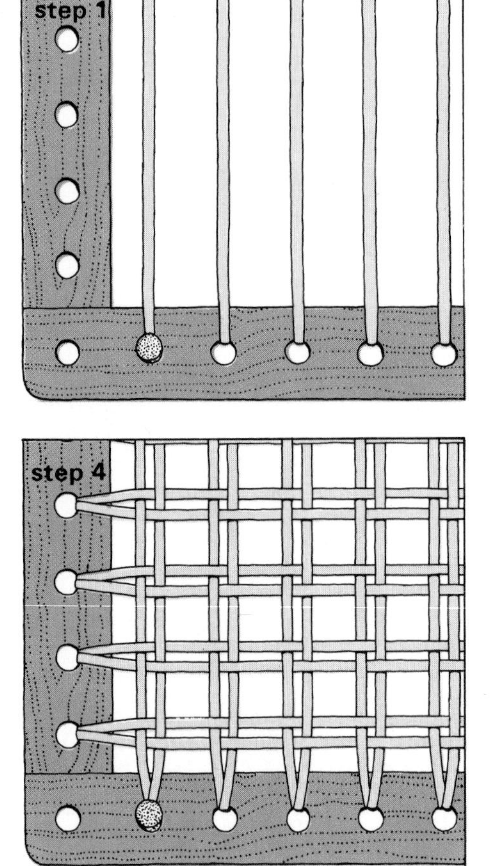


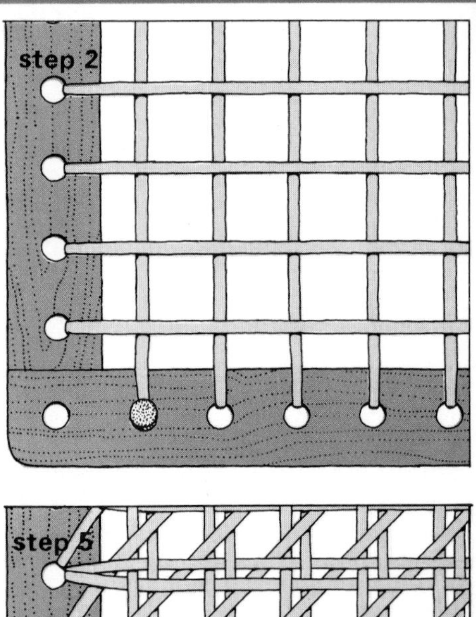


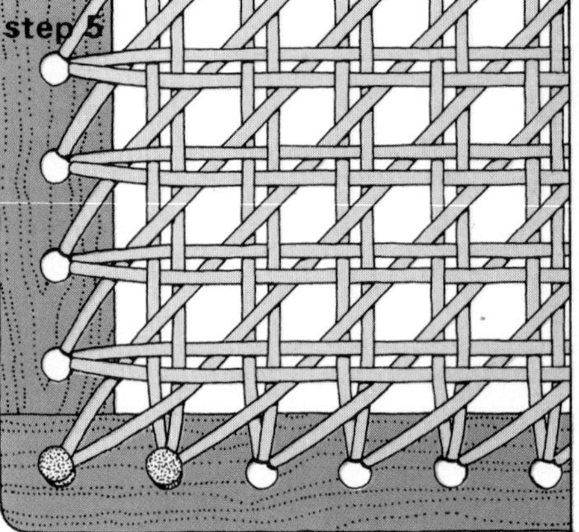


**Step 4**: *the second horizontal or second weaving*
This step follows the same pattern as the first horizontal but the cane is woven over and under the vertical steps.

There are some points to be watched when working this step.

**1.** You must see that the cane is pulled through the work in the correct direction. A weak spot is left where the leaves and thorns were pulled from the cane. If you feel one or two of these places with your thumb nail, you will find that one way is smooth and the other way chafes. The cane must be pulled through the work the smooth way otherwise it will not only tear itself, but it will also tear the other strands. If you really cannot detect any difference in the directions the trouble will not occur.

**2.** On the first three steps, you were able to twist the cane round in the hole in order to keep the glossy side on top. This time you must find the correct way by running the cane through your fingers before you start the weaving. Nothing is more frustrating than to find that the cane is twisted at the beginning of a long line of weaving and you have to take it out and do it all over again.

**3.** Do not pull the cane all the way through after each stroke. This will make the tension loose and the work bumpy. Thread through about 6 to 8 verticals with only a few inches of free cane and *then* pull the cane right through. This makes the fabric tighter and more even.

**4.** Do not worry about making the lines look neat and tidy and parallel with the first horizontal. Steps 5 and 6 (the diagonals) will do that for you.

**5.** Make sure that you start as you plan to continue – if you start this second horizontal in front of the first, all the second horizontal lines must come in front; if you start behind, they must all be behind.

Start as for the first horizontal and peg one end of the cane in one of the holes next to the corner on the left-hand rail. Weave the cane underneath the first vertical and over the second vertical all the way across. Make sure that you always do this under and over weaving in the same order. In other words you must see that the upper cane (or second vertical) is always pulled the same way. Work this step to the front of the first horizontal so that the instructions for the next step are easier.

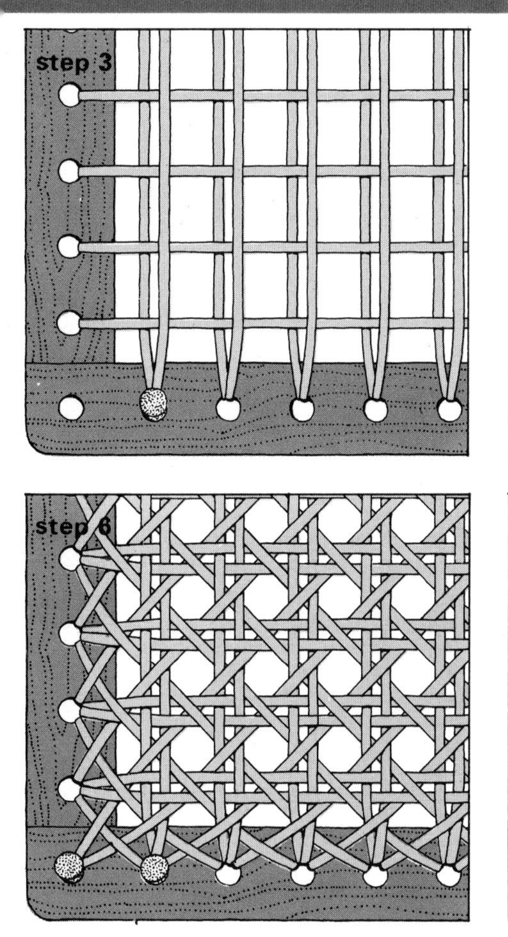


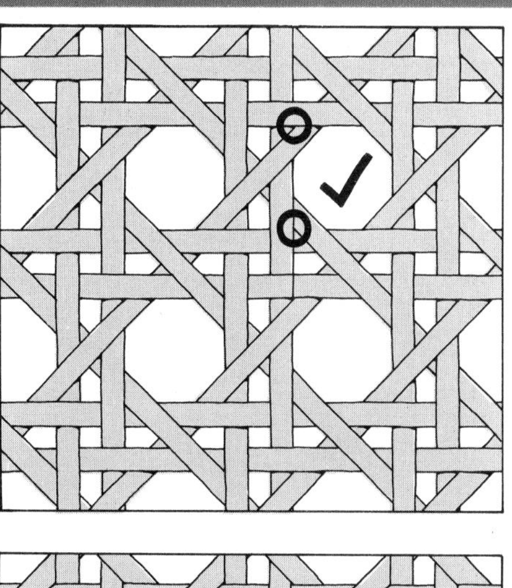

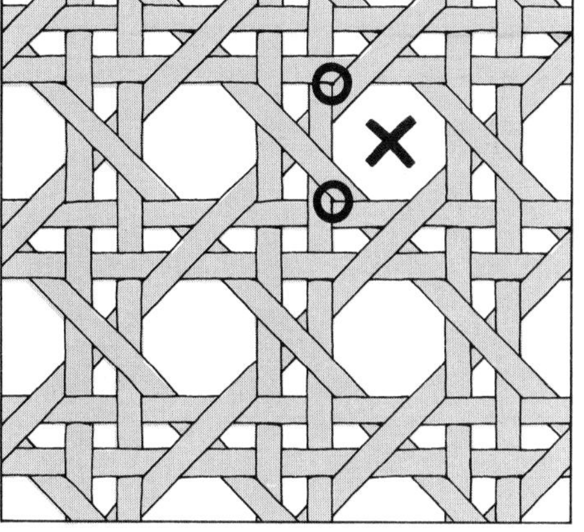

*Far left* The six steps of the traditional pattern.
*Left* The right (above) and wrong (below) methods of placing the diagonals.
*Below* Detail of the six step traditional pattern.

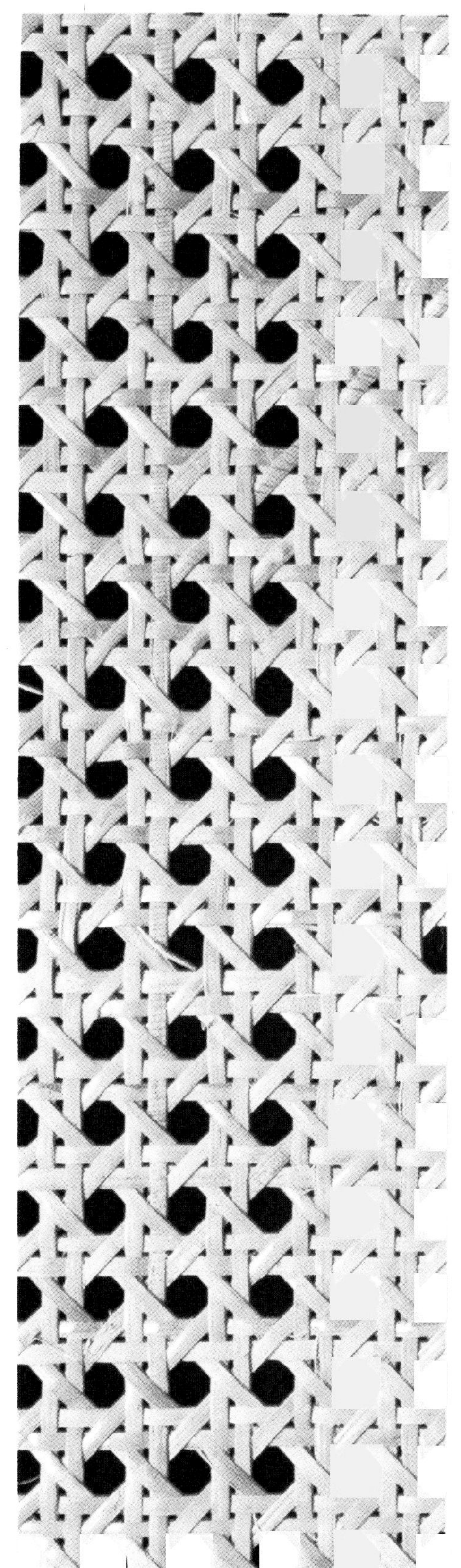

**Step 5:** *the first diagonal or the first crossing*
This is the time to change to the thicker of the two sizes that you have selected.

All the points concerning Step 4 must be observed for this step too. This time the corner holes are used twice.

Although this step becomes a diagonal it is worked in a series of right-angled steps – up (or down) one and then along one. When the cane is pulled tight it will automatically become diagonal.

Peg the cane into the back left-hand corner hole. Weave down over the first pair of horizontals (Steps 2 and 4) and then along and under the first pair of verticals. Now repeat – down and over the next pair of horizontals and along and under the next pair of verticals. Repeat all the way across the seat to the front rail. If the chair is quite square the first diagonal will finish in the opposite corner – otherwise thread it into whichever hole it reaches naturally.

Bring the cane up through the next hole to the left in the front rail and weave back to the top of the left-hand rail. The pattern of the over and under weaving should be exactly the same as the first line of diagonal weaving.

Continue to weave back and forth checking that the pattern is correct, until the front corner is reached and the cane is passed straight across the last two holes.

Go back to the top left corner, that is where you started this step, and peg another cane into that corner (the corners are used twice for this step). Weave the other half of the seat in exactly the same way as the first half, that is over the horizontals and under the verticals.

It is essential to ensure that the diagonals slip in between the horizontals and the verticals. This gives the finished fabric elasticity and the edges of the cane will not rub and cut each other. When you become more experienced you can decide for yourself which way the first four steps go as long as you strictly observe the fact that the diagonals are woven in the correct way so the edges do not chafe.

**Step 6:** *the second diagonal or second crossing*
This step is exactly the opposite of Step 5. Start in the back right-hand corner and weave at right angles to the other diagonal. This time weave under the horizontals and over the verticals. As for Step 5, the diagonals must slip in between the horizontals and verticals.

## Finishing off

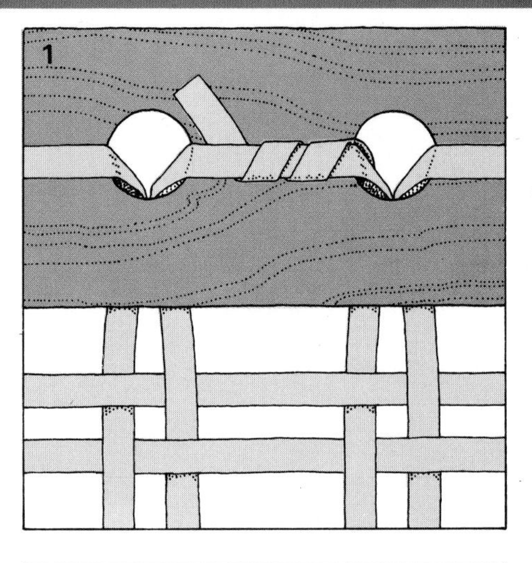


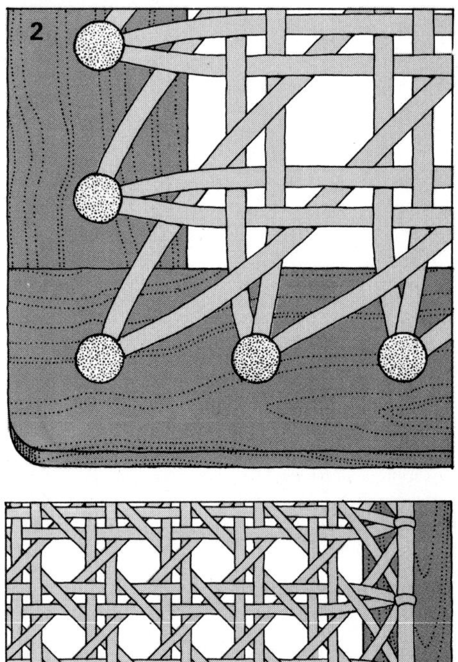


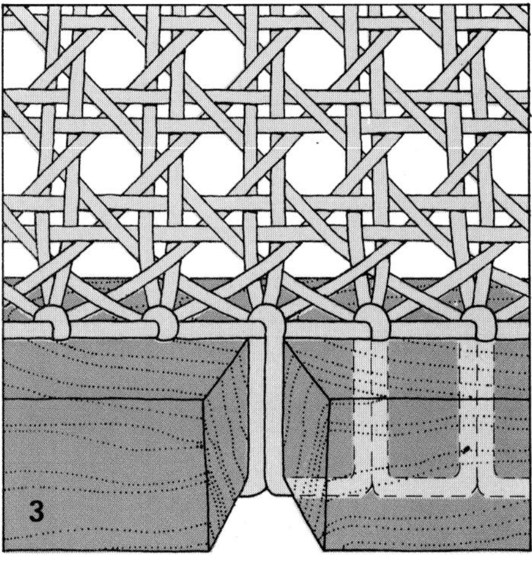


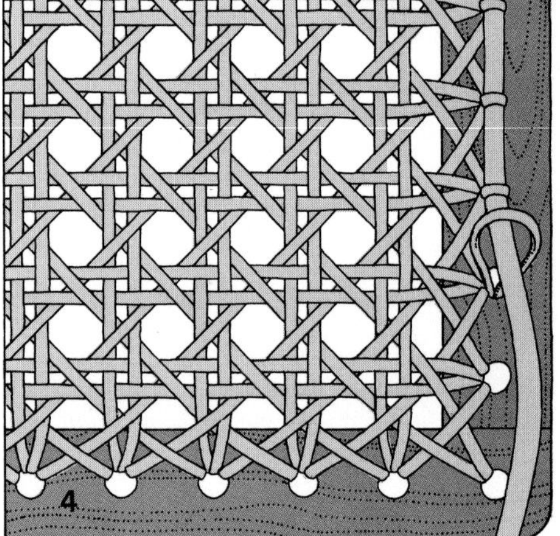


There are many methods of finishing off the ends of the cane which have been pegged at each end to the rails but tying in or pegging are the most professional.

**Tying in** Each end may be tied round an adjacent loop underneath the seat. It is a good idea to wet the cane first to get rid of its brittleness. Push the end of the cane under the loop twice and pull tight. A light tap with a small hammer will flatten the knot. This method is quick and easy but rather untidy, so do not use it on the back of a chair where the finishing off will be clearly visible.

**Pegging** Each hole may be pegged and all the ends securely held by cutting a piece of no. 10 or 12 centre cane or small pieces of soft wood, 3 mm smaller than the depth of the rail. Insert one peg into each hole, and using a punch, tap the pegs just below the surface. Make sure that these pegs really do fill the hole tightly; if not, use a thicker cane. Cut off all the surplus ends of the canes close to the underside of the chair after it has been pegged.

**Beading** This is a modern method of finishing off the upper edges of the seat. It consists of a length of wider beading cane (no. 5 or 6) couched down with a thinner (no. 1 or 2) couching cane. It is up to you whether you add it or not, but it should not be put on an antique chair.

First of all the ends should be secured by either tying them in (method 1 above) or by pegging every other hole. Any ends that finish in holes not to be pegged should be brought *up* through an adjacent hole to be pegged there.

Cut a length of the thick cane, long enough to span the side of the seat and down the corner holes with 7.5 cm to spare at each end. Insert it into one of the back corners. Add a long, thinner, couching cane into the same hole with only a couple of inches showing on the upper side. Thread this short end *down* through the first unpegged hole and the long end *up* through the same hole to make a short stitch to secure the end. The long end now passes over the beading cane and back down through the same hole, pulling it tight. Pass it along underneath the seat to the next unpegged hole and bring it up to the top again ready to couch in the beading cane. Continue until you reach the second corner, and insert the beading cane into the corner hole. Add in a new beading cane that will stretch across the front rail. Bend the new cane back and peg the corner hole so that the peg will be covered by this beading cane when it is put into position. Bead each side in the same way until you are back to the first corner. Peg this on the outside, catching in the thin couching cane also.

If you need to join in a new couching cane, loop it round the rail through the holes and underneath the beading cane to secure. The end of the previous length of cane is secured in the same way.

### Caning a shaped seat

If the chair is wider at the front than the back, find the centre holes or pair of centre holes (this will depend on whether there is an odd or an even number of holes). Start the first step here, working towards one side rail. When you have reached the hole nearest the corner at the back you will still have some holes left to fill at the front corner on this side, usually two or three. Continue with the verticals from these extra front holes, taking the cane into a hole in the side rail. Try to keep these canes quite parallel to all the others. Do not use the corner holes unless it is absolutely necessary. These extra canes are called short strokes. Return to the centre and work to the other side.

The first and second horizontals will be the same as for the square seat and the second vertical step will exactly follow the first.

When it comes to the diagonals, not only will the corners be doubled (two canes in one hole), but there will be one extra doubling along the side that the diagonals run *down* from, for each short stroke. On the opposite side there will be a hole missed out – again, one for each short stroke. If you have used the corner holes these are still counted as short strokes. Let your eye determine where these doublings and missings should come – you will soon get used to it. On the other diagonal the doublings and missings will come on the opposite sides, but they may not necessarily correspond exactly.

If your seat has a bow front and/or back, you will have some short strokes here too and therefore doublings and missings at the front and/or the back as well.

*Left* Bow-fronted cane chair with inset detail (bottom) of the shaped seat.

*Below* The first four steps for caning a shaped seat showing the missed holes and short strokes.

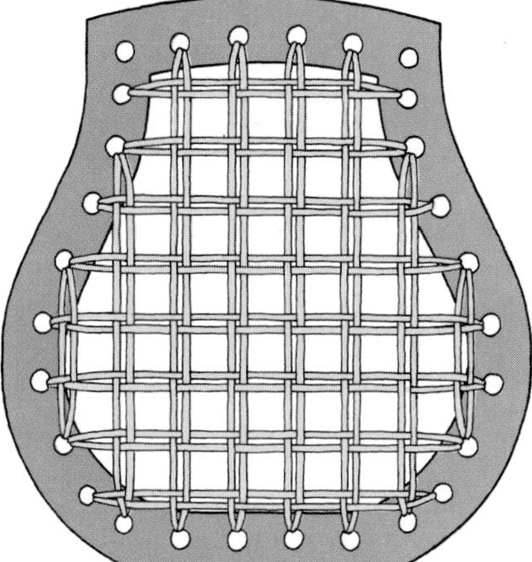

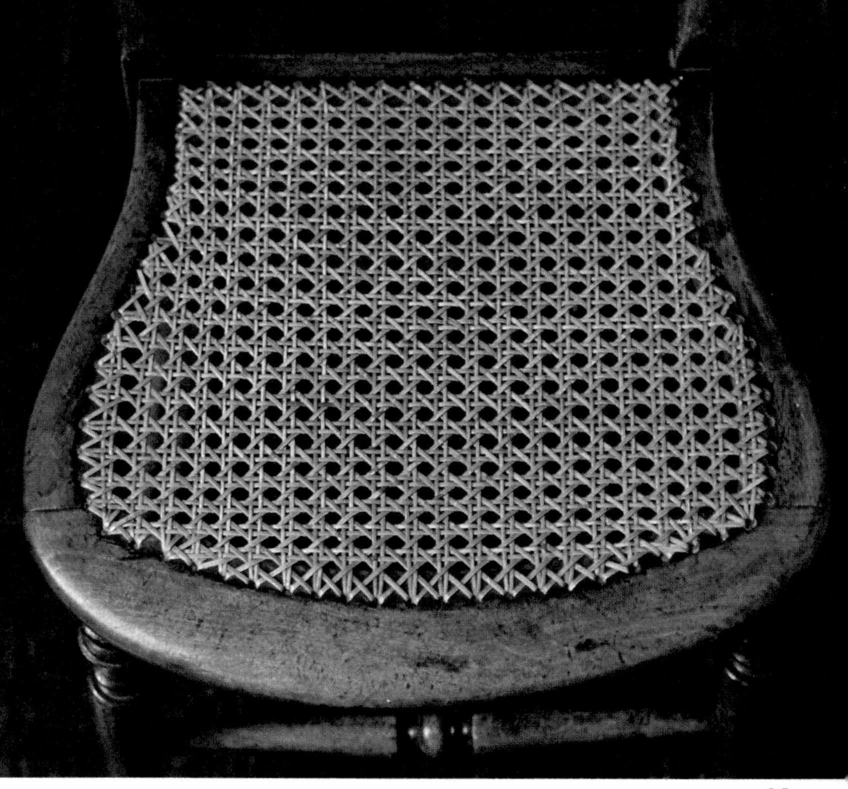

*Left above* Diagrams: 3 methods of finishing off the ends of cane. Top left: tying in on the underside of a chair. Top right: pegging each hole. Bottom left: cross-section of a beaded chair. Bottom right: couching down the beading cane.

# Rushing

Rushes have been used for seating for many hundreds of years especially in country districts. Many beautiful ladder- and spindle-backed chairs were made in the 17th and 18th centuries with such sturdy craftsmanship that all but the seats have survived. If you have one of these lovely frames in your possession, it is well worth learning to re-seat it yourself.

## Materials and equipment

**Rushes** Rushes are water plants that grow in slow moving rivers and shallow lakes. They grow to a height of 2 to 3 metres and need to be stored somewhere cool, dry and preferably dark (to keep their lovely colours). They are sold in bolts of approximately 2 kg in weight. An average-sized chair will need about half a bolt. The best time for gathering rushes is in July and August, and they are usually obtainable from suppliers up to January or February each year.

To prepare the rushes for use, wet them for 10 minutes, either by immersing them in cold water (a bath or garden pool is ideal), or by watering them with a hose or watering can. Make sure that the rushes on the inside of the bundle have had their share of water. Then wrap them up in a wet blanket or old towel for a further 2 to 3 hours to mellow. When they are ready for use they should feel soft and almost leathery. If they are still papery and brittle they need more time to soak or to mellow.

When the rushes have been wrapped for long enough, two more things have to be done. Firstly discard any weak tip ends – they will break anyway, so you might just as well get rid of them now, and secondly the rushes must be wiped down with a wet cloth to clean them and at the same time to expel all excess air and water. If you do not get rid of these, the rushes will shrink badly as they dry.

**Scissors** Any size will do.
**String** Soft sugar string is the best as it does not cut the rushes.
**A packing stick** Useful for pushing bits of rush into the seat during the work to pad it out. Any rounded piece of dowelling or even a garden stick will do if you cannot obtain a proper packing stick.

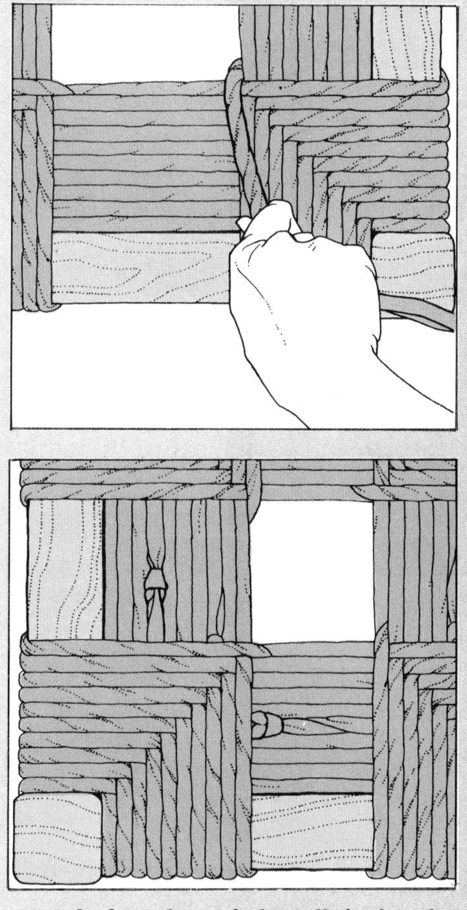

**A rush threader** to help pull the last few rounds through the work when there is hardly any space left. A large threading bodkin, sacking needle or a football lacing awl will do just as well.

# Working rushes

The aim of rush seating is to make a smooth but hard twisted cord which will be wound round the chair. It is attractive and very hard wearing. This cord of twisted rushes shows on top of the seat, but the rushes need not be twisted underneath the seat. In all, three layers will be formed, the top one twisted and the bottom and inner layers left plain.

*Left* Two miniature rush chairs in need of repair. *Above* Top: twisting rushes. Below: rushes joined with a reef knot.

Select the thickness of the cord to suit the size and fineness of the chair. Experience is an advantage here, but it will help to look at other rush chairs and then experiment with rush sizes. You must be careful to see that the cord stays the same size – nothing looks worse than one skinny cord half lost between two thick ones or some fat ones standing above the level of a fine seat.

Always have at least two rushes being twisted together (you may use more for a thicker cord), although the final cord should not look like one rush twisted round the other. This is achieved by pulling, stretching and stroking the rushes as you twist them. Place the rushes together, matching the tips (the thin end) and butts (the thick end) so that the size can be kept even.

Do not do all the work in one session. When the rushes dry out they will shrink a little and the cords may be pushed up closer and more added if necessary. When you stop at the end of a session there are two ways of finishing and then starting again:

**1.** Leave 30–40 cm of the old rushes lying loose. When you are ready to start work again, wet this tail for a few minutes to soften before tying on new rushes.

**2.** Tie the old rushes to the inner untwisted layer. When you are ready to start again, tie your new rushes in at the same place and travel in the same direction. Do not stop work with a corner half done.

## Joining rushes

Join in a new rush with a reef knot, but be sure to join it in so that the weight of the rushes is kept even. You may join in either the tip or the butt according to which end is needed to keep the thickness correct. At first the knot should always be tied on the inner layer and is therefore completely hidden, but later on when this becomes difficult and wasteful, you may tie on the bottom layer, but try to turn the knot so that it disappears into the inside of the rushing. If two or more joins come at the same place, do not knot all the rushes together (that would produce a very bulky knot), but stagger them a little so that the knots can lie happily side by side. Never join rushes on top of the chair or too close to the corners where the coils cross over. Ideally your chair should look just as neat underneath as it does on the top.

## Rushing a square seat

If possible start with a simple square seat to get the feel of it, or even a practice frame. An old but fairly sturdy picture frame is ideal for this.

Start by tying your selected rushes on to the left-hand side rail with the soft string. Tie as securely as you can so that the rushes do not just pull away.

The work will start by wrapping the cord round the front, left-hand corner. Twist the rushes to the *right* to reach the corner and down the side of the front rail, keeping close to the corner. Bring the cord up untwisted through the centre of the frame. Now twist to the *left* and take the cord over the left-hand rail and again bring it up through the centre of the seat untwisted. You will be able to see from this that the twist always goes away from the corner, and this pattern must be kept correct throughout the chair. At first it is easy to twist the wrong way, and this will spoil the lovely uniform fabric. Do not forget to pull-stretch-stroke all the time that you are twisting.

Now pass on to the front, right-hand corner. Twist again to the right to start with, just before you get to the corner, then take the cord over the side rail close to the corner. Bring it up untwisted through the centre of the frame and then twist it to the left ready to wrap the front rail. Keep these wrappings as close to the corners as possible.

Continue on to the next corner which will be the right-hand back rail and then the left-hand back rail, and so on round and round the seat.

As you build the corners up, you must be very careful to keep them absolutely at right angles. If the angle becomes too pointed, the centre of your seat will fill up before the rails are covered and you will be left with gaps at the edges. On the other hand, if the angle is too flat, the rails will fill up before the centre and you will be left with a hole in the middle of your chair. The sharp angle is caused by the work not being pulled tightly enough on the second part of the corner when the cord is pulled over the first half, while the flat corner is caused by pulling too hard. Adjust if necessary.

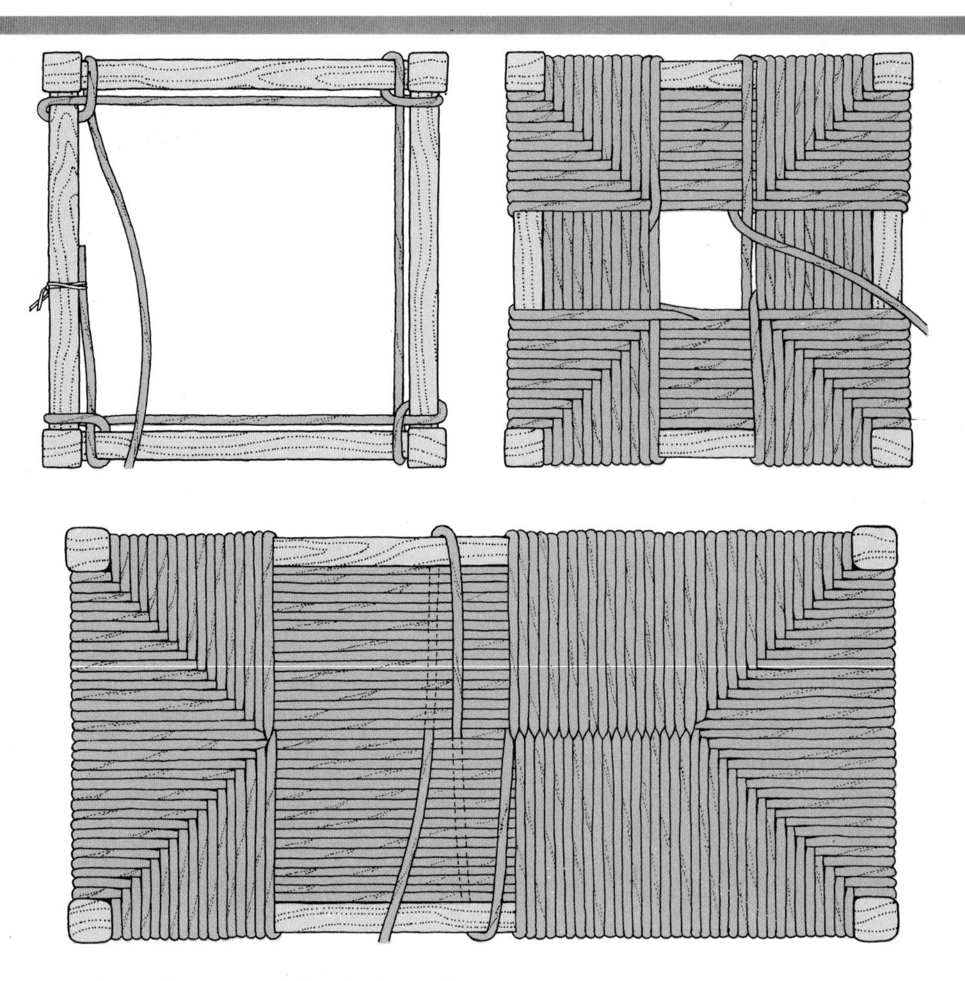

*Top left and right* Rushing a square seat.
*Above* Rushing a rectangular seat.
*Right above* Rushing a shaped seat.
*Right below* The two miniature chairs re-rushed.

As the work builds up, the twisted section becomes longer and therefore needs greater care. At the same time the untwisted layer at the bottom gets longer and is in danger of sagging below the chair unless you pull tightly.

There are two other things to be watched. Firstly the diagonal line formed by the coils crossing should be kept very straight and even. Secondly, try to keep the line of coils tidy and even at the lower edge of the rails.

### Padding

After you have completed a few inches you will find that pockets have been formed under the seat, two at each corner. These must be filled up with oddments of rush (you will find plenty of odd bits lying about that have been cut off and discarded) for three reasons: to thicken the seat, to press the inner layer up against the upper layer to help it to lie smoothly and to support the upper layer so that it does not press against the rails.

Cut the pieces into 5–7 cm lengths and use them nearly dry. If they are too wet they will have difficulty in drying out and may cause mildew but if they are too dry they will be stiff and unwieldy and will not pack tightly in. Push them firmly into the pockets using your fingers or the packing stick, pushing the inner layer towards the upper surface. Repeat this action after a few more inches and again just before the underside gap is closed.

Finally, when the rails and the centre are all filled, tie the last rush onto a rush on the opposite side underneath the seat. Use the threader to help you.

### Rushing an oblong seat

Work in exactly the same way as for a square seat until the short sides have been completely filled. The centre is then filled with a simple figure of eight movement, backwards and forwards between the back and front rails, keeping the direction of the twists going in the correct way. This time there will be no inner layer. Measure the space left to be filled by the figure of eight pattern, and mark

the centre of the remaining rails. When you reach the mark, the twist will change so that it will then match the other side. Be careful to see that the line formed by the coils crossing each other is really in the middle and very straight – do not forget that this will be a focal point of your chair. Press these crossings tightly together as the coils are double here but single at the rails.

## Rushing a shaped chair

You will soon find yourself able to progress to a chair that is wider at the front than the back. Coils must be added to the front only, until the shape that is left is a true square or rectangle.

First of all measure the distance between the corners on the front rail and between the corners on the back rail. Divide the difference between these distances in half, and mark the front rail in from each corner with that amount.

Start by tying your rushes on to the left-hand rail with soft string as you did for the square seat and work round the front two corners only. Tie the rushes on to the right-hand rail (quite firmly) and cut off any surplus ends. Go back to the left-hand rail and start again with fresh rushes. Work both the front corners and tie off at the right-hand rail once more. Continue with this method until you reach the marks that you put on the front rail. Tie in once more on the left but this time work right round the seat as for a square or rectangular chair. The pockets formed during this time may need filling (if the chair is much wider at the front) before you start going all the way round.

## Rushing a chair back

Sometimes the back of a chair may be rushed. The chair would need to have two rails at the back, a reasonable distance apart – not so close that the rush work becomes difficult to pass through and not so wide apart that the finished rushing looks heavy and unbalanced.

Start by looping one rush round the lower rail, bring the two ends together to form the double thickness. Use the figure of eight method of working, making sure that your twists match the twists on the seat. On the first round of the work go back over the single loop that you started with, which would look thin and flimsy on its own. Make all the knots come to the back of the chair, turning them in so that they are lost inside. You may twist the back of the rushing or not, as you wish. Pack it carefully as there is no inner layer to keep it smooth.

# Picture framing

Picture framing is another of the crafts that can be carried out in the home, with only a small amount of equipment, some or all of which may already be available.

Before making a start, it is important to consider the reasons for framing and the different ways of doing the job according to the type of picture.

The two main reasons for framing a picture are protection and presentation.

Oil paintings, and possibly some acrylics, will only need a frame which protects the edges and enables the picture to be hung.

With water colours, pastels, prints and etchings it is usual to protect the work behind glass, and in order to present it to its best advantage, to attach the picture to a specially cut mount, and to seal it in with a backing.

Collage, medals, and similar objects are presented in a box frame, also behind glass and sealed in for protection.

## Materials and equipment

**Mitre cutter**
**Tenon saw** to fit the mitre cutter. This should have a blade length of 30 cm and with a depth, from under the rib to the teeth, of 7.5 cm. Fine teeth are essential, so there must not be less than 5 points to each centimetre.
**'G' cramp** to hold the mitre cutter down
**Pencil**
**Rule** or **metre stick**
**Trysquare** (small)
**Light hammer** (about 100 g)
**Nail set** (2 mm diameter) or **pin punch**
**Bradawl** (fine)
**Panel** or **veneer pins** 1 cm and 2 cm, and 3.5 cm for securing canvases
**Wood-working adhesive**
**Craft-knife** with a supply of new blades, particularly if mount cutting
**Corner cramp** or set of picture framing corners on a nylon cord, for use in assembling the frame
**Pipe** or **water pump pliers** (optional)
**5 cm gummed sealing tape** and a **sponge**
**2.5 cm masking tape**
**Steel straight-edge** 1 metre long
**45° perspex or plastic set square,** the larger the better
**Polyfilla** or similar stopping for fine surfaces

**Mouldings** Many D.I.Y. shops sell mouldings, although their range is usually limited. Professional framers, understandably, are not often willing to sell lengths of mouldings.

## Choosing the frame

To get the best overall effect the frame should complement and enhance the painting's beauty, not draw attention away from it. Pictures with glass tend to look better with smaller section mouldings, whereas oil paintings will take the bigger, heavier mouldings. The smaller the oil painting, the wider the frame required, and to get this extra width, it may help to use a slip or liner, which is really a frame within a frame (1).

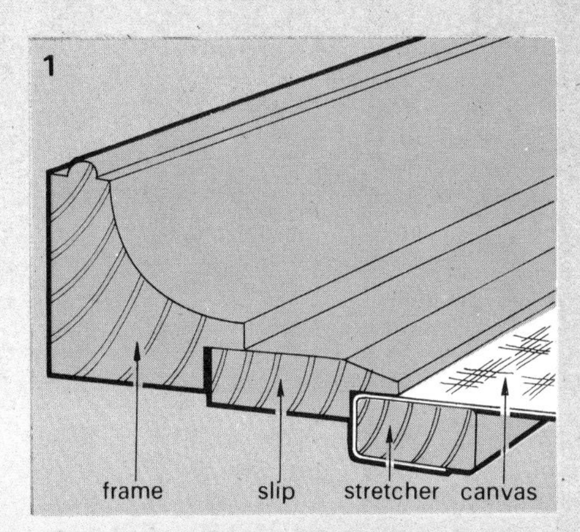

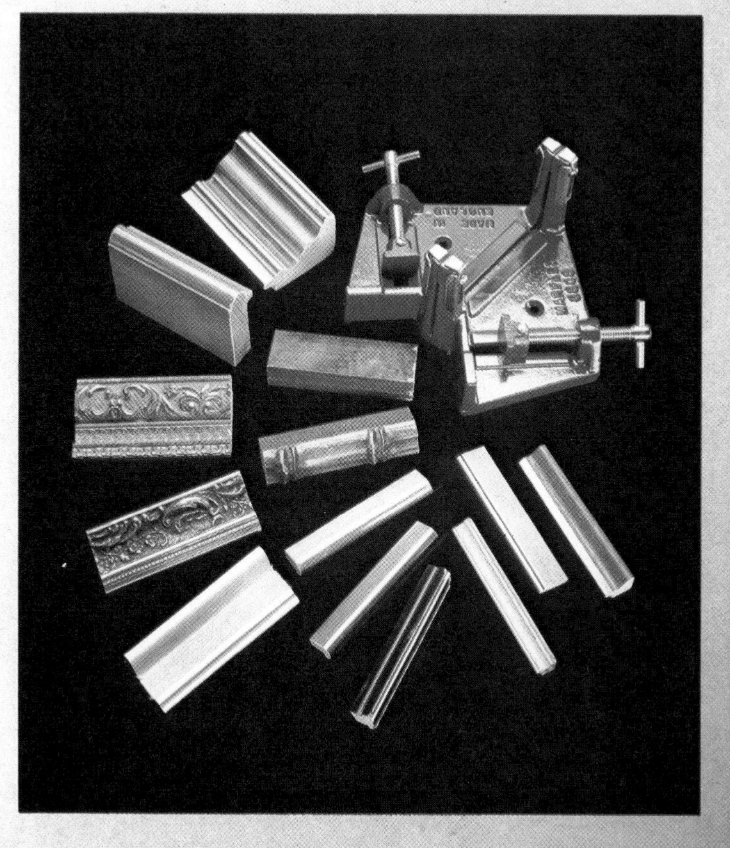

*Above* Pictures with a variety of frames, chosen to suit the subject of the picture. The watercolours are framed with mounts and protected by glass. The lower centre picture is framed with a slip (see (1), above right).

*Right* A selection of frame mouldings and a mitre cutter.

## Cutting the moulding

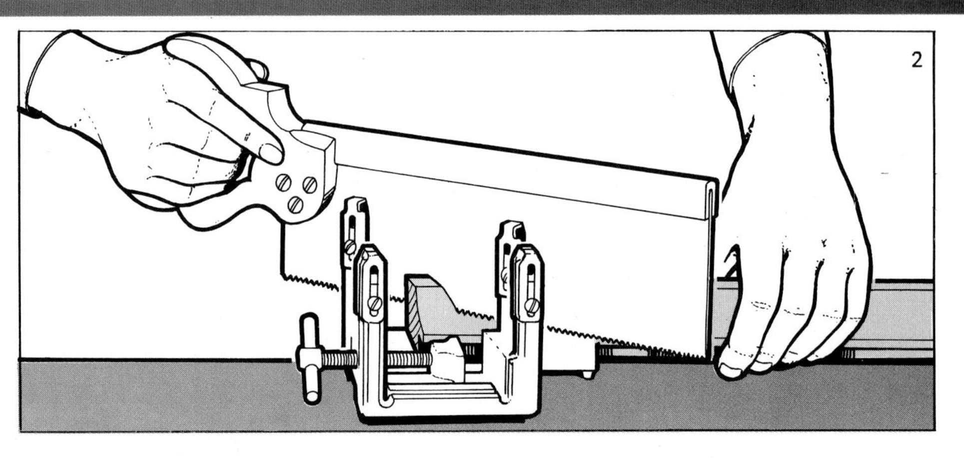


Armed with the overall measurement of the picture to be framed, the first calculation is the total length of moulding required, and the lengths into which it is to be cut up.

Each corner has a mitre of 45° so that every side member has a 45° cut at each end, and in every case, the overall side length is that of the picture plus twice the width of the moulding, measured from the inside of the rebate to the outside edge (2).

For example, when framing a standard Daler board 406 mm × 305 mm with a moulding which has a bottom width of 32 mm, it will be necessary to cut:

| | |
|---|---|
| 2 Lengths of 406 + 32 + 32 = 470 | 940 |
| 2 Lengths of 305 + 32 + 32 = 369 | 738 |
| | 1678 |
| Allowance For Saw Cuts | 50 |
| Total Requirements (mm) | 1728 |

There are eight saw cuts to make, and to ensure that the picture fits easily, add a further 1 to 2 mm to each length when marking out for cutting.

For best results the saw should be sharp. If starting with new equipment, adjust the depth stops on the cutting block to prevent the saw's teeth from touching the base. Maker's instructions will explain this.

Clamp the mitre cutter to the corner of the bench or table, put the moulding in with the rebate away from you, the top uppermost and with the long length out to the left (3). Cut the mitres from the top so that any splintering of the wood will be on the inner rebate edge and the bottom, neither of which should show on the completed frame. This first cut gives a small waste triangular piece (4).

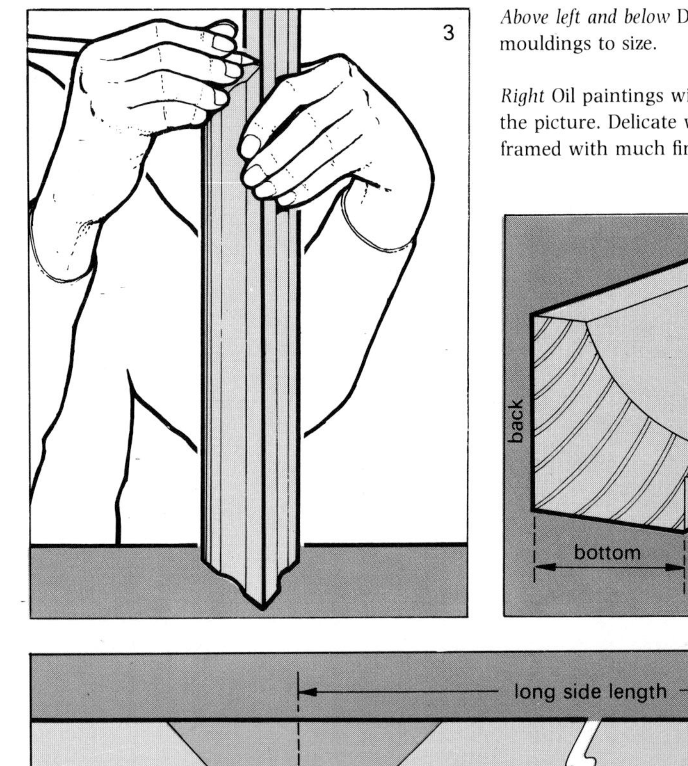


*Above left and below* Diagrams 2–5: cutting the mouldings to size.

*Right* Oil paintings with frames to suit the size of the picture. Delicate watercolours should be framed with much finer mouldings.

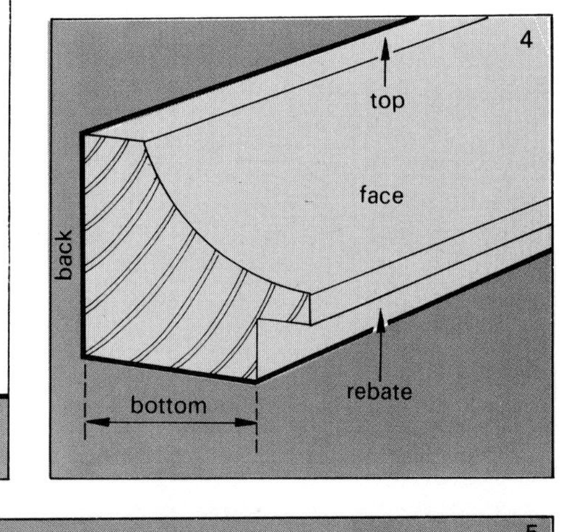


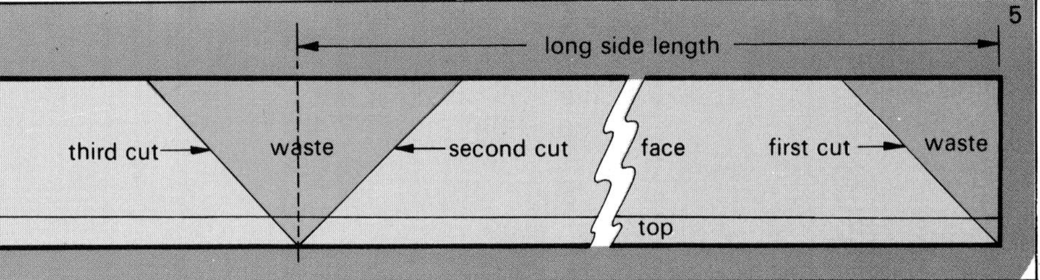


Remove the moulding and mark off along the back edge the length of one of the long sides and square the line with the trysquare across the back. It always pays to cut the long sides first, as if a mistake is made in the measuring, these pieces can still be recut for the short sides.

Replace the moulding in the mitre block, using the right-hand side, and make the saw cut just on the waste side of the pencil line.

Remove the moulding, replace on the left as for the first cut, and saw off the waste piece.

Place the mouldings back to back and with the tips of the mitres level, mark off the length of the first piece onto the second (5). Reposition again on the right and cut to the pencil line. Repeat the above procedure for the shorter sides.

Check each pair of sides, standing them up back to back on the bench, and adjust any variation of length.

This is best done with a wooden cutting block used with a small block plane, or put the two pieces back in the mitre block with the longer piece pushed across a little more than the shorter, and run the saw down the join. It should cut the longer one and be guided by the face of the shorter of the two lengths.

When the saw breaks through, there may be some roughness and small splinters. Remove these carefully with a knife, rather than with sandpaper, as you may end up with a rounded effect, which will spoil a neat joint.

On a flat surface, fit the four sides together, just to see that the frame goes in place correctly. If there is a slight gap in one of the mitres, try changing over one pair of opposite sides. They may fit closer the second way. A close fit at this stage is essential as glue does not fill gaps and you may have trouble assembling the frame later on.

## Assembling the frame

Put a long and a short section in the cramp and position them to get a neat close joint. Slacken the holding screw on one side, remove that piece of moulding and apply the glue fairly liberally. Replace, push the mitres up tightly together and reclamp. With a damp cloth wipe off any excess glue.

Choose a nail of a suitable length, probably 2 cm panel pins. With the bradawl make a small hole, and drive the pin in the corner until the head is almost flush, then punch it just below the surface (6). Two or possibly three nails, may be necessary depending on the size of moulding. Remove this section from the cramp and place it on a flat surface, then make the second L with the long and short sides relative to one another as for the first pair.

By handling these two L-shapes carefully, supporting the corners not in the cramp, they can be joined up together one corner at a time in the cramp, glueing and nailing.

Check the frame for squareness and put it back for the glue to dry. Rest it either on a flat surface or hang it up from the middle of one of the sides, not from a corner. Leave the frame to dry.

Another way of assembling the frame is to glue all four corners at once, then with pressure right round, applied by means of a loop of cord or a wire, assemble the frame and leave to dry. It can be nailed when the glue is dry.

The four corner picture cramp is ideal for the lighter type of frame. To use it, assemble the frame on a flat surface, adjust the corners on the nylon cord to fit the frame and pull tight (7). If all appears correct, slacken and take out one piece, glue both ends, and replace. Do the same with the opposite side. Carefully position each joint so that there is no step on the inside of the corners, and the top of the moulding is even. Pull up the cord as tightly as possible and lock it.

Check for squareness with the try-square, wipe off any surplus glue with a damp cloth, and put it back to dry.

The heavier wire cramps are more suitable for the larger mouldings, and as they have a screw to adjust the tension, they can be pulled up very tightly.

When the frame is out of the cramp, clean up any glue that may have been behind the corner pieces and in the rebate. Nail it, standing the frame on the bench for support.

If all measurements are correct the picture should fit easily.

Turn the frame face down and lay the picture, and backing board if used, in it. At about 75–100 mm intervals drive 13 mm pins half-way into the side of the rebate so that the head end holds the picture tightly against the top of the rebate. To avoid the possibility of breaking a corner joint it is advisable to hold a block of wood against the outside of the moulding opposite each pin (8).

To finish off, seal the joint between picture back and the frame with a strip of gummed paper. Cut two lengths about 12 mm shorter than the long sides of the frame, thoroughly wet them and put one on each side, about 6 mm from the outer edge and smooth down with a damp cloth, being careful not to rub the nail heads through (9). Cut two more pieces of gummed paper for the shorter sides and apply so that each corner has a double thickness.

The advantage of gummed paper is that it shrinks as it dries and gives a neat professional appearance.

For hanging, measure from the top a quarter of the way down the frame, and with the bradawl, make a hole for a suitable size of screw eye, on each side. Insert the screw eyes and attach a length of nylon cord or brass picture wire (10).

Before hanging, make good any slight damage to the frame, by covering nail heads with Polyfilla, or filling in any chips to the decoration. Tint to match the frame, using emulsion or acrylic paint, or mixtures of both to get the correct shade. For gilt, there are several types of paint available.

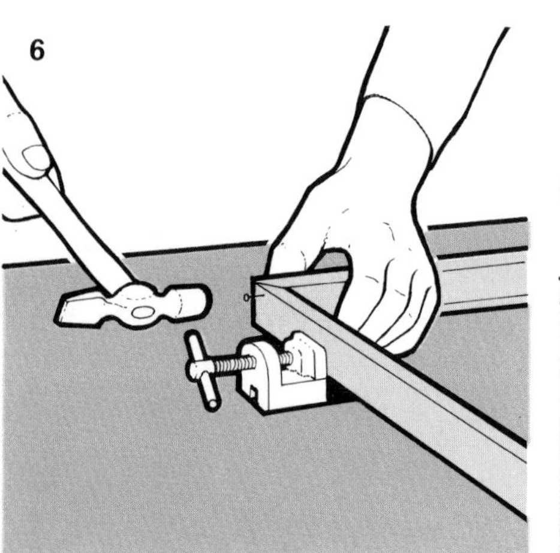
6

7

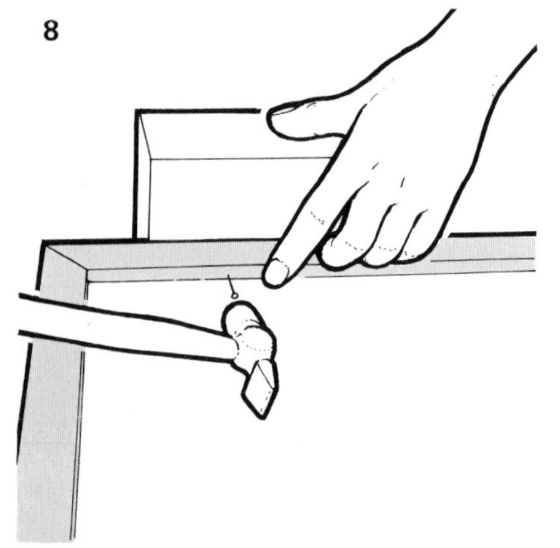
8

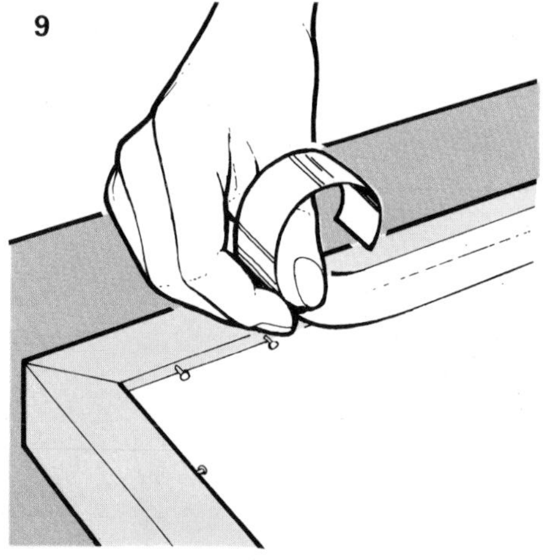
9

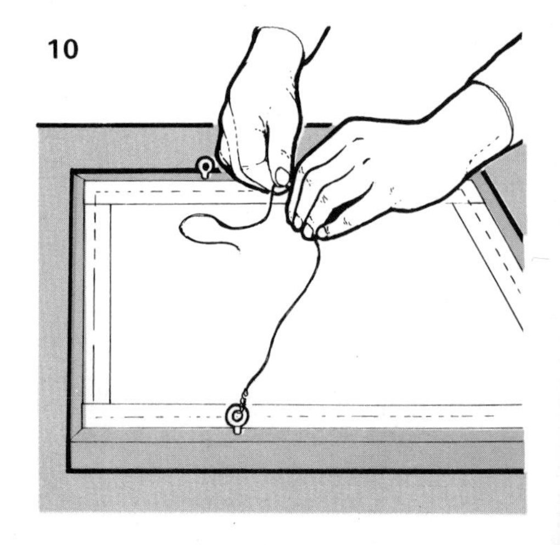
10

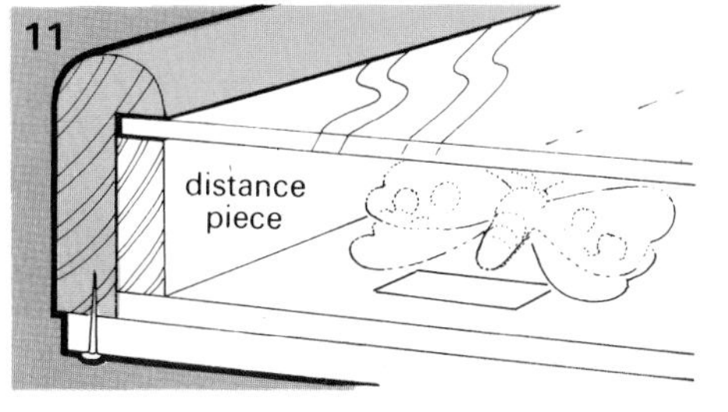


## Box frames

Box frames require a moulding with a very deep rebate (11). The glass is held up in the top of the rebate by small spacing pieces between the back board and the glass.

These frames are useful for three-dimensional objects, which are attached to the back board.

## Canvas with a stretcher

If the canvas is slack, it should be tightened. This is done by lightly tapping in the two wedges at each corner going round from corner to corner, until the canvas is reasonably taut.

To measure for the frame size, lay the canvas down on the bench and measure two opposite sides. Record the larger measurement. Measure the other pair of opposite sides, again taking the longer one.

Make up the frame to these dimensions, remembering to include the width of the moulding and add on 1 to 2 mm to each length.

If using a slip or liner, make up the slip to fit the picture first and then make the outer frame to fit the slip (see diagram 1 page 73).

When dry these two frames are joined together by nailing, before fitting the canvas.

To keep the canvas in place, special Z-clips are available but an accepted method is to drive 38 mm panel pins part-way into the frame and then to bend them over so that the top half holds the canvas down in the rebate. Do not seal in with gummed paper.

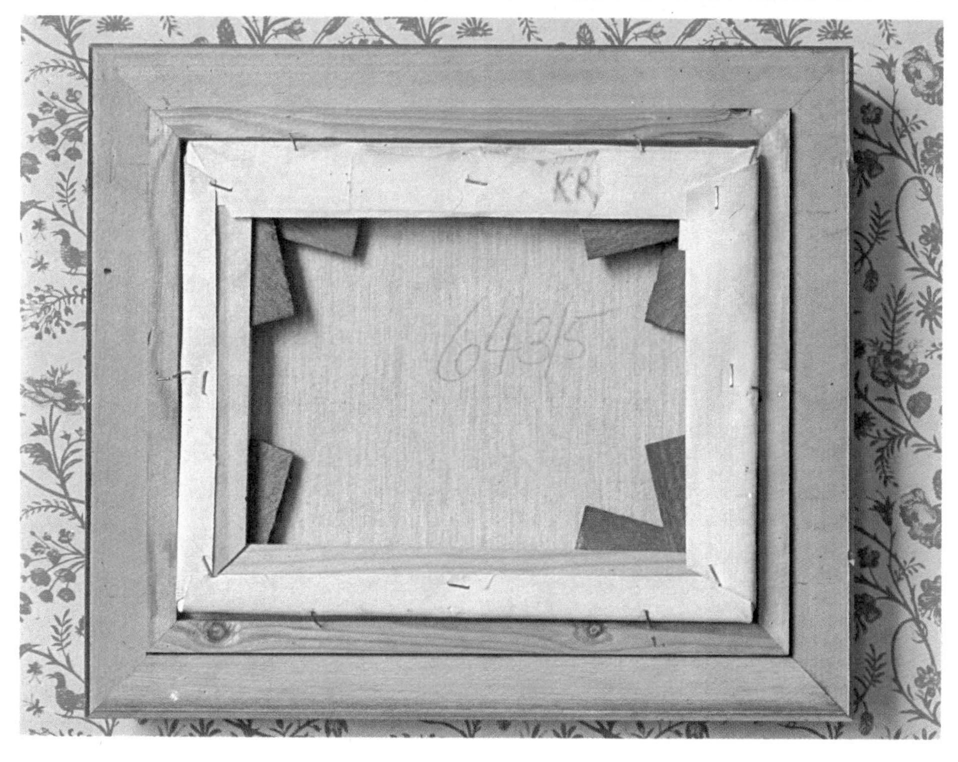


*Far left* Diagrams 6–10: assembling the frame.

*Above* (11): cross section of a box frame.

*Above left* Box frame.

*Left* The back of a stretched canvas framed with a slip.

## Framing with a mount

Framing a water colour or print involves the additional operation of cutting a mount.

There are many different shades and different textures of card for mounting. The colour chosen should tone with one of the colours in the picture itself or at least be complementary to the overall tone. Avoid a strong colour which might compete with the picture; the mount should only highlight the picture.

Generally, pastels and water colours go well with pale or cool colours such as ivory, pale beige, blue-grey or green-grey. Darker shades suit prints with bright colours and engravings.

The thickness of card is important, and to show to advantage the bevel around the window, it should be 6's (6 ply) or 8's (8 ply). It is worth hunting around to find the right supplier, as most art shops seem to stock nothing heavier than 4's.

### Size of mount

The window size must be slightly smaller than the picture itself. Two L-shaped offcuts of card are useful in helping to decide how much of the picture is to show (12). A note book or pad is useful to record all measurements.

The next decision is the overall size of the mount. To give the right effect and show the picture to its best advantage, keep the mount as large as possible but in all cases remember that about 6–9 mm of the outside edge of the mount will be lost in the rebate of the frame.

When considering the width of margins, it is usual to keep the sides and top the same, but to increase the depth of the bottom by between 5 mm and 15 mm. When hung on the wall, the picture will then appear central in the frame.

Dimensions are, to some extent, a question of personal preference, and possibly of available hanging space. However, narrow margins tend to give a mean, pinched-in look and some very small pictures can benefit from extra wide margins.

A word of warning when handling the card – keep your hands clean. A quick wipe over the straight-edge and rulers with a rag is a good precaution.

### Cutting the mount

Referring to your rough sketch, mark out with a pencil the overall size of the required mount, using the set square, to ensure right-angles.

With the straight-edge as a guide, cut with the knife along the lines, having placed a piece of scrap card, or newspapers underneath. Slight side thrust is necessary to ensure that the knife follows along the straight-edge. Make certain the blank is square by measuring the diagonals. They should be the same.

Now mark off the margin widths using two rulers to locate the four corners of the window (13).

Join up these points with a light pencil line, and once more check the diagonals and the window size. If they are all correct take the straight-edge and a really sharp knife and place the blank face up on scrap card as before. It is a good idea to make a few practice cuts on an offcut of card, before starting on the mount.

Place the straight-edge on the outside left of the window about 2 mm away from the line, holding the straight-edge down with the left hand. Lay the knife blade at an angle, repositioning the straight-edge if necessary so that the knife point will follow along the pencil line as the cut is made (14 and 15).

Start at the top left-hand corner and continue until the cutting edge reaches the bottom left-hand corner. Turn the blank 90° clockwise and cut again, repeating until all four sides are cut through. Usually the corners will hold, so they must be carefully eased out with the knife. Smooth with sandpaper.

### Attaching the picture

This operation can be quite tricky. Lay the picture down face up, and put the mount over it. Adjust as necessary making sure the horizon is level with the bottom of the window and any vertical object is parallel to the window sides. Put two small pencil dots on the picture in each bottom corner of the window and lift the mount off.

*Below* Diagrams 12–16: measuring, cutting and assembling the mount.

*Below* Cross section of a picture framed with a mount.

*Right* Three watercolours framed with a mount.

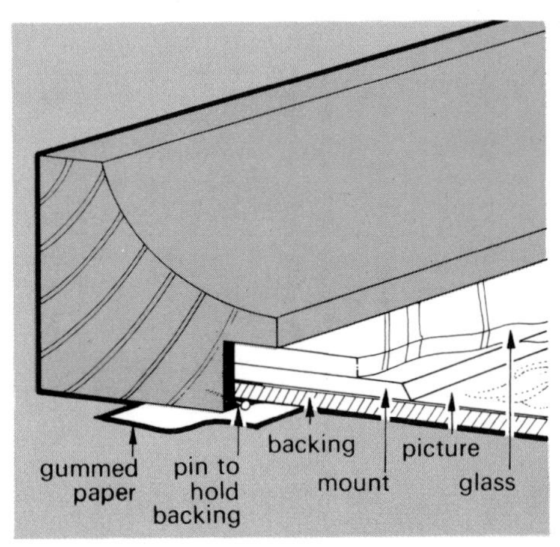

Using 2.5 cm masking tape, cut a piece the width of the mount and stretching it out on the bench sticky side up, place the top of the back of the picture along it, to cover half its width. Then taking the mount, keeping the top away from the tape, locate the two bottom corner marks and drop the top down, pressing along over the tape (16).

Making the frame first saves time, as while the glue is drying the mount and the backing can be cut.

## Assembling the picture

Picture glass is 2 mm thick. It is easy to order the glass from a supplier, but check the measurements inside the frame rebate before doing so.

The backing board acts as a support and holds the mount against the glass so it should be made of fairly rigid material. Strawboard or 2 mm hardboard are suitable, and are not too heavy. Cut to give a close fit and clean the edges with sandpaper to remove any loose particles.

Run a duster around the rebate to remove any loose dust.

Clean the glass on both sides making sure no white residue is left. Place it in the frame, put the mount and backing board in, and holding them in place, turn the frame over to inspect that they are correctly positioned and there are no specks of dust. It may be necessary to take it all out and re-clean several times to get rid of the dust.

Once you are satisfied, put the frame face down again, and secure the back in the same way as for the oil painting. Drive 13 mm pins at 75–100 mm intervals, half-way into the side of the rebate so the head end holds the picture securely.

Seal down with the gummed strip, and finish off with screw eyes and restore colour to any damage on the corners.

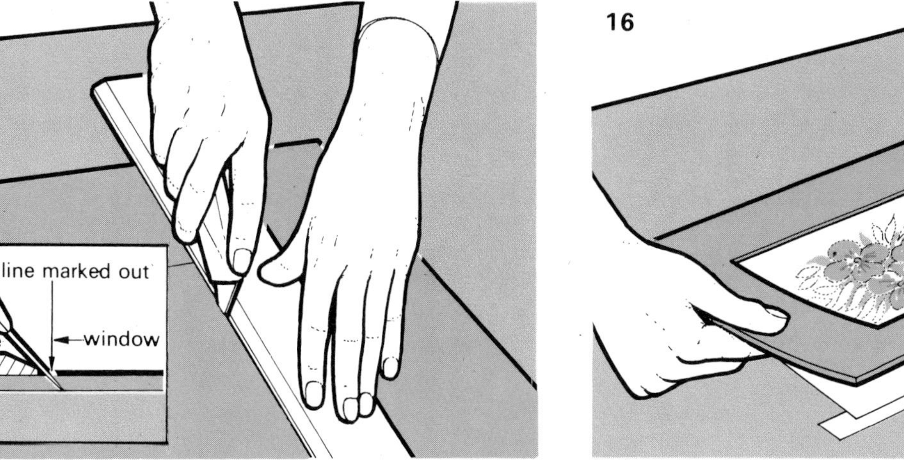

# Picture framing

The art of picture framing lies as much in successfully relating the subject to the type and colour of the frame as in hanging a group of pictures together to suit the general style and decoration of the room.

Pictures which are mounted without conventional frames can provide effective contrast with pictures which have rather more traditional frames.

*Right* A watercolour framed with a bright yellow moulding brightens up a group of pictures.
*Below* Silver and gilt frames to suit a modern décor.

*Left* Different shapes of framed and unframed pictures arranged together to form a square hanging scheme.

*Below* A wall filled with photographs and pictures lowers the height of the room, and alongside the fitted cupboards, has a military look.

*Left* An oval mirror is decoratively framed with painted twigs which are glued on. For suitable adhesives, see page 140.

# Furniture restoration

Restoring a piece of furniture is a craft which demands time and patience rather than money. The obvious places to find furniture to restore are junk and charity shops, markets and auctions.

## Assessing a worthwhile buy

**Will the piece be really useful?** Where will you put it and will it fit the space? Can you get it through your doors and up your stairs? Get into the habit of carrying a steel tape rule and a notebook with you even when 'just looking' – the eye can be unreliable in a shop full of furniture.

**Is the piece the right design for your room?** Study the possibilities and try to visualize the piece in your home, perhaps with a different finish or colour, or with a change of hardware. You could perhaps divide it up into smaller, more useful pieces, or cut down or change the legs.

**How much repair will it need?** Test for wobble and uneven lengths of legs, loose joints, warps and cracks, loose chair rungs, stiff or even locked drawers. Inspect the back, underneath and inside too. You can tackle surface flaws such as stains, dents, cracks, and holes up to thumb-nail size. If something is missing, how much will it cost to replace and is it too tricky for a beginner to tackle? If you have to invest in specialized equipment to make repairs, the job can cost more than the piece would be worth to you.

**Are your skills adequate for the task?** A beginner can refinish a piece of furniture but elaborate repairs take skill and tools. For your first attempt buy something that just needs a good clean up and a bit of first-aid – this only takes patience and some basic multi-purpose equipment. Success will build up your confidence and you can tackle more serious jobs as your skills develop.

**Will it refinish well?** Test with a wetted finger on an unpolished bit underneath to see if it darkens attractively. Is it made of more than one kind of wood? If the wood is solid you can match up the colour as part of the finishing process, but replacing pieces of marquetry is not a beginner's skill.

**Overall, will it cost less than a comparable piece of new furniture?** Unless it is really valuable and has investment and re-sale value, do not spend a disproportionate amount of money on it.

Keep a refinishing notebook if you get a taste for this worthwhile craft. It will save time and money and will help you estimate other jobs. When you are working, make notes about how long it is taking, which products you are using and how much is needed.

*Right* A typical junk shop with a variety of pieces which could be restored.

*Below* A junk shop table and chair before and after painting and a change of handles.

CLEARED OLD FURNITURE
PRICES PAID WANTED FOR

# Retaining the existing finish

The existing finish need not always be removed when restoring a piece of old furniture and in fact removing the finish can often lower the value of the piece. It is always worth considering just giving the piece a good cleaning first and then assessing whether it really must be stripped and refinished.

## Paint or varnish

If the piece is not valuable and it is painted or varnished solid wood, try scrubbing it clean – it is amazing what can be done by removing layers of grime and you may find it is not necessary to remove the existing finish. Use an abrasive pad, barely wetted in soap and water, and add a bit of household soda (not much) or even some scouring powder or ammonia for extra strength. Traditional recipes add vinegar or turpentine to the water wash. Do not flood the piece with the water mixture and always wipe it off straight away. Do not use this method for good or highly polished furniture.

## French polish and marquetry

Try rubbing gently with white spirit or turpentine to remove any layers of old polish and wax. Another traditional French-polish reviver is five parts methylated spirit, two parts boiled linseed oil and one part turpentine, shaken up in a bottle and rubbed on with a rag.

## Varnished or waxed furniture

Revive the surface of well-cared for furniture with white spirit and 000 grade steel wool; rub gently in the direction of the grain and then wipe off. On a dulled, mildly scratched finish, try a gentle abrasive rub using metal polish on a rag, followed by a restoring polish such as Topps Scratch Cover polish, choosing a tone to match the wood.

Sometimes all a piece with a traditional finish will need is cleaning and a reviving polish. Choose a polish that cleans the piece and gives a thin hard shine to protect the surface. The rubbing is the important part of polishing, so do not load on the wax with the idea you are feeding the wood – that is a myth. Too much wax just lies on the surface collecting dirt and fingermarks.

## Painting over a finish

If you are planning to paint over your piece, you may not need to remove the finish. Really effective rubbing down with coarse sandpapers will 'key' the surface enough to take the new coats of paint as the only problem when repainting is adhesion. If you have any doubts it is always best to strip the finish first, and wax and other polishes must always be removed before painting.

*Below left* A small pine cupboard before and after stripping and bleaching.

*Right* A French-polished mahogany table and a beech chair with a shellac finish.

*Below* A stripped oak sideboard with a semi-matt polyurethane varnish finish.

## Furniture woods and their finishes

Furniture wood can be difficult to recognize since there are many varieties of each kind and no two grains are quite identical. Furthermore, the wood may have been cut along the grain, straight across, or diagonally across the grain, and in some cases the piece has been so smothered with the finish that the appearance of the wood is quite transformed.

### Ash

This wood is most often used for tables and chairs. It is pale with an open grain and looks best with a clear natural finish. If you strip (remove) the existing finish, bleach if necessary and then use a clear finish, or for a colour change, either stain and give a clear finish or use a tinted varnish.

### Beech

This is pale with characteristic fine brown flecks and it takes most finishes well. Strip and bleach if necessary, then refinish with a clear or tinted varnish, or stain the piece and give it a clear finish.

### Mahogany

The favourite furniture wood of the Victorians. It has a characteristic reddish tone and a handsome grain. Traditionally mahogany was usually flattered by shiny French polish but nowadays a matt finish is sometimes preferred. To re-colour faded mahogany, strip the finish and restore the colour with linseed oil or stain, then French polish or use a clear varnish.

### Oak

This is the oldest, heaviest and toughest English furniture wood. Bargain buys are usually smothered in dark treacly varnish which can be stripped and bleached and then given a clear finish for a natural look or restained. Because of oak's open grain you cannot get a completely smooth surface with paint but the grain can be filled with a white filler to achieve a 'limed' look.

### Pine

Used for most 'cheap' Victorian furniture and usually painted. Nowadays it is fashionable to strip pine and then give it a clear finish. Sometimes, however, the paint hides defects and mis-matched wood. Look out particularly for unsightly round plugs replacing dead knots.

### Teak

This is an oily brown wood with a dark distinctive grain. In good quality furniture it is usually given an oiled finish for a matt, natural look. Because of the natural oiliness of teak, it is almost impossible to paint and difficult to varnish. Teak can be restored with a teak oil which is a quick-drying penetrating seal with a matt finish. 'Teak finish' can mean a veneer of real teak or a veneer with a reproduction of the teak look, or even a plastic laminate imitation.

### Walnut

Used for top quality furniture since the seventeenth century, walnut is usually polished and seldom stained. Walnut furniture normally has some value so it is best just cleaned and rubbed with wax polish (more elbow grease than wax) or finished with French polish – but soften the high shine by rubbing with fine wire wool and wax polish.

### Whitewood

This is a general name for the softwoods and you can often buy whitewood furniture unfinished. It is pale and bland but a dab of turpentine will show you the change a clear finish will make, or it can be stained. Alternatively, prime, then give it an undercoat and topcoat of paint for a good opaque finish. When finishing whitewood remember that the inside of the piece should be finished as well as the outside. Bare wood absorbs and gives off moisture at a different rate from wood which has a finish and you may get distortion. At the very least, rub the inside of the piece with a mixture of linseed oil and turpentine (page 98) or give it a couple of coats of thinned shellac.

### Varied woods

Marquetry is a patchwork of tiny bits of different woods, skilfully glued and inlaid, while veneer is applied in thin plates. Remove the finish carefully because the old glues soften if wetted, and sand down gently. Resurface with traditional French polish or a good quality modern clear finish. Do not attempt repairs on a nice piece until you have really mastered the skill of marquetry. Modern veneers are paper-thin, but the glues are stronger: treat any veneer with great care.

# Stripping the finish

## Sanding and scraping

If your piece is delicate and of some value, and perhaps decorated with nice touches like marquetry bands, it will probably have a fine, thinnish finish. Do not touch it with a liquid stripper or the old animal glues can soften and the wood will come loose. Instead, the piece must be sanded down using medium abrasive paper, rubbing with the grain: the finish will come off in a fine powder. Wet-and-dry papers (used dry) are the most suitable and economical, as the finest grades are finer than most, and a piece lasts longer if you wash it out after use and dry it to use again. Wrap the paper round a block (a child's building brick will do) as your hand is not flat and even enough. After sanding down, get a satin finish with the finest grade of glasspaper or fine steel wool.

Old varnish can often be scraped off with a flexible scraper – work with the grain and take care not to scar the wood. For turned wood like legs and spindles, cut strips of abrasive paper, and holding one end of the paper in each hand, rub it over the wood (with the same motion as you would use to dry your back with a towel). Be patient and work steadily and smoothly so that you do not damage the surface. A little finish will still be left in the grain, which means your own final finish will be smoother. Some people successfully manage to use a power tool with sanding attachments to abrade the finish without getting score marks on the wood. Electric sanders are suitable for multiple layers of paint on areas like doors and wardrobes, but do not try an electric sander on fine work.

## Blowlamps

Burning with a blowlamp is quick and cheap for big painted areas which you will paint over again so scorch marks will not show. Do not try it if you want to give the wood a clear finish. The way to use a blowlamp is to hold it in one hand, the flame correctly adjusted, and keep the flame moving enough to melt the paint without burning the wood.

**Safety note**
As you are working with a naked flame, be very careful to keep all inflammable objects well clear. Have a bucket of water nearby in case of accidents.

*Above left* Stripping a painted table using a blowlamp, hands kept well away from the flame. *Left* Using an electric sander.

## Spirit

Soften French polish by dabbing it with methylated spirit, and then rub off the dissolved finish with a rag, or scrape it off gently with a flexible scraper. When it is dry, sand carefully with fine steel wool as methylated spirit tends to raise the grain of the wood. Always remember not to wet marquetry or veneer areas.

If the piece is simply wax finished you can get down to the bare wood with white spirit and 000 steel wool, wiping down with tissues or an absorbent rag.

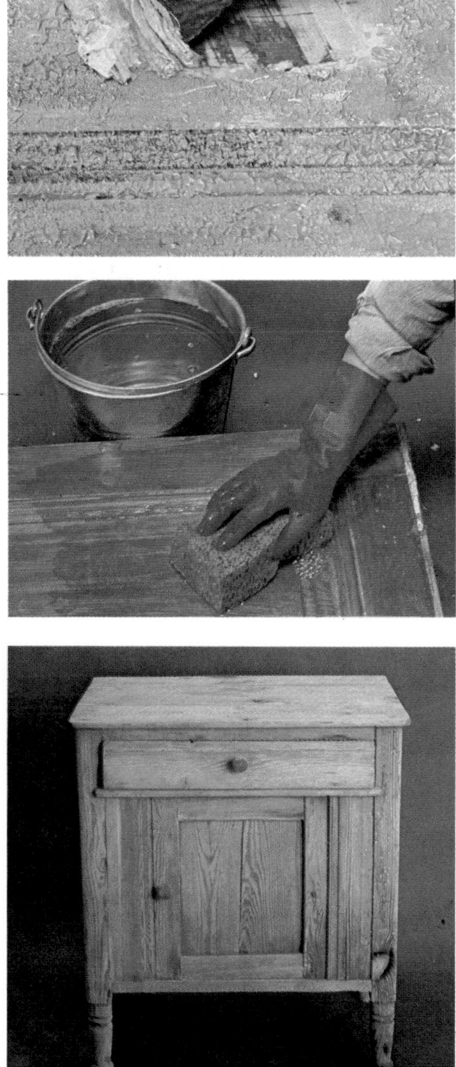

*Above* Six-step sequence to stripping a pine chest with chemical stripper, washing down with water and rubbing in wax polish when dry.

## Chemical stripper

If you are in doubt about the finish and the piece is solid, use a good modern chemical stripper. Remove all hardware and put it into a bowl so nothing is lost. Stripping with chemicals is a messy process, so wear old clothes and gloves and protect the area round the piece with newspapers, as the paint scraps can discolour anything they touch. Work in a well ventilated room, or better still, take the piece out of doors. Turn the piece over so that you work on the horizontal, one surface at a time. Apply the stripper according to the manufacturer's instructions. Usually you will need to use an old bristle paint brush to apply the stripper and wait until it softens the surface. Use your flexible scraper to push the loose surface across the wood in long strokes and collect all scrapings in a tin. Use an old toothbrush to work the stripper into crevices and carved areas and wipe it off with paper towelling and steel wool. Check manufacturer's instructions for any further treatment before refinishing as some strippers need a white spirit rub down and others require a water wash. Sand and smooth when dry.

## Caustic soda

Caustic soda is a cheap, wet, and drastic way to strip paint layers on solid wood such as pine furniture and doors. However, the process can loosen joints and cause wood to split and it also tends to darken the wood. Never use caustic soda on veneered or valuable pieces. Use caustic soda outside on a warm day, on a concrete area. It is highly corrosive so protect all skin areas by wearing gloves and old clothes and protect your eyes with goggles.

Fill a bucket with water and dissolve half a tin of caustic soda in the water, adding it slowly. Never add water to soda. Work on one surface at a time. Mop the solution onto the surface, preferably horizontal, wait about an hour, then scrub down with a wire brush and hose the solution off. Neutralize with a little white vinegar in the final rinse, which must be thorough to prevent white stains appearing on the wood surface. Dry slowly for several days. Be sure to rinse and re-rinse the working area, as even when dry, soda crystals can hurt animals' pads and children's bare feet.

**Safety note**

Methylated spirit, chemical stripper and caustic soda can be dangerous unless they are handled with caution.

Check manufacturer's instructions before using, and have to hand any substance recommended in case of accidents. Always phone the doctor immediately if an accident occurs. Keep all poisonous solutions in a locked cupboard, well out of children's reach, or better still, pour them down the drain and discard the container as soon as you have finished using them.

# Patching up the surface

When you have removed the finish you will see what minor flaws need to be tackled.

## Deep scratches, holes, cracks, cigarette burns

If the edges of the flaw have darkened with age and polish, you must either tint the filling to blend in and hope the repair looks like a timber vein, or gently abrade the darker edges with a scrap of abrasive paper. Cigarette burns must be carefully sanded to remove the char and the easiest way to do this is by winding some sand paper round a matchstick.

If the defect is on a surface which gets little wear, you can fill it with wax. Scrape a little beeswax (available from craft shops) or a child's wax crayon of a suitable shade of brown into an old teaspoon and melt it over a candle flame. With the surface of the furniture piece horizontal, drip the wax into the defect and when it is hard, level it off gently with a razor blade. A dab of artist's oil colour helps blend in the repair – raw and burnt umber, and raw and burnt sienna match most wood colours. When it is dry, dab on some shellac to seal the repair before refinishing the entire surface.

Surface damage can also be repaired with wood stopping, obtainable in woody shades and it can be tinted with water colours. Press the filling into the hole, level it off (it will not shrink) and when it is dry sand it smooth with fine abrasive paper to avoid damaging the wood round the repair and seal with a dab of shellac.

Plastic wood is useful for building up damaged edges as it dries extremely hard and can be tinted with oil paints. It shrinks on drying, so fill holes a little above the surface, but be careful not to damage the wood when sanding smooth. Plastic wood looks woody and you can imitate grain lines with a needle before it dries. Patient sanding and increased skill in tinting can make these repairs almost unnoticeable under a clear finish. As a beginner, tackle only holes up to thumb-nail size. Beware of trying to over-repair the damage – better a real old hole than a clumsy repair. Remember you only need a smooth surface and not a colour-match if you plan to paint over the piece.

To avoid over-repairing, work in stages so you can assess your progress at regular intervals.

## Ringmarks

Black ring marks on French polished surfaces happen when liquids sink into the wood under the finish. Try removing them by stripping the finish, then gently sanding with medium, followed by fine abrasive paper. A solid wood surface can be sanded, or you can bleach the mark gently. Old craftsmen swear by oxalic acid, which is cheap and gentle but deadly poison, so take great care if you use it. Buy a minimum quantity (from chemists) and pour it down the drain immediately the job is done. Telephone 999 immediately in case of any accidents. Drop the white crystals into a cup of hot water until no more will dissolve, then swab the preparation onto the entire surface, putting extra on the marks, and leave for ten minutes. Wipe off and repeat the process until the

mark goes. Several gentle treatments are better than one drastic one. Neutralize with white vinegar (ordinary vinegar might stain the wood). Alternatively, Rustin's make an effective two-part bleach – follow their instructions and neutralize its action the moment the mark goes. You may then need to stain the surface to restore its original colour.

## Fading

Sunlight bleaches wood colour, particularly mahogany, through French polish. Remove the finish with methylated spirit, then try rubbing in some warm linseed oil and turpentine to restore the colour as linseed oil tends to darken woods. Very gently warm the oil in a jar set in a saucepan of hot water, watching it all the time. Do not let the oil get hot and keep testing with your finger. As soon as the oil is lukewarm remove it from heat and add turpentine in the proportion two parts linseed oil and one part turpentine. Rub this into the surface with a soft cotton rag for fifteen minutes, then leave the piece to stand for a day or so. Keep the mixture and the rag in a screw-top jar and rub a little in each day until dark enough.

## Dents

If the wood fibres are not broken and the surface is solid wood, put a thick pad of damped towelling or brown paper over the mark and put your iron, set to medium heat, on top. The steam should swell the wood fibres and encourage them to rise back into place.

*Left* Four-step sequence to filling a hole with beeswax.
*Below* Active woodworm: the adult beetle (bottom) lays eggs and the grubs which hatch out bore into the timber (top).

## Woodworm

Look for the holes left by these wood-boring insects as they escape. If they are dark, the beetle has gone. If they are powdery and new-looking, the grubs may still be active and you should not bring the piece into your home until you have treated it. Put it in your garage or shed on a piece of paper and watch it for the dust that will show that the worms are still active. Paint the piece all over with woodworm killer, then inject woodworm killer into each hole with the fine spout on the can. Repeat the process after a day or so.

## Damaged veneer or marquetry

Replace tiny bits of marquetry with wood filler. If marquetry is loose, clean the surface with white spirit, put a damp cloth over the loose parts and press the cloth with a hot iron to remove the loose pieces. Clean off old glue while warm. Stick the pieces back in place with a modern wood-working adhesive, then cramp or weight until dry.

Cutting patches of new veneer to size and replacing them artfully so the repair does not show, is a very skilled job. Go to evening classes, or practise on a non-precious piece before you tackle something you value.

If your piece has blistered, carefully slit the blister with a razor blade and slide some glue under the veneer with the edge of the blade. It is important to keep the veneer as flat as possible during this process and you must put a weight on it or cramp it until the glue has dried.

# Hardware repairs

## Handles

To give the right period touch to your junk shop buy or bit of modern whitewood, get a good book out of the library and look at the knobs and handles our forebears favoured. Most of the famous shapes are still made – at a price. Visit a specialist shop like Beardmore's, 3 Percy Street, London W1, or choose from a catalogue of a mail order specialist like Woodfit, Whittle Low Mill, Chorley, Lancs.

It is important to choose hardware of the right size and proportion for your piece. A shallow drawer looks best with a lightweight handle, such as the classic swan neck. A deeper drawer can take a handle with a plate back which looks heavier. On a small area, a simple ring handle looks best. Plain knobs, beloved of the Victorians, can look unpretentious, but it is important to get the size in the right proportion for the piece. Brass gives a touch of sparkle while wooden knobs finished like the furniture are unobtrusive. Cut out bits of paper with the knob size you fancy and try it on your piece to check the correct proportion. Some hardware is screwed from the back of the drawer front, otherwise it is either screwed, dowelled or bolted from the front. If a change of hardware means that old holes must be filled, be sure to blend the repair with the wood if you plan a clear finish. Choose knobs or handles which have to be recessed into the wood surface only if you have the tools and skills to fit them.

Hardware is often most attractive when kept sleek and simple, as ornate knobs can cheapen the look of your piece. A modern classic shape is the 'D' handle – it goes vertically on a door, horizontally on a drawer.

## Castors

Castors with screw fittings can get wobbly when the screw works loose in the wood of the leg. Ideally you should remove the wobbly castor, plug the hole which this leaves in the leg with a piece of dowel cut to size and glue it in position, then re-drill the hole. If a leg has split, work adhesive into all the cracks, bind up tightly and leave to set. Remove excess glue with a damp cloth or solvent, according to the manufacturer's recommendations.

For larger surfaces modern castors have a plate fitting, and for legs, a peg and socket fitting which goes into a hole drilled in the leg is available. Traditional castors cannot generally be fitted on splayed legs. Castors which fit over the leg and have worked loose can be taken off, and the leg built up with plastic wood before screwing the castor back on again.

**Screws** Screws which have rusted in place are sometimes tricky to remove. Brush the screw head with a wire brush to take off rust and dirt and clear the centre slot. Sometimes a stubborn screw will shift if you screw it a turn deeper into the wood or if you put the screwdriver in the groove and hit it firmly with a hammer. Be sure to use a screwdriver that fits the groove exactly. Alternatively, if you heat the screw-head with a soldering iron, the metal will expand and force the wood round to expand. When it cools, there will be a minute gap between metal and wood, and the screw may loosen when you turn it. If the slot or head is broken you will have to drill the screw out with a metal twist bit. If screws have worked loose and the timber is damaged, take out the screws, plug the holes with plastic wood and then re-drive the screws.

*Below* A selection of furniture handles.

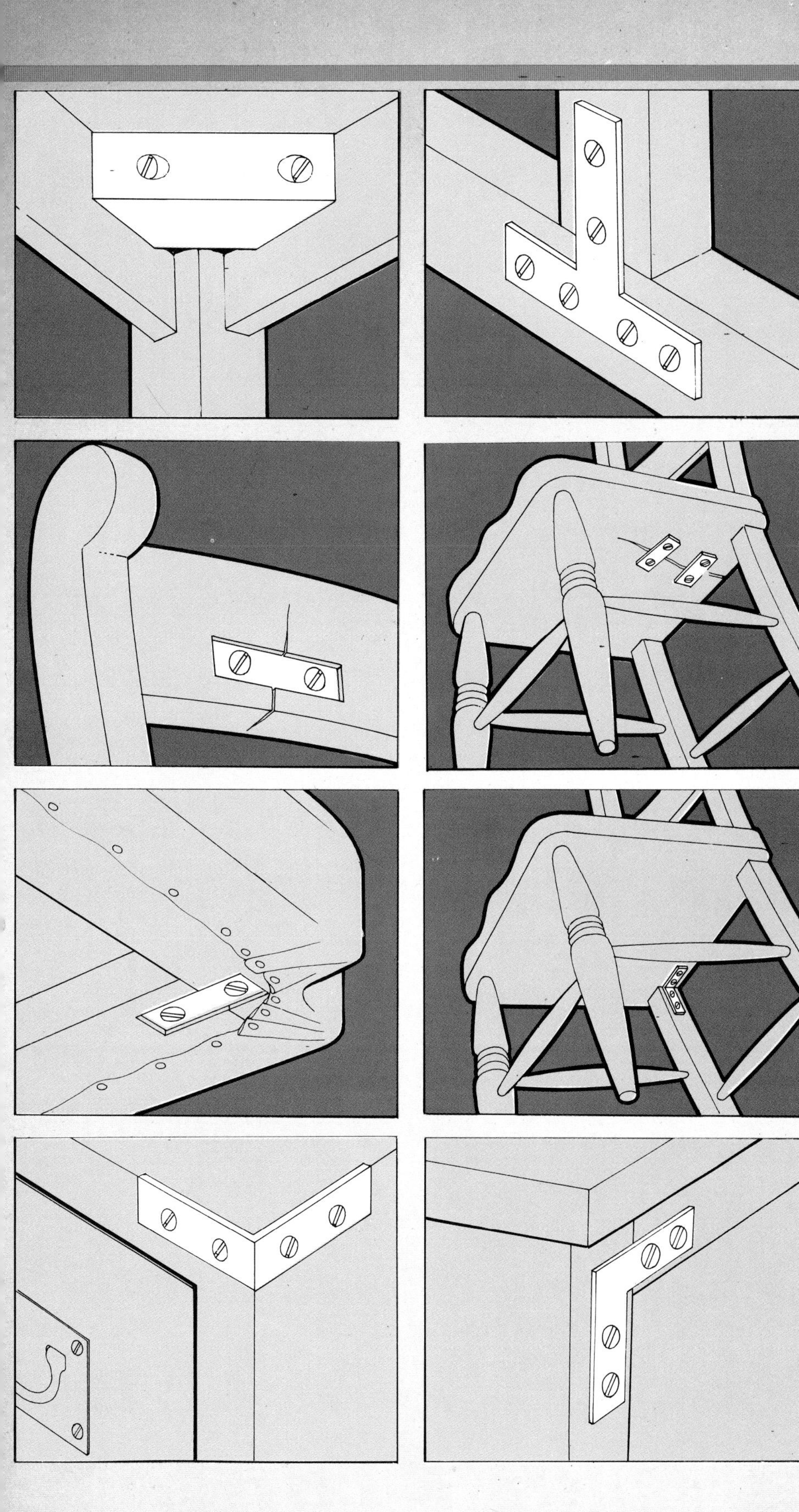

## Structural repairs

### Repairs with plates and blocks

Under seats and table tops the best repairs are made with triangular hardwood corner blocks. Cut squares of one-inch thick hardwood, then triangles, making sure the wood grain runs parallel with the long edges of the triangles. Plane to fit the corners exactly. Drill two holes through the long side at an angle into the other two sides, glue and then screw into position with No. 10 wood screws.

Repairs can be done to non-valuable furniture with easy to find, easy to use, metal angle-plates, placed carefully out of sight. Choose a right-angle T-shape or straight plate to fit the repair and glue the metal in place with epoxy resin. After making pilot holes with a bradawl, screw the plate in firmly.

Repairs on the outside of a piece are less unsightly if you chisel a recess slightly deeper than the depth of the plate, screw the plate in place, then fill the recess and carefully tint the surface to match the wood. Or you might make a decorative feature of a repair by choosing brass-finish angle-pieces and placing them to get a fashionable military-chest look. For dark woods, consider the iron-bound old oak chest look. Fix your angle-plates on the outside and paint them with rubbed down antique-looking black paint.

*Left* Eight methods of structural furniture repair using a block (top left), and L-shaped, T-shaped, and straight metal plates.

*Far left above* A selection of castors for different leg shapes. Top row from left to right: straight square leg; straight round leg; cabriole leg. Bottom row left to right: tapered leg; dowel-fitted castor.

## Regluing joints and splits

Chairs and tables can get wobbly as their joints get a lot of stress in everyday living and it is sometimes best to pull the piece apart and reglue the joints. Modern glues set rock-solid and do not disfigure your piece, so it is unnecessary to use screws.

Old animal glues can be softened by soaking with warm vinegar and water, or by the steam from a kettle. Then loosen the joints by tapping gently with a mallet, protecting the wood with a thick pad of newspaper. If you have never dismembered a piece before, be careful to mark or number each bit as you remove it so you can get it back together again. Be careful not to break any part by forcing it out of position. While the wood is warm, scrape off the old glue with a chisel, clean off grease, wax, and dirt, and wait for the wood to dry thoroughly. The surfaces must be lightly sanded and scraped so that contact is exact – glue does not fill gaps. If the joint is dirty, the glue will just hold the dirt together – it will not bond the woods. If the joint is loose, wind a scrap of cheese-cloth soaked in glue round it to fill the gap, or drive glue-soaked tooth-picks into the joint, cutting them off when the glue is firm. Sometimes a wood-shaving helps pack a joint, or you could choose a glue with a gap-filling property. Epoxy resin glues are expensive for all but small jobs, but they set so fast that you can sometimes hold the joint together instead of having to cramp it. Some sort of cramp must be used with most wood-working glues. You can improvise satisfactory tourniquets with a clothes line, rubber bands (cut up an old inner tube, luggage straps, and so on. String wound tightly round can hold legs, rungs or chair rails together if you are repairing a split. Panel pins can hold a joint temporarily together: do not drive them home so you can pull them out when the glue is hard.

If you cannot get a joint apart without damaging the piece, you can sometimes work glue into the joint or even drill a tiny hole where it will not be seen and, using a woodworking adhesive applicator that has a nozzle, inject the glue until it shows round the joint.

## Levelling legs

Check first whether it is the leg or the floor that is uneven. Put the piece on something genuinely flat, such as a sheet of non-warp chipboard. To correct uneven legs they must all be cut to the same length. Put bits of wood under the short leg or legs until the piece stands

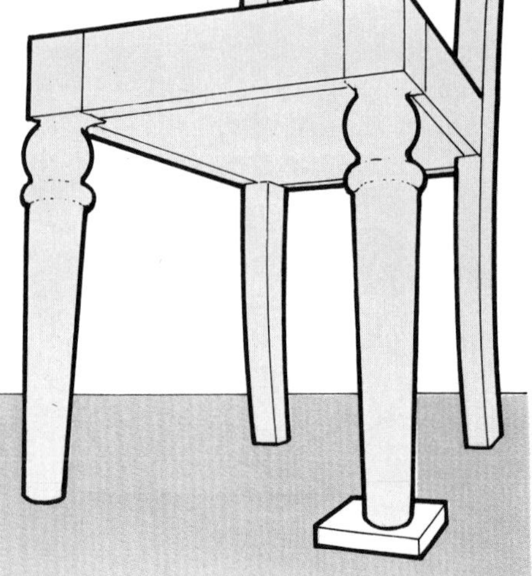

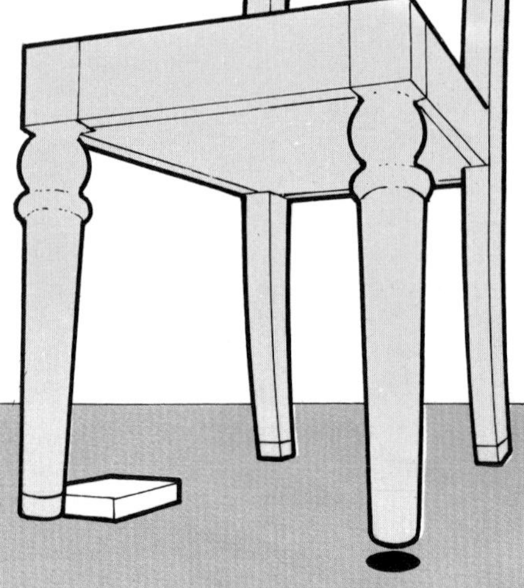

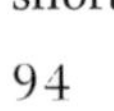

firm. Mark the thickness of one packing piece on the longer legs and cut off. Make sure the legs are cut square, and be careful when legs are set at an angle. Alternatively, build up the shorter leg with a scrap of wood, glued on and shaped when it is hard.

## Drawer repairs

Candlewax rubbed on the drawer runners can sometimes stop drawers sticking, but if this fails, look at the sides of the drawer. Smooth any shiny bits which are sticking with tough abrasive paper or a plane. Remove worn drawer runners with a chisel and replace with new strips of hardwood. Make the runner slightly oversize for a tight fit and then gently sand down to fit exactly. If the joints at the drawer corners are loose you can take them apart and re-glue them.

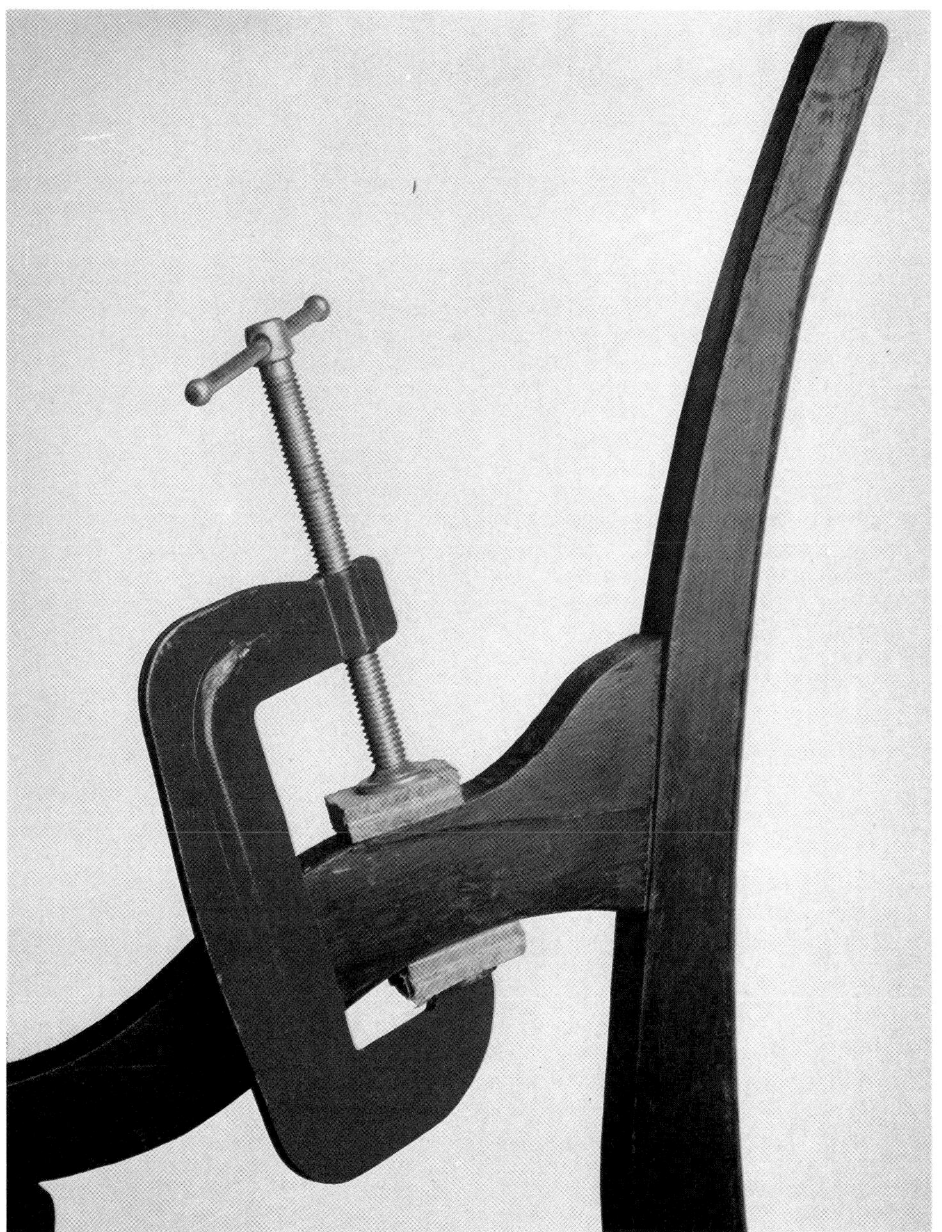

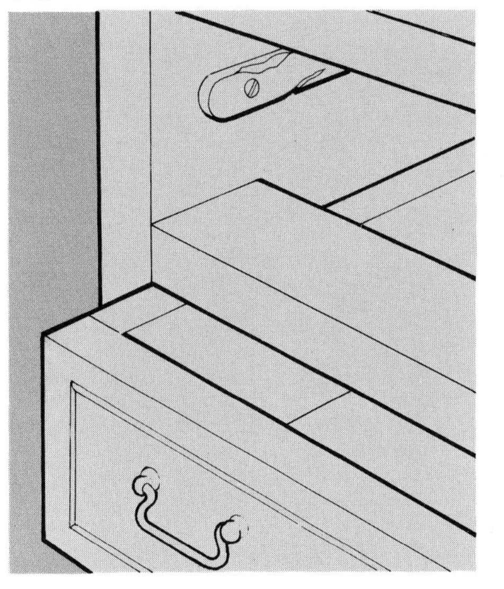

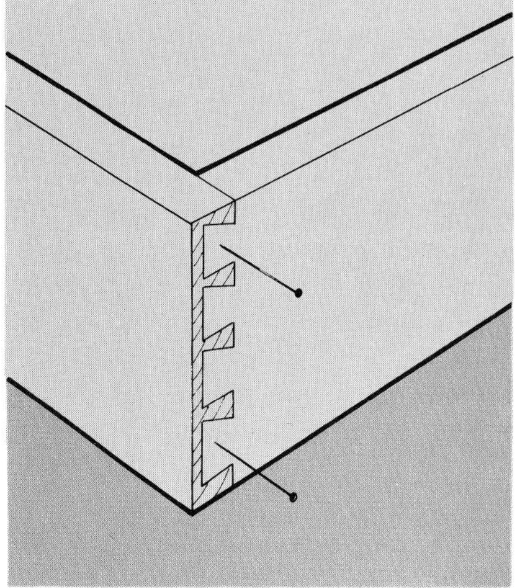

*Above left* Keeping the legs of a stool in the correct shape while the glue dries. The tourniquet is made by winding a length of string or rope twice round the legs. A wooden block is then inserted between the pieces of string and wound round and round until the string is tight enough.
*Left* Levelling chair legs.
*Above* Decorative, shaped legs such as these, would be best levelled by building up the shorter leg with a scrap of wood.
*Above right* Cramping a broken joint until the glue sets.
*Right* Repairing drawers: worn runners should be replaced (left), and loose joints can sometimes be repaired by panel pins (right); otherwise take joints apart and re-glue them.

## Clear finishes

There is a bewilderingly large selection of commercial finishes on the market but do not be confused by all the labels on tins and bottles. For do-it-yourself purposes, there are three families of finish: water-based, oil-based and spirit-based. Products within the same family are compatible and go safely on top of each other. If you cannot recognize the family base by the smell, look at the instructions for cleaning brushes. Brushes must be cleaned in white spirit for oil-based products, in water for water-based products, and with methylated spirit for spirit-based products, and all finishes can be thinned with their base liquid.

Very broadly, the choice of wood finish lies between a clear finish which will show off the grain or an opaque one for a colour accent. Modern finishes give a family-proof top coat to your furniture. They are more heat-proof, spill-proof and scratch-proof than any of the traditional finishes.

Varnishes have now been replaced by products such as polyurethanes, and these come with gloss, satin or matt finishes and are applied with a paint brush. Choose a good brush as the bristles are softer and fuller and they shed less. Look after it well, for once a good brush has been broken in, it will help all your fine finishes. Spend at least fifteen minutes cleaning it at the end of every job and do not stand it bristle down for any length of time or you will deform it.

If you can deal with one surface at a time on the horizontal, you will lessen the risk of drip marks. Brush on the finish lightly and let the surface level itself out. If you do 'brush out', you must make your strokes lighter each time to break up the original brush strokes you made. If you choose polyurethane, remember that it tends to yellow in time. Rustin's two-part plastic coating dries chemically and gives a very hard finish which can be used to restore plastic laminate surfaces. It can also be tinted with wood stain.

### Shellac

The classic clear top coat used to be shellac. It is still a useful finish, sealer and intermediate coat. It is comparatively cheap, quick drying, and easy to apply with brush or pad when thinned with methylated spirit. Shellac goes over or under anything, enhances the look of wood, and does not devalue antique pieces. Its only snag is that it gives only minimal protection against scratches, hot plates, water and alcohol, and it comes off with spirit-based drinks as easily as it goes on, so it is not really practical for surfaces such as table tops which get heavy wear.

Another easy and cheap shellac finish is three coats of shellac rubbed on with a French polish pad and sanded with fine paper between coats, taking care to wipe the dust carefully away each time. Dull the final coat down to a glow with 000 steel wool and a little wax polish to act as a lubricant.

Different kinds of shellac go on different wood tones: garnet is the deepest tone, button polish a medium golden tone, and for the least colour change, try clear or white shellac.

*Right* A pine sideboard which has been stripped and then waxed to show off the clear grain and wood knots. To wax furniture, apply a liberal coat of antique wax polish using a stiff brush, leave for several hours then polish with a clean brush and a soft cloth.

*Far right* A stripped mahogany dressing table. Mahogany darkens considerably when it is given a finish, see page 98.

## Filling the grain

If you look at a wood surface carefully you will see tiny hairline grooves in the surface. For a flawless clear shiny finish you must use filling. You may find that two coats of shellac adequately levels out the surface of a fine-grained wood, such as beech. With an open-grained wood like oak, you must rub in grain filler for a really smooth surface. Thin a proprietary woodfiller (they are made in several woody tones) with white spirit, brush it on to the wood, allow it to dry partially, and then rub it off so as to leave the filler in the grain. Let it dry for twenty four hours, seal with a thin coat of shellac, then add a clear finishing coat of your choice.

For a special effect you can choose a lighter or darker filler – this will emphasize the grain. Limed oak is a finish that exploits oak's open grain. Brush the wood with a stiff wire brush along the grain to open it. Fish out the thickened pigment at the bottom of a can of white undercoat and rub it *across* the grain to fill it. Let it stand for fifteen minutes, then wipe it off *across* the grain with a rag damped in turpentine. Let it dry thoroughly and then give a clear finish. For a fumed oak look you can use a diluted walnut stain on the oak after stripping the old finish and then fill the grain with an undercoat either darker or lighter than the oak tone.

## Bleaching

To lighten the look of your wood you can use cheap and easily available household bleach, but remember that it will wet and possibly split your wood. A bleached piece will need a clear finish to protect the wood.

## Linseed oil and turpentine

The easiest and cheapest traditional finish you can give wood is the linseed oil and turpentine formula (page 98) rubbed hard into the wood every day until you get the colour you want. It flatters the grain, darkens the wood, gives some protection and smells authentic, but it does require patience and elbow grease. A more modern version of this process is Rustin's Danish Oil.

*Below* Linseed oil and turpentine rubbed into raw mahogany with a French polish pad.

*Right* Three steps to French polishing.

*Far right* A French-polished mahogany table top.

## French polish

There is much mystique about this classic finish which is extensively used on valuable furniture, but it is cheap and quick and if you make a mistake you can always take it off in minutes with methylated spirit.

French polishing is best done in clear daylight, in a warm, dust-free room. Hands can be protected with barrier cream (not gloves), and do not wear wool as this might shed hairs and fluff on the work. An efficient pad fitting snugly into your hand is essential to ensure the surface goes on smoothly. Cut a 15 cm (6-inch) square of cotton wool, fold it in half to form a triangle, then fold the corners in to make a pear shape. Cut a piece of lint-free cotton about 18 cm square – for example a large old handkerchief is ideal. Soak it in methylated spirit and wring it out. Put the cotton wool in the middle of the soaked cotton rag and pour enough shellac on to it so it is soaked through but not dripping, then wrap the edges of the rag round it, flattening the pad and making sure that there are no creases. Press the pad on a piece of wood so the polish oozes through – by twisting the rag at the back you can control the flow of shellac. It is very important to put the right amount of shellac on the pad, as too much causes ridges and blobs which you cannot remove except by taking all the finish off and starting again. For the same reason do not press too hard when the pad is full of polish.

**Step 1** Lightly rub the pad across the grain of the surface, never letting it pause on the surface, and never going back on your work. Work in long strokes from one side to the other; this will deposit an even coat of polish on the surface and fill the grain. Let it dry for about twenty minutes, then sand it down carefully with fine paper and dust it off. Repeat the process, until by looking at the work against the light, you can see that the grain is reasonably well filled. Let the work dry overnight, keeping the pad in a screw-topped jar. Next day, rub the surface down again and dust it carefully.

**Step 2** This step builds up the coat of polish. Undo the pad and pour a little more shellac on the cotton wool. Starting at one corner of the work, methodically rub in little circles right across to the other side, then back again overlapping the circles and covering the piece evenly over the whole surface. As before, do not pause or go back on your work, and never glide the pad on and off the work. The shellac dries in minutes and after a few coats you will see the polish building up. Should the pad feel as if it is sticking, smear a fingerful of linseed oil on it to lubricate it. If in doubt, stop, as it is better to have too thin a surface than a thick sticky one.

**Step 3** Undo the pad and pour some methylated spirit on the back of the cotton wool. Apply this in long smooth strokes along the grain from one side of the surface to the other. Again, never pause or go back and never skim the pad on and off. Let the methylated spirit dry, and repeat the process until the surface is glassy smooth. Let it stand overnight. If you prefer a satin finish, the gloss can be softened down with 000 steel wool plus furniture polish for protection.

SHELLAC
METHS

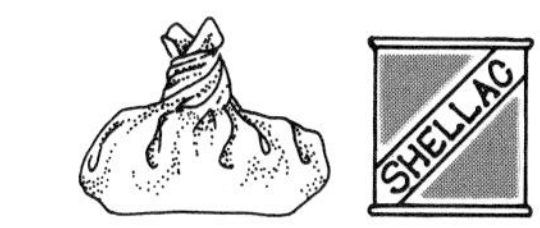
SHELLAC

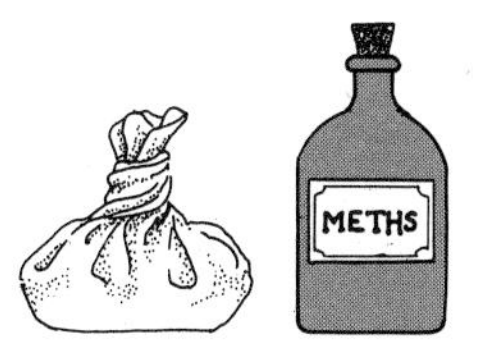
METHS

## Staining

While a fine piece of wood needs no artificial colouring, the pale, bland look of whitewood can be made to tone in with a roomful of existing furniture by staining with bright colours which do not spoil the woody texture. The colour of a piece can be matched up or restyled after you have stripped it or bleached it. Each manufacturer has its own stain formulation and makes a compatible clear finish to go with the stain, as the stain itself does not protect the wood. For the colour you want, experiment on a hidden bit, inside a drawer front, for example, to see whether the stain needs thinning or mixing.

Apply the stain in daylight, with straight strokes the full length of the surface, and finishing one surface at a time. Do not pause, and do not go back on your work, and do not let the liquid collect in one place.

## Tinted clear coatings

You can change the look of your wood with either a natural or a bright colour and give a glossy finish at the same time. The snags are that any scratches on the surface go straight through to the original wood and may make unsightly marks. Also the colour build-up with each coat can be unpredictable and this is tricky if you are trying to match one surface with another. The craftsman's method is to stain first and then clear-coat the work separately.

*Above left* A stained whitewood wardrobe. The four centre panels have a motif stencilled (see page 104) in wood stains. The piece has been given a proprietary clear finish.

*Left* A whitewood chest of drawers, stained and given a clear finish.

*Right* Six steps to painting a chair. Unless you work methodically, you often find you have missed part of a rung.

1 side edges of rungs
2 upper side of rungs
3 underside of rungs
4 inside of front legs, outside of back legs
5 outside of front legs, inside of back legs, underside of seat
6 chair back and seat.

# Opaque finishes

## High gloss paint

The first job is to prepare the surface. New wood should be sanded and then given a coat of primer following manufacturer's instructions, before putting on the undercoat.

To prepare a previously painted surface, wash it with soap and water, rinse it off, and while it is wet, rub it with 320 gauge wet and dry paper. The paper will cut and dull the peaks of the surface, so keep rubbing until the surface is uniformly matt. Then change to a finer paper, such as 400. Fill any holes with an oil-based filler, which must be left to harden properly and then rubbed absolutely smooth with fine paper.

Put on the undercoat evenly and smoothly and allow it to harden completely – two days at least. Wet sand the undercoat then rinse the surface. Let it dry and take off every speck of dust with a damp rag or a tack cloth. A tack cloth is a piece of rag soaked in equal parts of oil-based clear finish and turpentine and kept in a screw-top jar so that it stays sticky. For the most flawless finish choose a gloss paint of the traditional kind (oil-based), not a thixotropic one. The latter drips less and takes less skill to put on, but the finish is never so free of brush marks. Gloss paint takes some time to dry and in that time dust from the air can settle and stick. One way of avoiding this is to hang the piece upside down and paint it from underneath. This would be feasible for something small such as the top of a small coffee table for which you require an immaculate finish. Otherwise, work in as dust-free a room as you can, with no air flow and few people coming and going, and never wear wool. Pick off bits of dust with a needle when you see them. Allow each gloss coat to dry completely – do not be deceived by surface hardness, as it takes at least three days for each coat to dry. Between each coat, wet sand with fine paper, rinse, dry, and finish with a tack rag before the new coat. Clean your brushes scrupulously. Avoid getting dust into the paint by pouring the required amount for each coat into a dish or paint kettle, never taking the paint from the tin. Once you have opened the tin, strain the paint each time through an old stocking to make sure no dust has got in. All this may sound extreme, but it is how those glossy doors in the paint advertisements are arrived at! If you do not have the patience, settle for a matt or eggshell finish.

## Satin finish paint

Look for a modern formula paint like Vymura Colour Sheen which goes on like a traditional oil-based paint – that is, it needs spreading carefully and evenly but only minimum brushing out, and goes on any surface, walls as well as furniture. Brushes are easy to clean and it gives a dense, almost matt finish which flatters even an imperfect surface.

An emulsion paint is the easiest of all paints to put on and dries to a satin matt finish (according to type) but it is vulnerable to finger marks. Add a coat of acrylic sealer like Mander's Gard which looks milky as you paint it on but dries clear. Gloss emulsions are also available but are neither as shiny nor as durable as traditional oil-based gloss paints. They are, however, much easier to use.

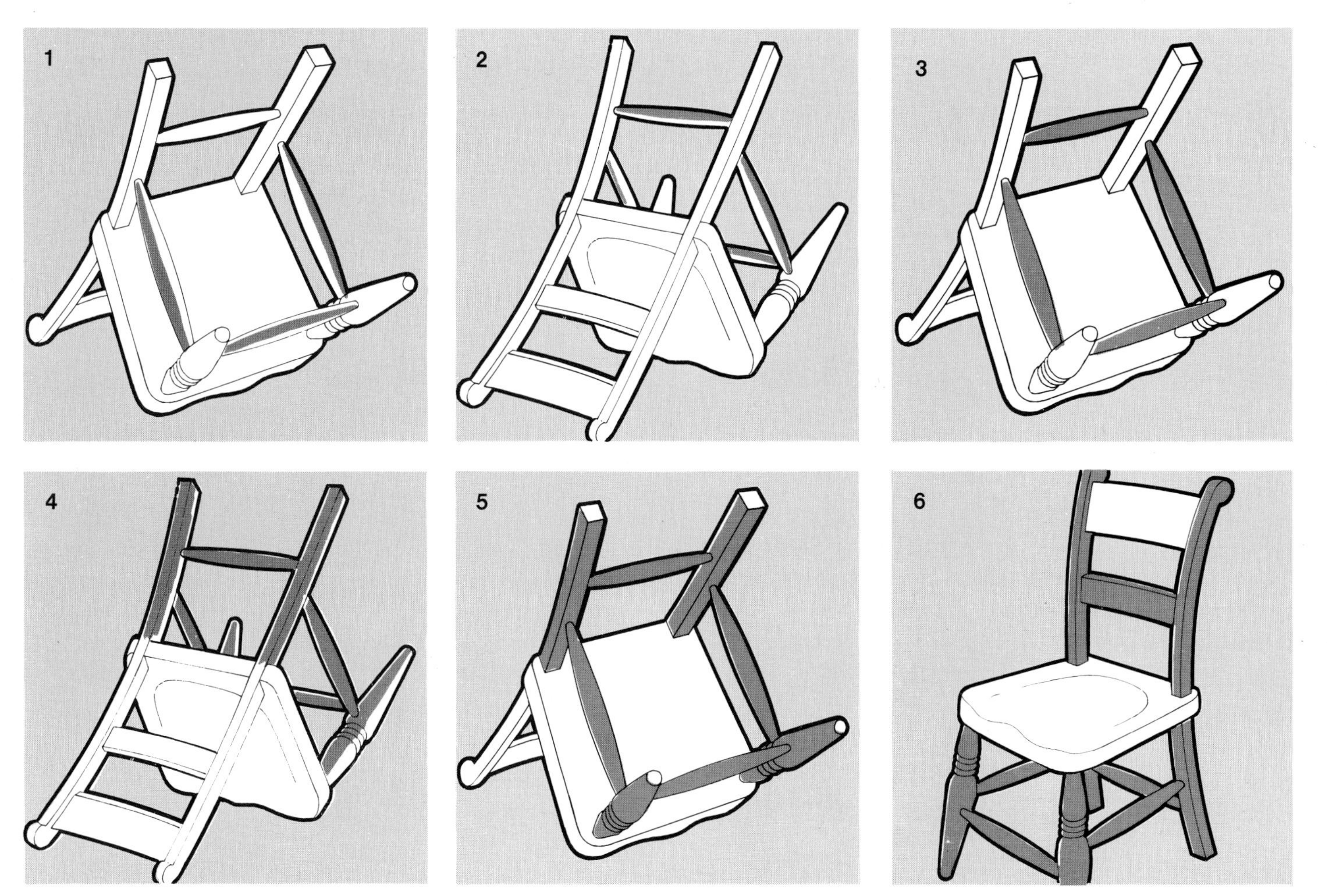

## Lacquer look

One of the smartest finishes for a plain piece, such as a modern coffee table, is satiny red or black lacquer, and it is a finish which looks right in modern or traditional rooms.

The surface of your piece must be perfect so it must be filled meticulously and smoothed and you must soften the hard edges of the piece with a Surform tool. All this is time-consuming, but not really hard work. Keep looking at the surfaces against the light, and when you are satisfied, give the wood a thinned shellac sealer coat. When it is dry, sand the piece again with the finest abrasive paper and go over it with 000 steel wool. Make sure that there is no dust by blowing, brushing, wiping and finally using a damp chamois leather. The perfectionist will coat with shellac again and repeat the process.

Put on the first coat of gloss – either black, or red dulled down with a teaspoon or so of black paint stirred in thoroughly. Turn the piece over as you work so that you are painting each surface on the horizontal. Let it dry for an hour and then rub it down and add a second coat. If you prefer a non-shiny finish, in three days' time, when the gloss has dried, rub the piece down with 000 steel wool and a wax polish, taking about a minute per square foot.

# Wood finishes for whitewood

## Antiquing

If you do not want your furniture to have a newly-painted look, consider antiquing. In a brown colour it can make a piece of whitewood fit into a roomful of period furniture. It can also give a different look to a really boring or battered piece. It particularly flatters pieces with a lot of mouldings and turnings. Use water- or oil-based paints.

**Water-based paints** After stripping or rubbing down, coat the piece with a light-coloured emulsion paint so that the old finish is obliterated. If you need more than one coat, allow it to dry between coats. Then tint some emulsion to a deeper tone with watercolours or poster paints – experiment for the right shade, remembering that the paint will dry lighter. Thin the tinted emulsion with an equal amount of water, and paint a thin but even glazing coat over your base colour. Then wipe it off the mouldings and turnings, leaving the deeper tone in the crevices; or drag a dry paint brush along each surface so you can pick off the deeper tone in lines that look a little like woodgrain. Alternatively, you can dab this coat on with a sponge or cloth, or spatter it on with a toothbrush. Work on a small area at a time, but do not overwork the piece and make sure that the effect matches up on all the different areas. Lively effects can be achieved with white emulsion base and a brightly or deeply coloured glaze, while more subtle effects come from a near-match shading – obtained by tinting the glaze with raw umber water colour over a clear or pale undercoat. When you have a satisfactory result, finish the piece with a clear coat of shellac.

**Oil-based paints** For a more substantial finish on a piece which will get heavy wear, you could use the same method with oil-based paints. Coat the piece with an oil-based undercoat or eggshell paint. Mix an oil glaze (three tablespoons turpentine to one tablespoon warm linseed oil) with a squeeze of artist's oil paint in a deeper shade than the base, such as raw umber. Choose a paint which dries slowly and so gives you more chance to manipulate the effect.

## Graining

This gives a woody look on a painted finish and is particularly useful in cases where the wood might be too patched and filled for a clear finish. The process is simple, and the possibilities are limitless. Paint the piece with Matsine undercoat – it comes in woody shades. Then paint on a thin coat of scumble. Matsine and scumble are available from specialist paint shops/trade suppliers. Take off the coat of scumble with a graining comb (Dryad's make one) or a coarse-toothed hair comb to make it look like wood grain. Alternatively, use a rubber graining roller (Ridgeley Trimmer Co., 117–119 Clerkenwell Road, London EC1 make them), and with practice you will be able to imitate knots and different grain effects. The scumble stays manipulable for up to an hour, so if the effect does not please you, you can smooth it out and start again. Allow twenty-four hours between each coat and protect the final result with a clear finish. The old skilled grainers were able to imitate any kind of wood but it is not difficult for an amateur to achieve a general 'woody' look.

# Furniture restoration

*Far left* A whitewood coffee table, painted to achieve the lacquer look.

*Left* When antiqueing is done with brightly coloured paints, the piece acquires a modern look. However, if dull brown shades are used modern furniture can be made to fit in with antique pieces.

*Bottom* A modern chest which has been effectively grained.

*Below* The materials used for graining: the rubber graining roller is in the foreground.

# Decorative finishes

## Patterns with masking tape

A simple way to give a plain painted surface an interesting pattern is by using a roll of masking tape. With this method you can brighten up a bit of modern whitewood or give a period piece a narrow band of colour such as gold or black round the edges for a simple finishing touch. Test first by pressing a small bit of tape on the piece in an unobtrusive place to make sure it will not damage your existing finish when removed.

For a simple stripe, decide how wide it is to be and where it is to go, and if possible turn the piece over so the surface you will be working on is horizontal. Smooth a length of masking tape along one edge of the proposed stripe and a second length along the other edge. Place the tape down firmly in place with the back of a teaspoon in order to prevent paint running underneath. Using acrylic paint, which adheres to most surfaces straight from the tube, apply the colour with a brush or cloth on the space between the tapes. When it is dry, peel off the tape carefully and slowly. When you have gained confidence, you could try this method with gloss or gold paint.

*Above* Trunks with a repeating stencilled motif.

*Right* A plain chair has been given a cheerful new look with spongeing. Tone-on-tone spongeing is particularly effective, and here, one tin of red paint has been mixed with different quantities of white paint for the two tone effect.

## Stencilling

This decoration technique needs patience rather than skill, and can be as simple or as elaborate as you choose. You can buy ready-made stencils at stationery shops or you can trace your own shapes onto thin card, cut them out with a craft knife and coat the card on both sides with shellac to stiffen it.

The design need not be elaborate; simple shapes can be used in a variety of ways. Draw your motif in the centre of a piece of card and cut it out on glass (a picture flat on its back is ideal), holding the knife more or less vertical. It is often easier to cut straight if you hold the knife steady and move the card.

When stencilling it is essential for the paint to be thick (acrylics work well) and for the stencil to be held tightly against the surface so the paint does not run underneath – work on the horizontal if you can turn the piece. Use a paint pad, a sponge or a stumpy paint brush and dab the paint into the stencil holes, starting in the centre and working up to the edges. The colour need not be solid, you can get some subtle effects by shading or dabbing the paint. Unfinished whitewood can be given a country look by coating the raw wood in shellac, stencilling patterns in acrylic paint and then giving the whole piece a clear finish. Subtle effects can be achieved by tone-on-tone stencils (for example dark green on a light green background) or gloss paint on a matt background.

## Découpage

Traditionally, this was a craft needing exceptional patience. On a surface carefully prepared and finished you neatly glued paper cut-outs. Coat after coat of clear finish – thirty or forty in all – were then applied until the edges of the paper were completely incorporated in the finish. The piece had to be kept in a dust-free room, preferably under a little tent of sheeting, and every day it was given another coat until the desired finish was achieved.

Fortunately, there is now a method more in keeping with our hurried times. First, paint your piece with emulsion paint. The motifs you choose should be small ones and it is not advisable to take them from a book or magazine or you will have see-through problems. It is better to take them from something like an uncoated wallpaper, and to choose

*Left* A plain chest is given a 'Chinese look' by a coat of lacquer-coloured paint, an appropriate change of handles, and the découpage technique has been used to apply decorative motifs.

the thinnest paper you can. Cut out the motifs painstakingly with curved nail scissors. The easiest way to cut is to hold the scissors still and guide the paper into the blades. Arrange the motifs, pencilling in their positions if necessary. Spread adhesive smoothly and evenly on the back of the cut-out. Place the cut-out in position and press firmly – a wallpaper edge roller is useful here, as there must be no bubbles. When the glue is dry, give the whole piece two or more coats of a water-thinned acrylic glaze like Unibond or Mander's Gard, allowing it to dry between each coat. This protects the paper and gives the emulsion something of a protective sheen at the same time. This method works well on doors, sides of furniture, backs of chairs and little-used surfaces, but you will need more coats of finish for areas of wear such as table tops.

## Spongeing

This is an economical way to make whitewood furniture look more interesting. Buy a natural decorator's sponge (from a local shop which supplies the trade – in London John T. Keep, 15 Theobald's Road, London EC1 is a useful address). Paint your piece with white emulsion paint. Mix a cupful of Mander's Gard in a basin and tint it with Universal Stainer to the colour of your choice – ten intermixable pastel tones give you an infinite range of soft subtle colours. Dip your sponge into the mixture, squeeze it out and then pat the colour onto the emulsion so you get a natural irregular mottle. As the finish dries fast, blob first in the corners of a surface, then the middle, then fill in so the base-coat shows evenly and the mottle is regular. If in doubt, give a light coat first and let the piece dry. It is easier to add more than take it away. Another trick is to mottle lightly with a pale tint, then add some more stainer to the mixture and mottle again. A coating of Mander's Gard gives the piece a surface which can be wiped clean when dry.

The possibilities of a tin of white paint (any kind) and a tube of stainer are infinite. You can get the subtlest gradation of colours from soft pastels to deeper tints by altering the proportions of paint to stainer, and you can always be sure that the tones you create will go together.

# Woodwork

Wood evokes immediate response; fine timber and traditional crafting brighten and beautify our existence. Much pleasure can be derived from learning how to become proficient in handling the tools used for woodworking, and as with all crafts, it is helpful first to understand something of the nature of the material to be worked.

## Wood structure

Wood is the flesh of the tree, and just as there are many different kinds of tree, so there are many types of wood, and each piece of wood has its own recognizable family features – a particular texture, grain and colour.

As a tree grows, new wood forms just beneath the bark. Each year's growth repeats this process and this causes the ring patterns on a cross section of a tree trunk. The alternating dark and light rings show the spring and summer development of the tree. Slow growing trees such as oak have a closer ring patterning (grain) than faster growing trees. The closer the grain, the denser and heavier the timber, and wood from fast growing trees which has a widely spaced grain (such as pine), tends to split along its length much more easily.

## Classification of wood

Wood is classed as either hard or soft. The distinction is botanical, hardwoods coming from broadleaf trees and softwoods from coniferous trees. Hardwoods are heavier and more difficult to work than softwoods, but there are certain exceptions, notably balsa wood which is used by modellers. It is probably the lightest and softest timber in general use, yet it is classed as a hardwood.

**Hardwood** The great furniture makers of the past used mostly hardwoods – Chippendale, Sheraton, Hepplewhite and Adam designs were mainly carried out in mahogany, a strong wood that has an attractive colour and fine graining. It is still used today, but more often as a veneer.

Native timbers, particularly oak, have been part of our heritage for so long that they are often unregarded nowadays. Oak grows slowly, matures slowly and is seasoned slowly – the perfect recipe for a durable timber. It finishes beautifully, and if the examples of the past are anything to judge by, it lasts forever.

**Softwood** Common softwoods include both home-grown and imported pine of several varieties, often grouped under the general heading of deal.

Softwoods are used extensively for structural woodwork and for do-it-yourself purposes. They are cheaper than hardwoods and are easier to rip (saw along the grain). However they generally do not last as long and they have less resistance to surface damage.

Sawn softwood comes in standard lengths from 1.8 metres to 6.3 metres, and it is generally available in a number of widths from 25 mm to 225 mm and in thicknesses from 16 mm to 38 mm.

Tongued and grooved boarding can also be bought: strips of pine, commonly 20 cm wide, are grooved one side and have a tongue on the other which fits into the groove on the next sheet.

## Buying wood

Wood sizes are quoted in measurements of the width by the thickness by the required length.

The sizes at the timber yard refer to *sawn* timber. If you buy wood that has been *planed* after sawing, it may be fractionally smaller than the quoted size, so it is essential to measure accurately the actual piece you are working on. It is possible, but more expensive, to order timber sawn and planed to 'finished' size.

Timber brought in from an outdoor store into the home may react. Warping and twisting can be minimized if the wood is bought a week or two before it is to be used, and stacked flat indoors while its moisture content dries out further. Better at this time than after construction!

Avoid heavily knotted timbers, particularly in hardwoods, but do aim to select timber that has clear grain markings. Always buy lengths that will allow you to cut what you need with minimum wastage.

## Man-made boards

Various types of boards are usually sold in sheets measuring 2440 mm by 1220 mm. Many shops will cut exact sizes to order.

*Chipboard* is made from wood particles bonded together by heat and pressure with special resins. It is heavy, and if used for book shelves, needs supporting every 45 cm along the length. Chipboard must be used with special double-threaded chipboard screws. It is available in thicknesses from 4 mm to 25 mm and is often veneered.

*Plywood* is much stronger than chipboard and therefore thinner. It comes in thicknesses from 3 mm to 32 mm. Plywood is made by bonding together 3 or more veneers of wood (hardwood or softwood or a combination of both) so that the grain of one piece is at right-angles to the next.

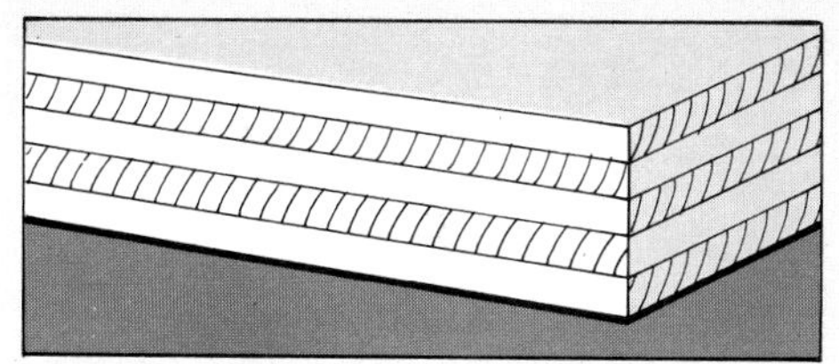

*Blockboard* is made from strips of wood up to 25 mm wide, bonded under pressure between single or double ply sheets. It comes in thicknesses from 12.5 mm.

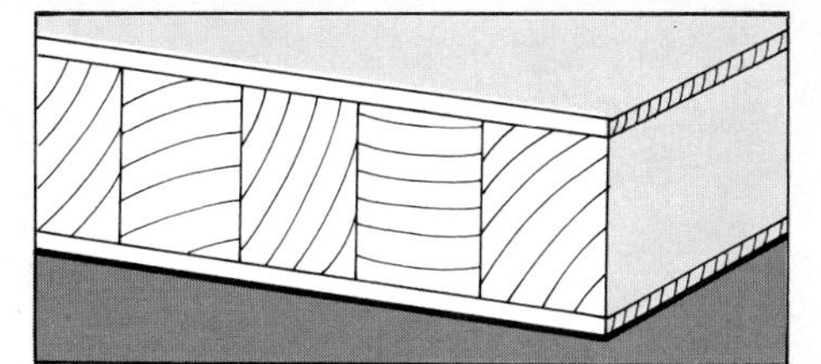

*Hardboard* is a thin sheet material made of pressed pulp. Although flexible, it is reasonably strong when supported, and is suitable for backings for pictures, collages etc. One side is smooth and shiny, the other textured or 'meshed'. It is also available cut with decorative fretted designs, reeded or fluted, and perforated as pegboard.

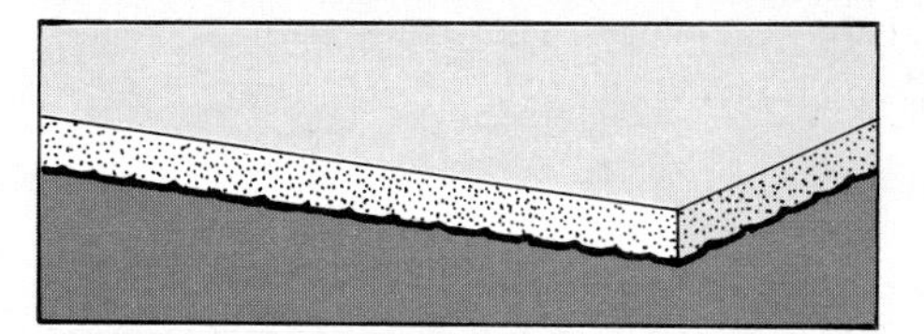

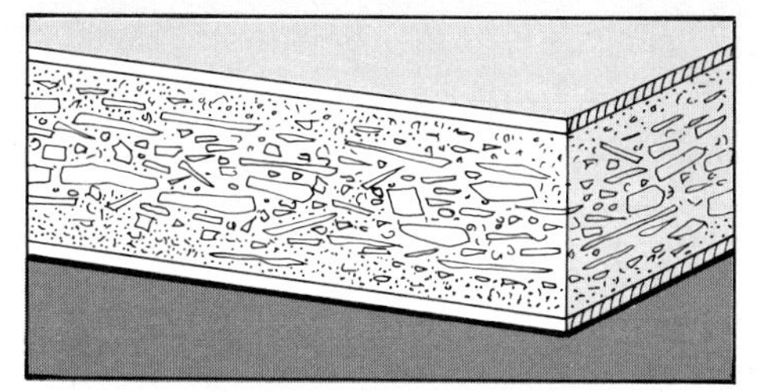

*Left* Wood samples. From top to bottom: mahogany, pine, oak and redwood.

*Above* Cross section of a tree trunk, showing the alternating dark and light growth rings.

*Right* Cross sections of man-made boards. From top to bottom: plywood, blockboard, hardboard, chipboard.

## Basic equipment

Every household has at least a rudimentary toolbox (see page 138) and this will probably contain the few tools that are needed to construct the basic cube. While it may be true that a bad workman always blames his tools, an afternoon bodging along with the wrong weapons can be exasperating.

**Workbench** A good workbench is probably the most essential tool that is required. A firm kitchen table is satisfactory but it is advisable to protect it with a sheet of blockboard cut to size, as any surface to be worked on will sustain severe damage.

**Vice** Ideally, a woodwork vice should be available; later, when more ambitious projects are tackled, it will be essential. It should never be tightened enough to damage the work, indeed, a wooden block should be placed between the timber being worked and the jaws of the vice to avoid bruising the held timber.

**Saw** Saws come in many shapes and sizes but their use is confined to two basic functions: ripping wood along its grain or cutting across the grain. The main difference lies in the number and size of teeth that the saw needs to rip or crosscut efficiently. A general saw which will do both jobs will have 8 teeth to the inch.

**Plane** A plane is the tool that most rouses uncertainty in the beginner but sharpening and setting a blade correctly is not the mystery that legend would have you believe and for the job that you are about to tackle some sort of small plane is necessary. A popular substitute for the professional thing is a proprietary shaping tool (such as a Surform) but do not be misled – such tools are designed to shape wood and other materials but can never achieve the effect you will be attempting when, for example, smoothing end-grain. A jackplane is what is needed.

**Trysquare** In all this work, square-on precision will be impossible without a trysquare or something which you know has a *guaranteed* 90 degree angle between two *straight* sides – do not be tempted to rely on the corner of a book – accuracy is essential.

**Steel tape** A steel tape is essential for accurate measurement.

**Drill** Holes can be driven with a hand drill (or wheelbrace as it is often called) fitted with a twist drill bit of the correct size.

**Screwdriver** Screws need to be tightened home with a screwdriver.

**Bradawl** A bradawl helps to locate and start the screw in the right way.

### Using tools

Useful tips will be picked up with practice in the use of these and other tools but there are one or two essentials to observe, both for safety and ease of operation.

**Saw** A saw cuts only on the downward stroke but heavy pressure is not needed if the teeth are correctly set and if the saw is sharp. Always saw *outside* your cutting line, on the waste side of the material then plane to size.

**Plane** When using the plane, stance is important – good balance on feet set slightly apart and the weight of the shoulders directly over the plane means that the tool can be operated by shifting weight from foot to foot, keeping elbows well tucked in to the body. The major difficulty when planing across the grain on the end of a timber length is that the far edge splits and tears. A simple solution is to clamp a piece of offcut to the far edge and plane right across both pieces of wood.

**Drill** Before using the drill, mark the point at which the hole should be made – punching the timber with a blunted nail will stop the drill bit from skidding across the work. While it is essential to hold the hand drill vertical at all times, remember that the left hand is for support only – do not press down too firmly – a sharp drill bit will do all the work.

### Woodwork joints

These fall into three categories; overlocking, interlocking and butted joints. The butt joint is the simplest, most basic way of joining two pieces of wood at right angles to each other (1).

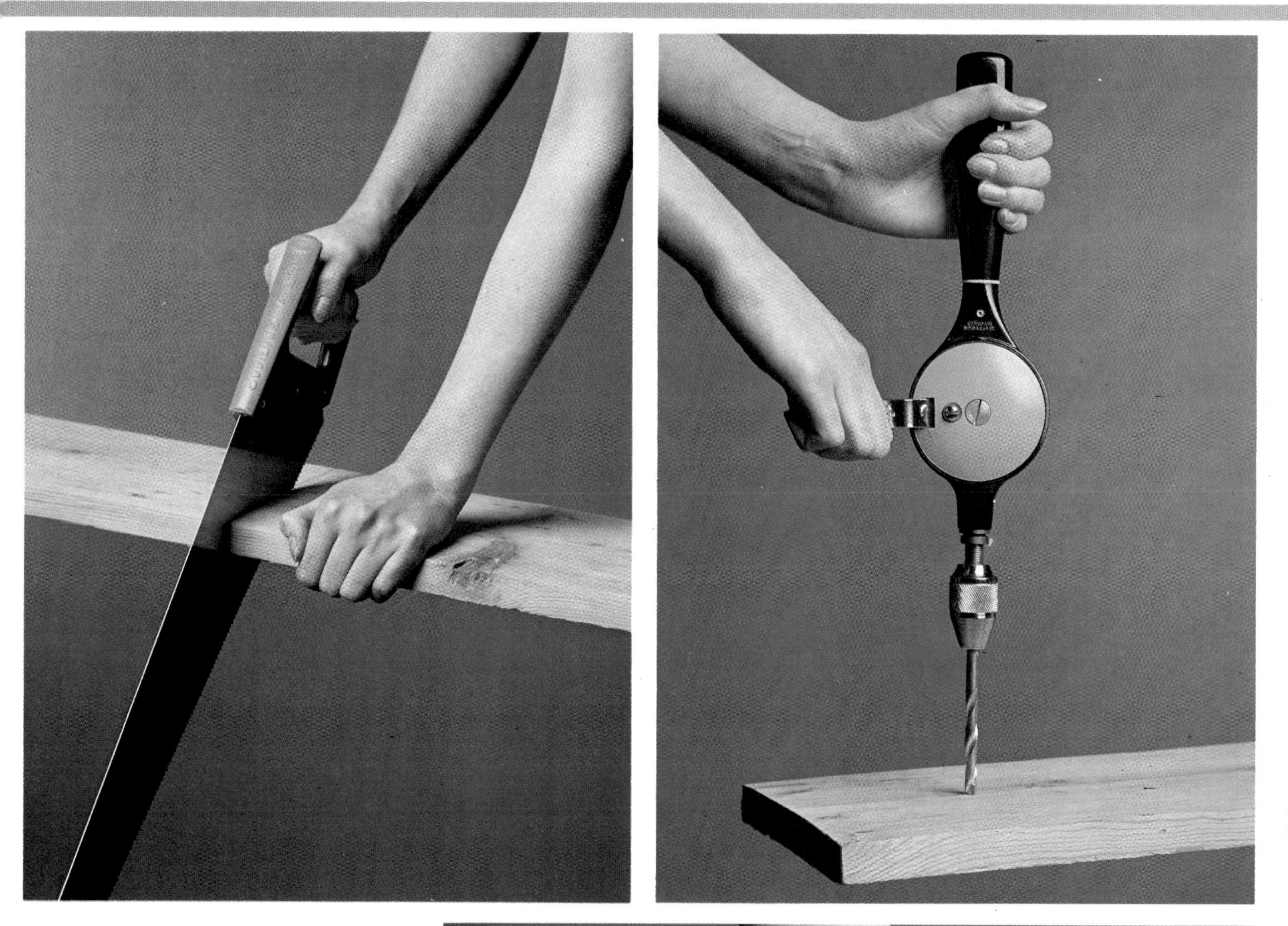

*Above left* Shelf unit constructed using L-butt and T-butt joints.
*Above* Using a saw.
*Above right* Using a drill.
*Below right* Using a plane.
*Below* L-butt joint.

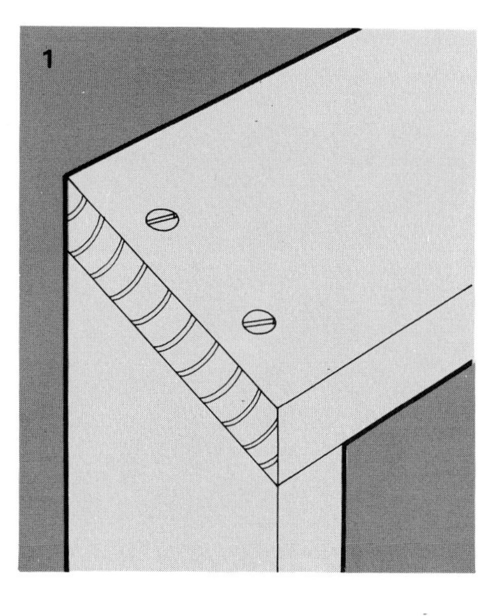

# The versatile cube

Modern designers have coped with the constant demand for more and more storage space with modular units. A simple box-shape 50 cm square allows a remarkable number of permutations within the home and as each unit is completed, the system can be moved or given a new function. Deeper units can be made with simple joining methods, using the basic module. The simplest and most professional joint is made by cutting a groove into the facing edges of the pieces to be joined and inserting a tongue of ply (2), gluing and clamping the boards *before* making up into the final cube. Proprietary faced block or chipboards will extend the range and size of the basic cube.

Each unit will be either free-standing or wall-hung, depending on its purpose within a room. Cubes may also be subdivided or compartmentalised for specific purposes. Doors, lids, and interior shelves are all simple additions.

Planning the use of each module and its effect on the space around it is all-important before setting out to achieve the finished result. What is needed? A toybox? Spice cupboard? Tape deck housing? Hideyhole for the wellies? Thoughtful decisions at this stage can save time and effort and possible disappointment. Make rough sketches of what you would like to achieve, or try placing cardboard boxes of about the same size in the situations you envisage.

## Making up

Using a trysquare and rule, carefully measure and mark off 50 cm on the chosen wood. Do not imagine that sawing a straight line is beyond your capabilities – practice will give you confidence. Remember that even professional craftsmen mark their timber accurately and have to concentrate to keep a handsaw square to the work!

Four of these 50 cm lengths are needed for the sides of the basic unit. Remember that wood sizes quoted by the retailer are always nominal. Timbers were once sawn to 20 cm at the yard but since then they have been smooth-planed and prepared so that a certain amount of width is missing. Keep this in mind while working and planning and always measure accurately what you have actually got on the bench in front of you.

Mark four points at one end of each of the lengths and drill through, 12 mm from the edge. When all sixteen holes are drilled, change the bit to a countersink rose and burr out. The countersink rose cuts out a conical shape at the top of the hole so the head of the screw can sink below the surface (3). At this point, square off the edges of the drilled ends with the jackplane if necessary. Match up a drilled and an undrilled end and mark through each hole with a bradawl. Change from the $\frac{5}{32}$ inch to a $\frac{3}{16}$ inch bit and drill at these points to a depth of 2.5 cm. When all four corners are prepared apply woodworking adhesive to the edges which will be butted together and screw down, one corner at a time, tightening screws equally. To check that the shape is square, measure diagonally across the framework – if both diagonals are equal, you are on target.

Measure the unit sides and mark up and cut from a sheet of $\frac{5}{32}$ inch plywood the square that is to form the back or base and complete the basic open unit. At each corner and at two intermediate centres of each side drill $\frac{5}{32}$ inch holes, each 12 mm from the board edge. Match up the backing ply to the cube shape and mark through the twelve holes with the bradawl. Change to the $\frac{3}{16}$ inch bit and drill out these points to a depth of 12 mm. Match ply and basic cube shape, glue and screw into place using 16 mm (No. 8) screws. Extra tightening into the plyface is safer than risking the countersink rose because ply is laminated and the rose could make the surface ragged.

**Castors** The cube can be made movable by fixing castors to the underside. The variety that slide will do for a cube that is not to contain great weights but if bottles or books are housed, wheel or roller castors, of the plate-fixing variety, should be used.

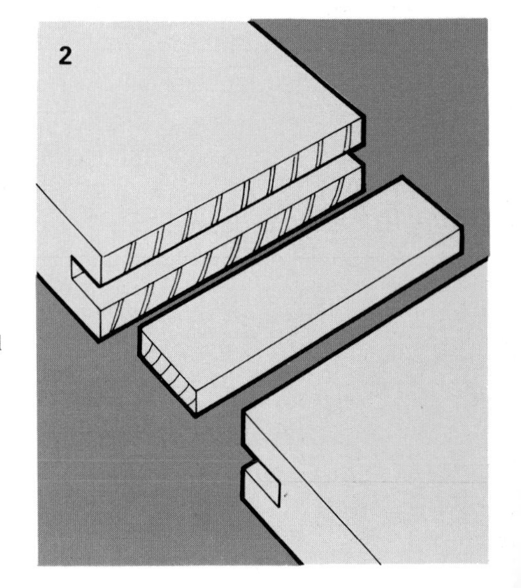


*Right* Diagram 2: making a tongue and groove joint. Diagram 3: using the countersink rose.

*Far right* Making up the unit. left: the diagonals are equal for a square shape. right: the completed unit.

*Above right* A modern furniture system based on the modular unit.

*Far right above* This wardrobe is just a large-scale version of the basic unit, subdivided into compartments.

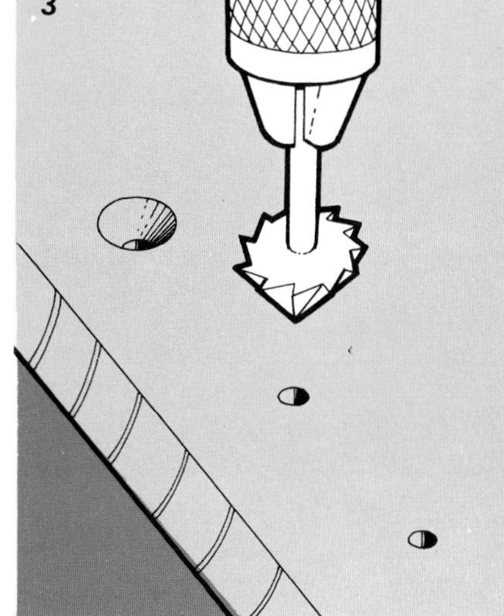
3

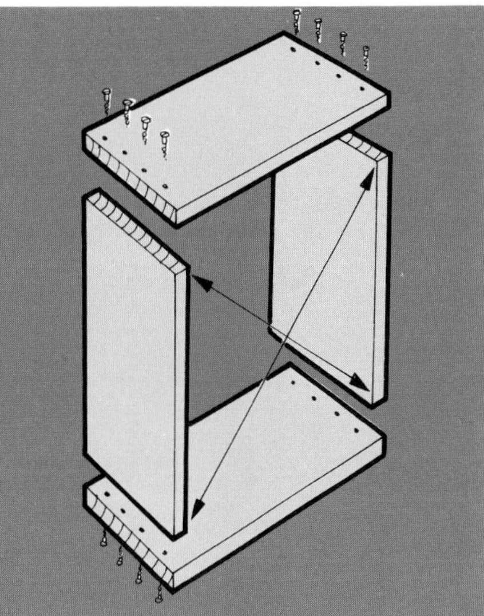

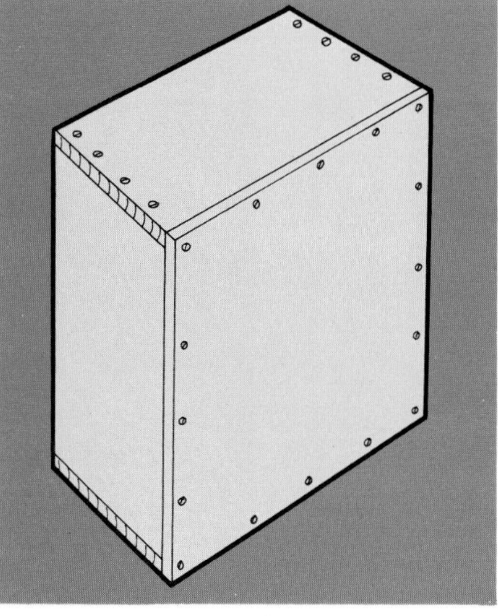

**Shelves** Shelves may be added to divide the cube in a number of ways. Cut timber for a tight fit within the unit and on the outside of the cube mark carefully the proposed shelf position on both sides. Drill four equally spaced holes along these lines and glue and screw the shelf into position (4).

**Compartments** To make compartments you will need a slightly more ambitious fixing called a halving joint. Cut two shelf timbers to the interior horizontal/vertical measurements of the cube and mark the points at which you want them to interact. Draw a line down the centre length of each shelf piece. Place one shelf across the other centred exactly on the chosen point and lightly pencil its actual thickness on the other shelf as far as the centre line (5). Reverse the shelves and repeat. Saw *inside* the pencil lines to the centre line. Use a chisel to remove the tongue of wood that you have cut (6) and glue and slot the two timbers together at right angles (7). They can then be fitted inside the cube, glued and screwed from the outside as before.

**Doors** Measure carefully the inside edges of the cube and cut a square of $\frac{5}{32}$ inch birch ply accurately to size. This panel must now be backframed with 19 mm × 50 mm timbers. Cut two lengths to exact panel size and glue and pin them to opposite edges of the panel, driving pins from the face of the ply through into the frames. Measure distance between frame timbers and cut two more lengths to complete frame, butting them in on the ply panel between the already fixed frame rails (8). When the work has quite dried, use small corrugated fasteners to complete corners (9). Pins may be driven below plyface with a punch and the holes stopped with wood filler.

There are many face-fixing hinges available in ironmongers and department stores which can be fitted without rebating. Simply screw them into the edge of the cube and into the face of the doorframe. Magnetic catches are a favourite for this type of light cabinet and are face fixing on the inside of the cube. One particular type is of the push-opening variety, a spring device thrusting the door open when the door is given a firm push.

If you intend to close the unit with a door, cut the shelf/compartment narrower so that it stands back from the front edge of the cube.

The care and attention that is lavished on the original material is reflected in its finish (see page 114): the time spent on finishing will transform the basic unit into a bright addition to your home.

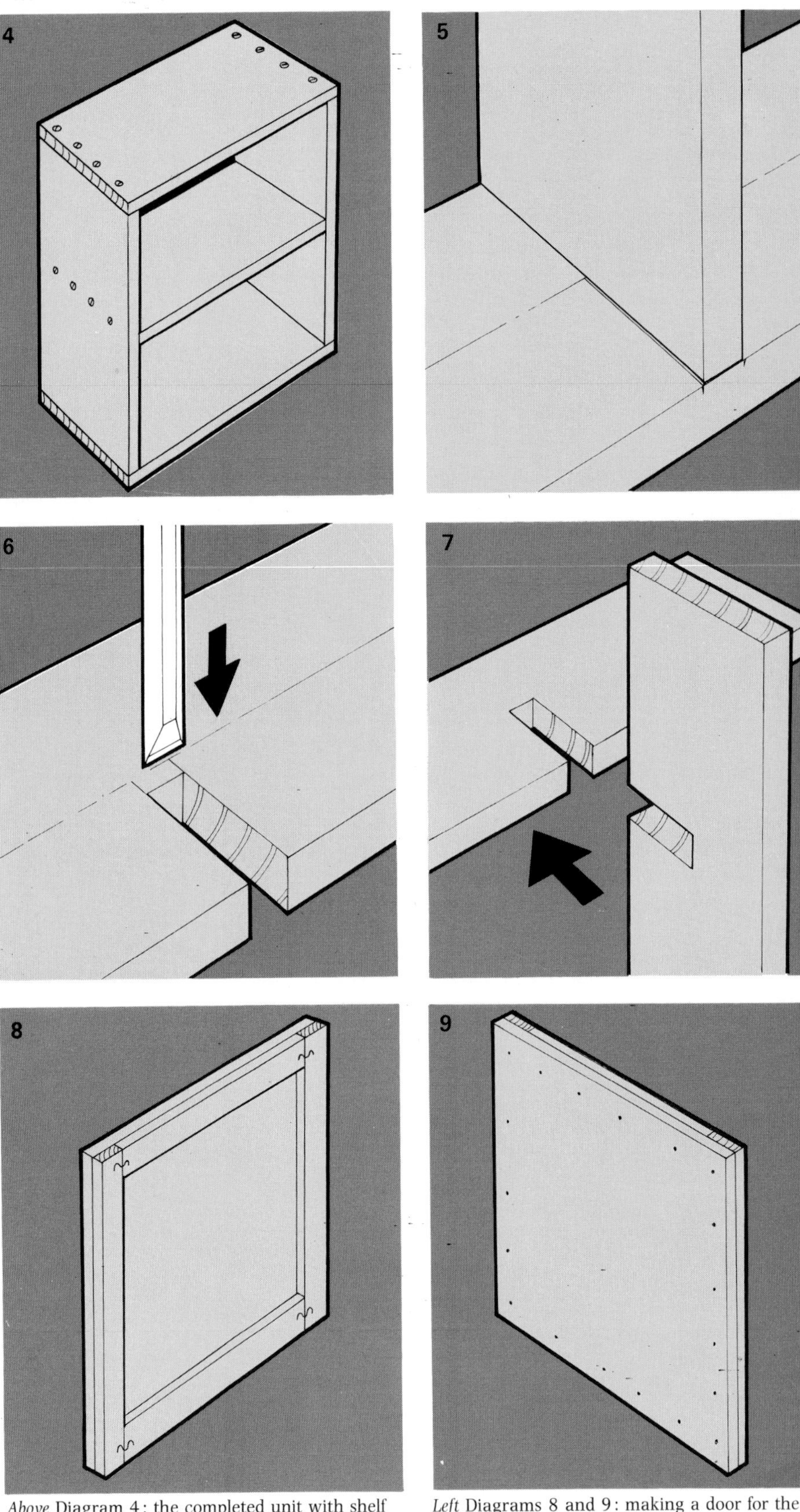


*Above* Diagram 4: the completed unit with shelf added. Diagrams 5, 6, 7: making a halving joint for the compartment.

*Left* Diagrams 8 and 9: making a door for the unit.

*Right* Cubes with doors, shelves, compartments and castors, showing a variety of uses to which the basic unit may be put.

WHITE HORSE
Scotch Whisky

## Shelves

No house ever seems to have enough shelving, there is always a demand for more! Proprietary units are the best answer for freehanging shelves on a plain wall but if you have a niche beside a chimneybreast or a corner to fill, it can be simple to make your own shelves. Using standard 2.5 cm × 25 cm deal, cut accurately to the exact length to fit the space and fix in place with flush mount fittings or mirror plates. For this use a masonry bit in the hand drill and plug the wall holes with rawlplugs.

More permanent fixing can be effected by cutting battens from 16 mm × 50 mm deal and fitting one along the wall at the required height and butting the two short pieces beneath the ends of the shelves – again, drill and plug the wall, screw on the battens firmly and slide the tightfit shelf into place on these supports (10). Screw shelf onto battens. Timber of these measurements can be expected to support reasonable weights over a distance of about one metre – most niches will be wider and support can be effected by following the instructions for fitting shelf and compartment divider in the cube unit. Dowels are sometimes drilled and fitted at intervals along the front edge of shelves to form pegs for hanging cups, outdoor clothes and so on. When working with timber of only 2.5 cm thickness, cuphooks would seem to do the same job more effectively. Dowel holes need to be drilled at least 25 mm into the timber using at least an 8 mm bit. Dowels cut from hardwood can then be glued and driven home, projecting at least 50 mm.

## Finishing wood

With the construction of the work completed, finishing can begin – the more care and planning that has gone into the work so far, the less tedious the tidying and completion will be. All screws are countersunk and the holes filled with a matching wood stopping.

Today's varnishes and polishes save a great deal of time and effort when compared with traditional French polish or ebonizing finishes but beneath the final buffing there is still a need for old-fashioned elbow grease! Two grades of glass, sand or garnet paper are required to bring the unit to a satisfactory state for polishing. The one absolute rule in the use of these medium and fine grades of paper is that you must always rub with the grain. One swirl cutting across the grain will take an age to sand out and will look even worse when varnished. Wrap the paper around an offcut block of wood and work with the grain using not too much pressure. As the work feels smoother, change to the fine grade paper. Rub with the grain as before.

Clear polyurethane varnish will pull out the beauty of the wood grain and will cause some surface darkening but the result on deal should be a rich honey colour. The unit will also look good stained and sealed, or painted (see also Furniture Finishes pages 96–105).

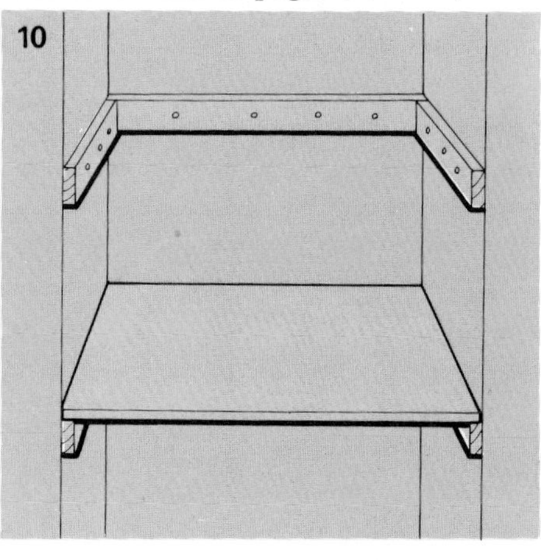


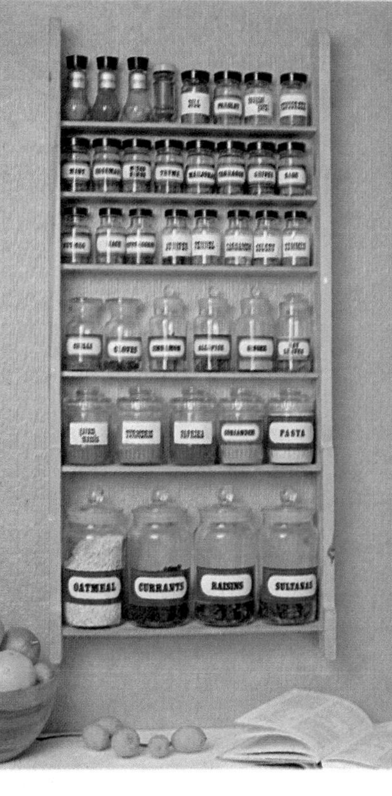

# Doll's house

Overall dimensions: 2440 mm long, 1470 mm high, 225 mm deep.

**Materials required**

**A** 2440 × 1220 (backing panel)
**B** 2440 × 380 (roof)
**3 × C** 2440 × 225 (C1, C2, C3)
**3 × D** 1840 × 225 (D1, D2, D3)
Chimney constructed with offcuts C3, D1, D2.

The 3 'C' pieces of wood, C1, C2, C3, and the 3 'D' pieces of wood, D1, D2, D3, are each cut into smaller lengths as detailed below (retaining their width of 225 mm), and used as indicated in the diagram.

**C1**: 1220; 1220
**C2**: 920; 920; 600
**C3**: 1220; 920; offcut for chimney

**D1 and D2**: 1470 on one side, tapering to 1220 on the opposite side; offcuts for chimney
**D3**: 920; 920

All measurements are in millimetres.

Assemble using the simple butt joint method which was used for the cube.

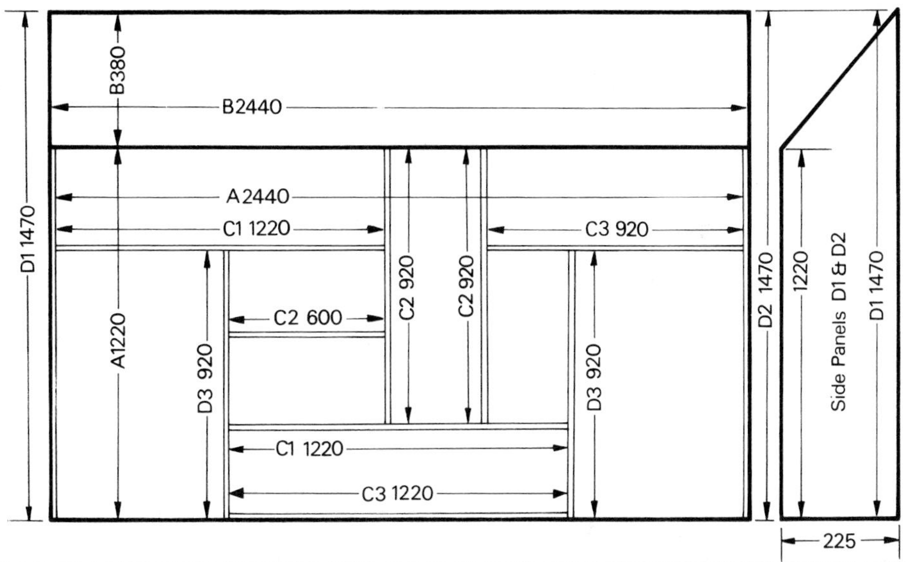

*Above* Shelves supported by wooden battens.

*Far left* Diagram 10: constructing the shelves.

*Left* A spice rack made by the glue and screw T-butt joint method. The rack can be made to the exact size to suit your jars.

*Right* A doll's house shelving unit constructed by the screw and glue T- and L-butt joint method. Blackboard paint has been used for the bottom left hand section, other surfaces have been stained with wood-stainer and given a clear finish.

# Lampshades

Making lampshades is a really absorbing craft as well as being a great money-saver. Ready-made lampshades can be expensive to buy, and it is not always possible to find exactly what you want. Lampshade-making gives scope for creating something practical and attractive for the home at a comparatively low cost. Existing lampshade frames can sometimes be used again, provided they are not out of shape or rusty, and as long as they have enough struts to support the fabric. Remnants of curtain fabric and pieces of material left over from dressmaking can often be made into attractive lampshades that fit into the décor of the home.

## Choosing the base

A large selection of bases is available in all shapes and sizes, but the main thing to consider is whether the base is solid and firm enough to support the shade. Some bases can be top heavy and then it is necessary to weight them with sand or pebbles. If possible, select the base first and then find a lampshade frame to balance with it.

Special converter kits are available which make it easy to transform such things as vases, bottles, candlesticks into attractive lampshade bases.

## Equipment

The tools and equipment for making lampshades are simple and apart from the frames and tape, readily available in the work basket. For binding the struts and rings of the lampshade frame use 1.3 cm wide loosely woven tape. Coloured bias binding can also be used if it is necessary to match the struts to the lining fabric, as for a tiffany style lampshade. Pins play an important part in the construction of a lampshade and can easily mark some fabrics, so be sure to use best steel dressmaking pins that are free from rust and dirt. You will also need scissors, needle and sewing thread.

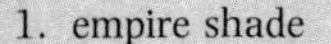

1. empire shade
2. tiffany shade
3. wall-size empire shade with scalloped top and base
4. wall-size empire shade
5. cone-shaped shade
6. square cone shade
7. empire shade with scalloped bottom

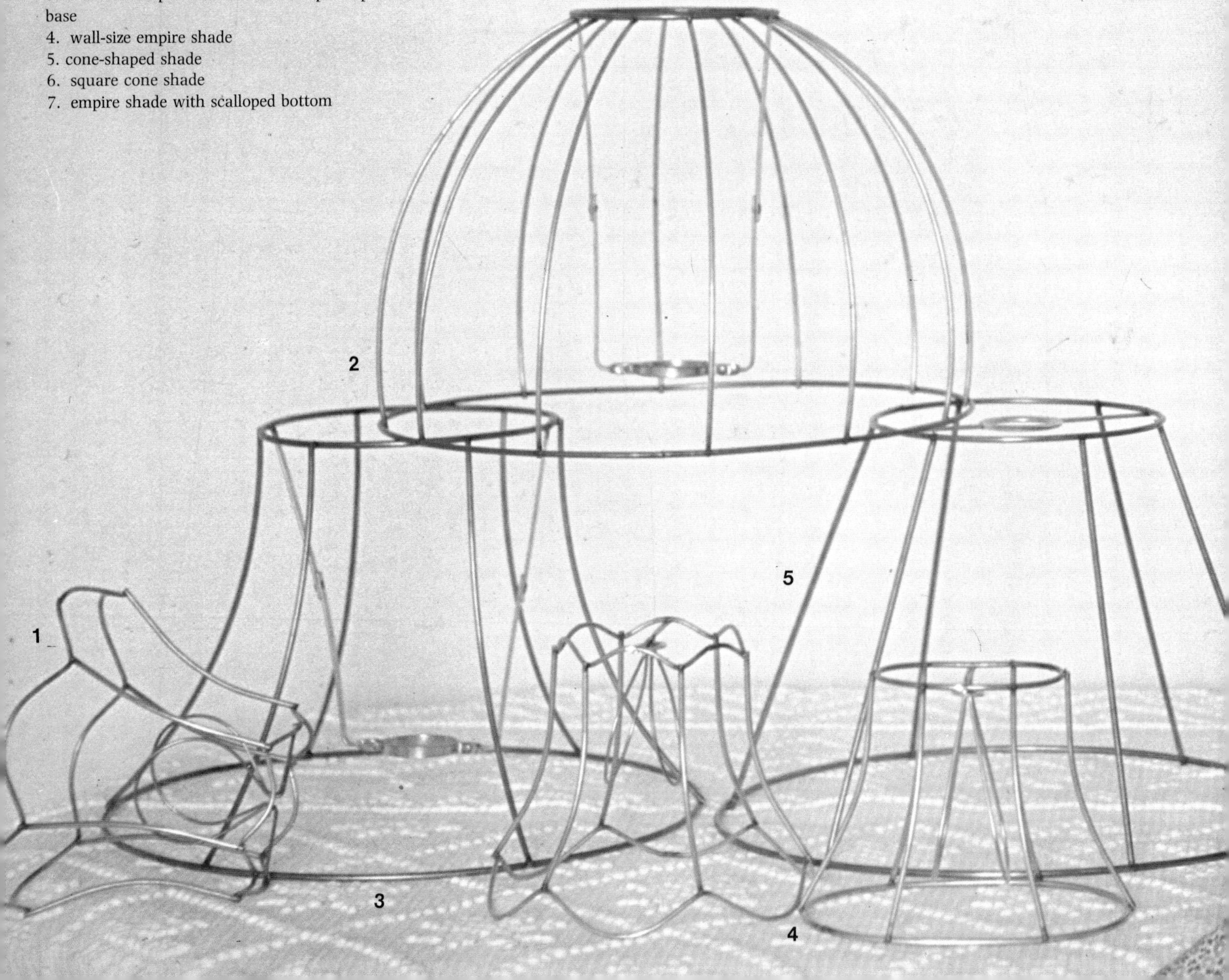

**Frame** It is important to choose the right shape of frame bearing in mind the purpose for which the light is needed. Some shades shed more light than others; some distribute the light evenly, and some produce small pools of light which illuminate only a limited area. There is a shape of lampshade to enhance every type of décor, whether it is of a traditional or a contemporary style.

Frames are made with various types of fittings – when buying your frame make sure you choose the correct fitting for your light so that the bulb is far enough away from the shade to avoid any possibility of burning, and choose one that is made from a firm strong wire. If using an old or existing frame remove all the binding tape, clean it with wire wool and paint it with a quick-drying enamel paint or lacquer. This helps to prevent the frame from rusting when the lampshade is washed. Make sure though that the paint is thoroughly dry before binding with the tape.

6

7

## Fabrics for soft lampshades

There are two types of lampshade – soft and hard. Soft lampshades are made with soft flexible fabrics and hard lampshades are made from special lampshade card or parchment.

For soft lampshades choose fabric that is flexible and that stretches easily. Crêpe-backed satins, rayon dupions, silks and man-made fabrics that have 'give' all make up well. Many dress fabrics and lightweight furnishing cottons can be used most effectively and can look very attractive when matching other furnishings. Broderie anglaise over coloured linings can be particularly successful when used on tiffany-style shades.

Avoid particularly inflammable fabrics such as nylons. Heavy furnishing fabrics are also unsuitable, as they are too thick and do not diffuse the light well. They are also difficult to work.

When making pleated lampshades take care to choose a light-weight fabric that drapes well such as silk and cotton chiffon, shantung silk or fine cotton lawn. Generally, if you choose patterned fabrics, small designs are the most suitable for making lampshades as large patterns can lose their impact or fail to show up to advantage.

Patchwork, macramé and lace are some of the other crafts that can be successfully adapted for use when making lampshades. With a little imagination and skill many original effects can be achieved.

**Lining** For lining soft lampshades, crêpe-backed satin is very suitable as the shiny surface reflects the light and repels dust. Do not use rayon taffeta linings as these are very difficult to stretch over the frame successfully.

**Washing soft lampshades** Most soft fabric shades can be washed successfully with a little care. Use a gentle detergent, swishing the shade in a bowl of warm water and rinsing in fresh water. Dry the shade as quickly as possible to avoid rust forming on the frame.

*Left* A luxurious pleated cone shade, made in a fabric which matches other soft furnishings in the room.

*Right* A fitted empire shade.

*Far right* Diagrams 1–4: binding the struts.

## Binding the frame

It is important when taping the frame to make sure that the binding is tight and firm, on both the rings and the struts. If the binding is loose the stitching will slip and the lampshade will be spoilt. Keep the tape as smooth and as even as possible to avoid it showing through the fabric when the lampshade is complete.

To work out how much tape is required for the lampshade, allow twice the circumference of the top and bottom rings and twice the length of each strut. Bind the struts first and then the top and bottom rings.

**1.** Take a piece of binding tape twice the length of the strut. At the top of the frame fold the tape over the top ring and start to bind the strut, tucking in the end so that the tape is secure (1 and 2).

**2.** Continue to bind the strut until the bottom ring is reached (3). Complete the binding by winding the tape first to one side of the strut and then to the other (a figure of eight) and finish with a knot round the bottom ring (4). Trim off excess tape.

**3.** After binding all the struts, tape the top and bottom rings in the same way, making a figure of eight turn round each join in struts and ring.

**4.** When taping a ring set for a hard lampshade it is necessary to secure the end of the tape to the ring with a little adhesive tape to prevent the tape from slipping. When finishing the binding, secure the ends with a few stitches on the outside edge of the ring.

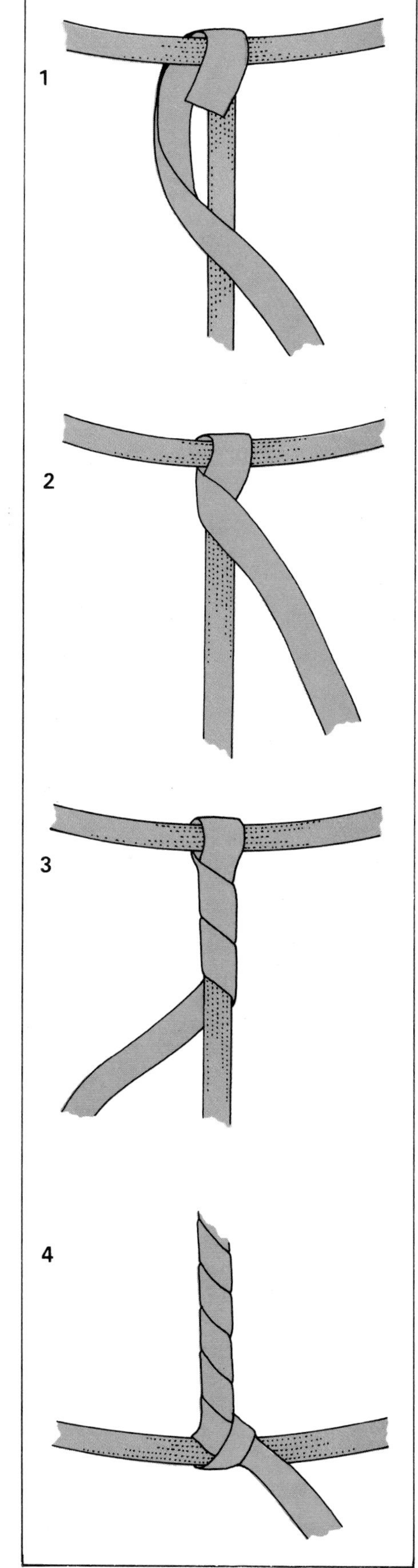

## Classic fitted shade with balloon lining

*Above* A classic fitted shade in a plain fabric with braid trimmings (see page 123).

This method of making lampshades can be used for making most styles of shade where the measurement round the smallest part of the frame is not greater than the measurement round the top ring. By pinning and fitting the fabric on the straight grain onto the frame, a very good fit should be obtained. This method can be used for curved-sided frames as well as straight-sided ones.

To estimate the amount of fabric needed for making this classic style of lampshade, measure
1. the depth of the longest strut and to this add approximately 10 cm
2. the circumference of the bottom ring and add approximately 12.5 cm

This gives a generous allowance for stretching the fabric to the frame.

For a 25 cm frame, for example, you will need
50 cm cover fabric 90 cm wide
50 cm lining fabric 90 cm wide
1.3 cm wide lampshade binding tape.

### To make the outer cover

1. Prepare and tape the frame.
2. Fold the cover fabric in half with the right sides together. Lay it on one side of the frame, being careful to keep the straight grain X to Y running vertically (5). Pin the fabric to the frame by inserting pins on the top ring at the two side struts, and on the bottom ring also at the side struts.
3. Start pinning the fabric to the two side struts, stretching the fabric gently outwards at the same time. Place the pins approximately 2.5 cm apart and keep stretching the fabric and adjusting the pins until all the fullness is removed (6).
4. Pin the fabric to the top and bottom rings, placing the pins 2.5 cm apart and stretching the fabric gently until all the wrinkles disappear.
5. Adjust the pins on the side struts and fill in until they are 0.5 cm apart (7).
6. With a pencil, mark down the side struts over the pins from A to B and from C to D (8), extending the line 1.3 cm at the top and bottom rings. This is the stitching line. Make a 1.3 cm horizontal guide line at the top and bottom rings. Tack through the double thickness of fabric approximately 5 cm away from the pins.
7. Remove all the pins from the fabric and machine down the stitching line from A to B and from C to D using a medium-size stitch. Trim the seams to 0.5 cm and cut along the fold line at the top edge (9). Do not cut away any fabric at the bottom edge. Press flat.
8. Prepare the balloon lining in the same way and press flat.
9. With the right side outside, slip the outer cover over the top of the lampshade frame and match the side seams to the side struts. The horizontal guide lines should be placed on the top and bottom rings and pinned into position. Pin the cover to the top and bottom rings, adjusting it until it fits snugly.
10. Sew the cover to the frame using matching thread (10). Use short lengths of double thread and work from right to left keeping the stitches to the outside edge of the shade. Trim off the excess fabric close to the stitching at the top and bottom rings.

### Inserting the balloon lining

1. Fit the lining into the upturned shade, matching horizontal guide line marks at top and bottom rings. Make sure that the seams of the lining match up with the seams of the outer cover.
2. Pin the lining to the top and bottom rings, adjusting the fabric until the fullness has been removed and the lining is tight (11). Unstitch the side seams in order to fit the fabric round the gimble, or if necessary slash the fabric carefully to neaten round the fitting (12).
3. Stitch the lining in the same way as the outer cover, using matching thread and keeping the stitching on the outside edge of the rings.
4. To neaten the gimble cut a piece of lining fabric 10 cm by 2.5 cm wide. Turn in 0.6 cm at each side and press. Place the strip underneath the gimble fitting and oversew into position taking care to keep the stitches on the outer edge of the ring so they will be hidden by the trimming (13).

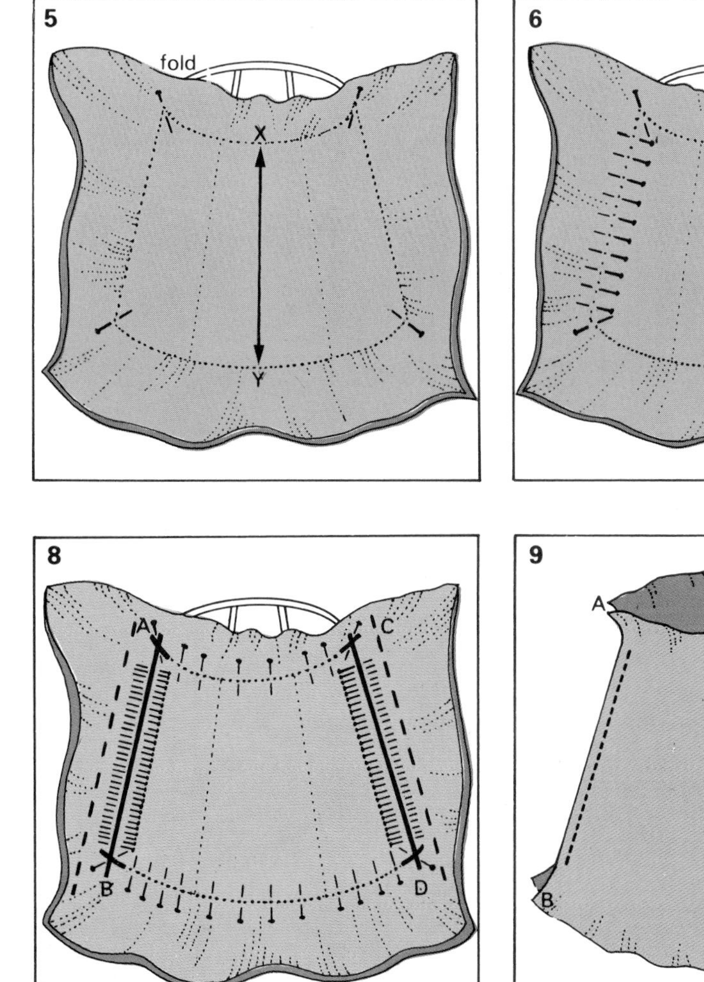


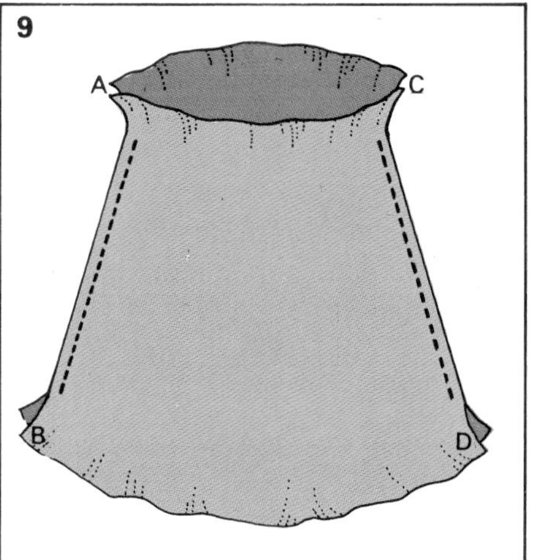


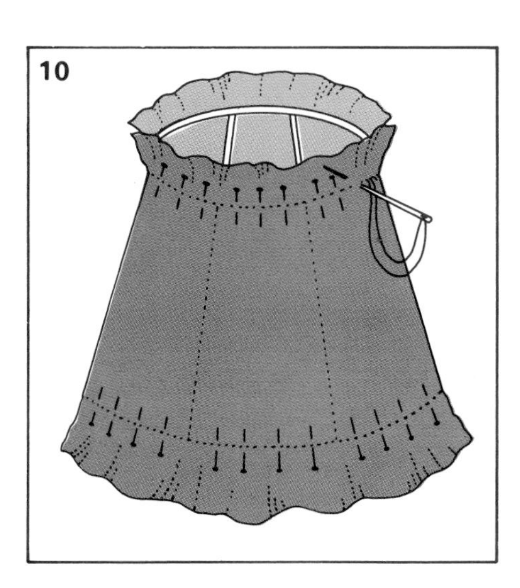


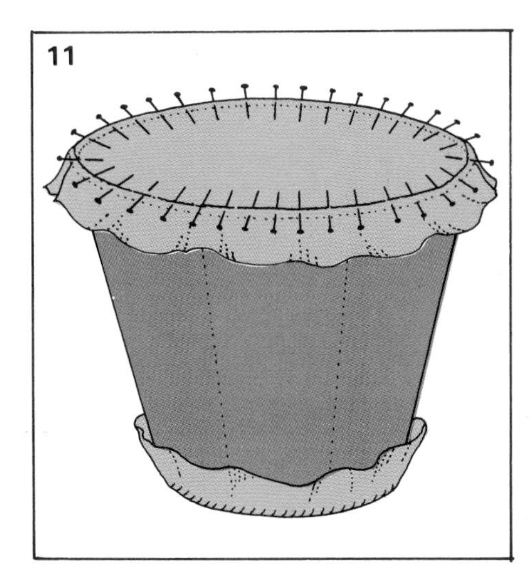


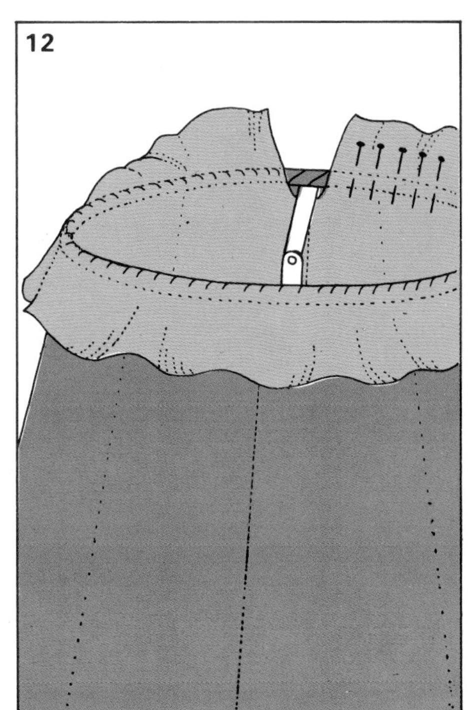


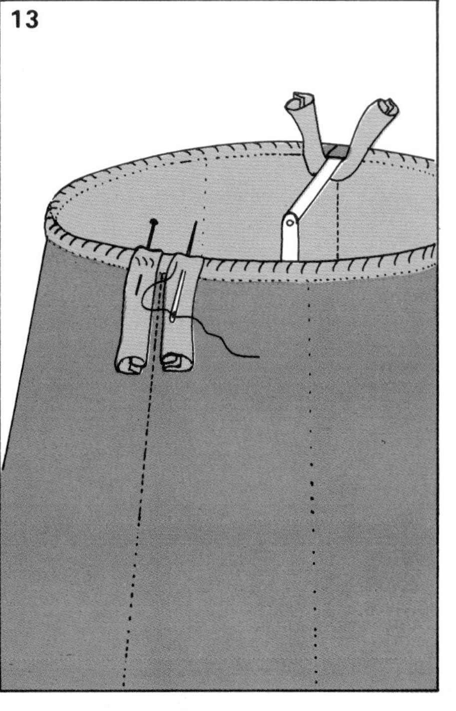


*Above* Diagrams 5–11: making the outer cover for a fitted shade.

*Right* Diagrams 12 and 13: making a neat finish at the gimble.

## Pleated shade

Pleated lampshades look extremely attractive when made in soft fabrics that drape well. The secret of a professional finish lies in the accurate pleating of the material.

1. For a straight pleated lampshade choose a frame that has straight sides or struts. Prepare the frame and tape the struts and rings.
2. To estimate the width of fabric required for the pleating measure round the bottom ring of the frame and multiply by three. For the length measure the depth of the frame and add 5 cm working allowance.
3. Prepare the balloon lining as for the classic fitted shade (page 120).
4. Cut or tear the fabric for the pleating into strips of the depth required (see no. 2), making sure that the selvedge runs from the top to the bottom of each strip to help the pleating to set well.
5. Starting at the bottom ring of the frame and at one of the side struts, fold in the raw edge at one end of the strip of fabric to the width of the pleat required. Pin to the bottom ring, having a 1.3 cm overlap below the bottom ring (14). Then pin this first pleat into position on the top ring, making quite sure that the grain of the fabric corresponds to the fold of the pleat.
6. Continue to pleat and pin the fabric to the bottom and top rings until reaching the next strut, taking care to keep the 1.3 cm overlap at the bottom edge straight. Oversew this section at the top and bottom rings (15).
7. Continue pleating and sewing each section of the shade in turn, making sure that the same number of pleats are worked into each section. When it is necessary to join a fresh piece of fabric do not sew the fabric together but turn in the raw edge and lap it over the end of the previous strip of fabric, so forming the next pleat.
8. When you reach the first pleat unstitch it at the side strut and tuck it underneath the very last pleat made. Finish oversewing in the usual way.
9. Insert the balloon lining as for the fitted shade and attach trimmings.

When working pleating on cone-shaped frames, care must be taken to keep the centre pleat in each section exactly at right angles to the bottom ring (16). With this style of shade the pleats at the top ring will automatically be closer together than at the bottom ring. They can be adjusted if desired by leaving a small space between each pleat on the bottom ring. Slightly less fabric is used if this method is adopted.

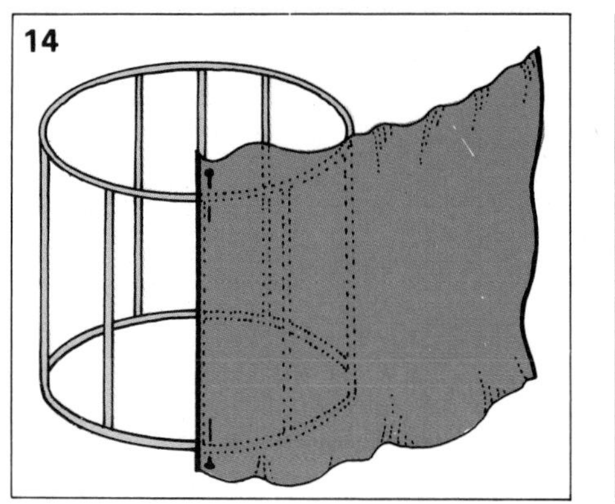


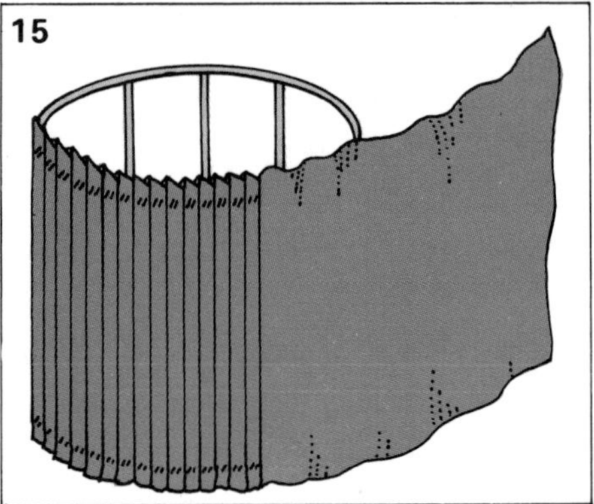

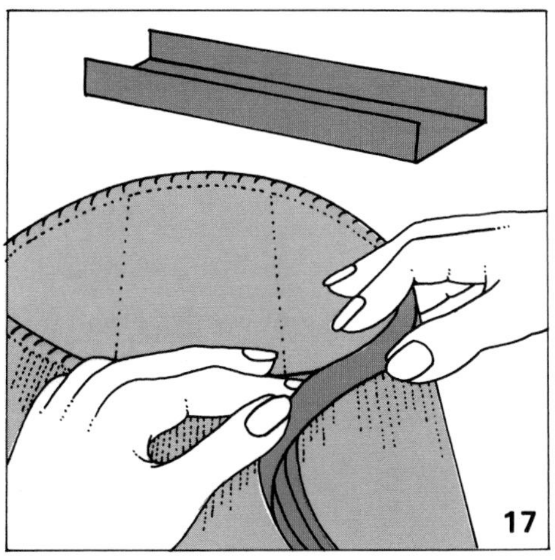


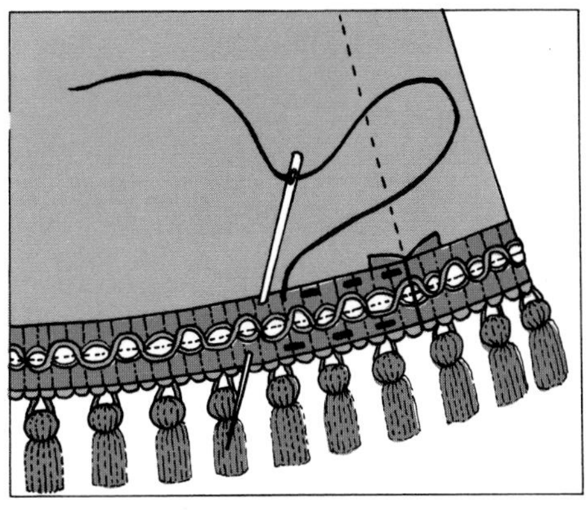

*Left* A very wide cone-shaped pleated shade.
(14–16): making a pleated shade.
*Above* Attaching trimmings.
*Below* An empire shade with simple trimming.

## Trimmings

Trimmings for lampshades can be plain and tailored or elaborate and frilly and this should depend on the fabric being used for the shade and its style: delicate trimmings suit fine fabrics.

A simple trimming can be made by cutting a bias strip approximately 2.5 cm wide, and long enough to fit round both the top and bottom rings of the shade. Turn in the long edges 0.6 cm and press. Starting at one side seam and spreading clear adhesive carefully and evenly over the wrong side of the strip with a small knife, apply the strip to the top and bottom rings of the shade. Stretch the strip slightly as you press it down firmly with your fingers. Turn in the end of the strip 0.6 cm to make a neat finish. Take care that the strip does not extend to the inside of the shade but make sure that it covers the oversewing stitches. This method is also used when applying a bias strip to cover the stitches on a tiffany shade.

Attractive trimmings can be made using such skills as crochet, macramé and machine embroidery and many can be bought ready-made. Braids and fringes should always be stitched to the shade, except in the case of hard lampshades where they are best applied with adhesive. Stitch the trimming with small stitches, being careful not to let them show on the inside of the shade. To finish, turn in the braid 1.3 cm and butt the ends together (17).

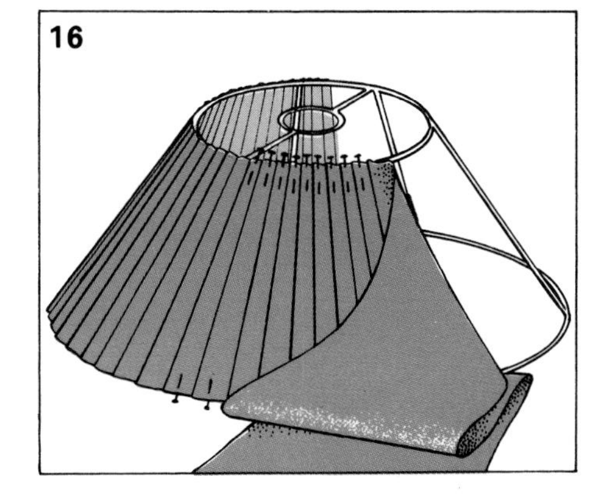

## Tiffany lampshade

Tiffany lampshades spread the light well because of their shape and many different types of fabric can be used to make them. When making a tiffany lampshade, motifs and patterns can be positioned accurately.

For a tiffany lampshade approximately 25 cm across the base, you will need
75 cm of 90 cm lining fabric
75 cm of 90 cm cover fabric

**1.** Tape the lampshade frame using unbleached tape, dyed to match the colour of your lining or a matching bias binding, as the struts will show on the finished shade.

**2.** Using the lining fabric on the cross of the grain place it onto one quarter of the frame (18). Pin the fabric into position at the top and bottom rings and also down the two side struts AB and CD. At the same time as pinning, gently ease and stretch the fabric so that it fits neatly over this section of the frame.

**3.** Oversew the fabric to the frame using matching double thread. Trim off the fabric close to the stitching.

Fit the remaining lining to the other three quarters of the frame in the same way, pinning and stitching each quarter in turn.

**4.** When the lining has been completed pin the top cover on in the same way, centralizing any motif or pattern where necessary. Pin and stitch to the same struts that were used when fitting the lining (19).

**5.** Trim off the cover fabric close to the stitching and cover the stitches with lengths of bias strip (see page 123). Fringing or other braid can be sewn round the bottom ring of the shade, with matching braid on the top ring.

Alternatively, make a double frill in matching fabric (see page 22), and sew to shade with neat stitches.

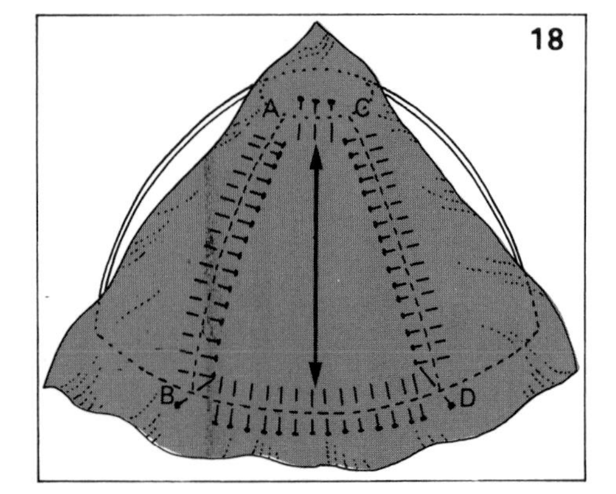


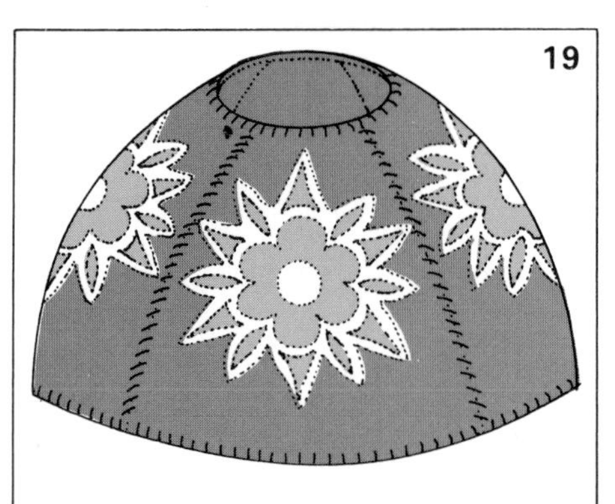


*Above* A tiffany shade with matching frill.

*Left* (18 and 19): making a tiffany shade.

*Above right* A shaped hard shade. The base for this lamp is made from an old cider jar, converted by means of a simple conversion kit.

*Right* (20 and 21): making a hard shade.

*Far right* To mark out the lampshade card for a cone-shaped frame, roll the frame along the card and draw lines to mark out its course.

# Hard lampshade

Hard lampshades are quickly and easily made if one of the specially prepared lampshade cards is used. These cards are available at craft shops and department stores and are made from fabric bonded onto a stiff card. The range of patterns and plain colours is wide and a good choice is usually available. Selapar and Parbond can also be used for making hard shades. These are stiff cards with an adhesive on one side. Your own choice of fabric can be ironed onto this side using a hot iron; remnants of suitable furnishing and dress fabrics can be used to advantage in this way.

Buckram and parchment are two other materials that can be used for making 'hard' lampshades. Simple arrangements of dried flowers and leaves can be mounted and stuck onto buckram to make attractive and original shades. Cover these with acetate film (available from art shops) to protect them from dust and dirt.

Do not wash hard lampshades – they are best kept clean by brushing regularly with a soft brush.

## To make a hard drum shade

Prepare and tape the rings. Measure round the taped rings to find the circumference of the drum, and decide on the depth of shade.

Cut out a pattern on stiff paper to these measurements plus 2 cm seam allowance. Try the pattern on the rings, holding it in place with clothes pegs (20). Adjust pattern if necessary.

Cut out fabric from pattern and fix to rings with clothes pegs. Sew shade to rings using blanket stitch with double thread (21). Trim seam to 5 mm and stick firmly with adhesive. Add trimmings as required.

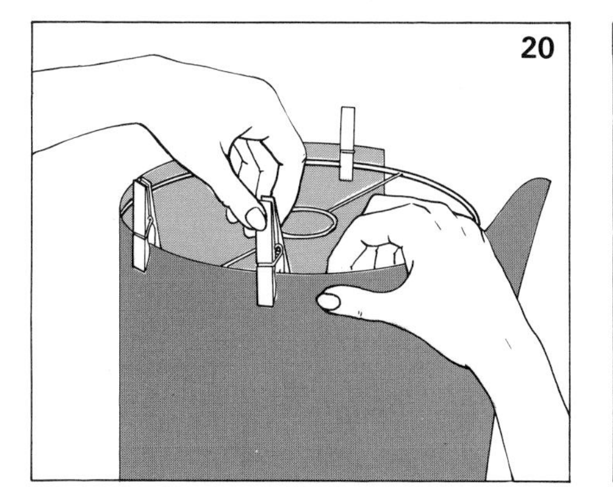

20

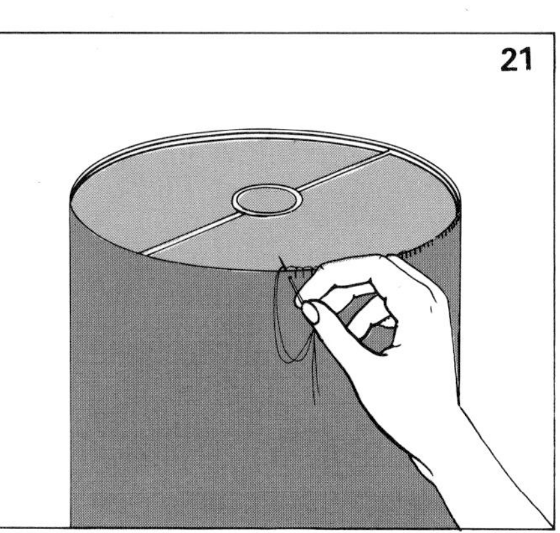

21

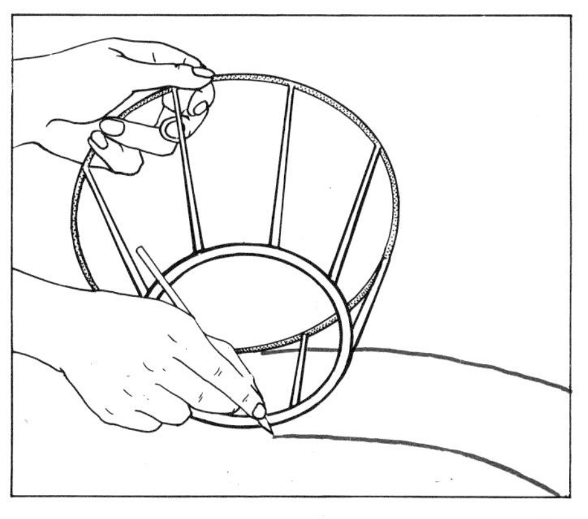

# Rugs

Rugs are a special feature in the home: they can add character, colour and comfort to the humblest of surroundings.

Many techniques are simple and offer the rugmaker plenty of room to develop his or her own special style. Appliqué, quilted, braided and rag rugs can also be adapted to make wall-hangings, bedspreads, cushions and many other attractive additions to one's home.

## Design

Designing is a creative and personal experience, a chance to express oneself in terms of scale, colour, pattern and texture. A good design is one that feels right, that will be interesting to undertake and will be enhanced by the medium and materials used.

Rugs can be planned in detail for design, colour and materials, or you can decide on the size and shape, and work out the design as the rug grows. The right approach is the one that suits you.

If one has a particular place for the rug, its size, colour, shape and function can be determined by its position in the room. Alternatively, you may choose to design and make a rug simply for your own satisfaction and there are certain practical considerations which may be helpful in understanding how a design works.

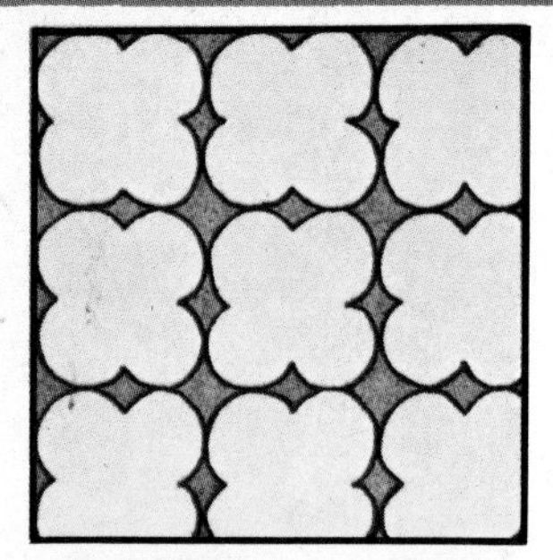

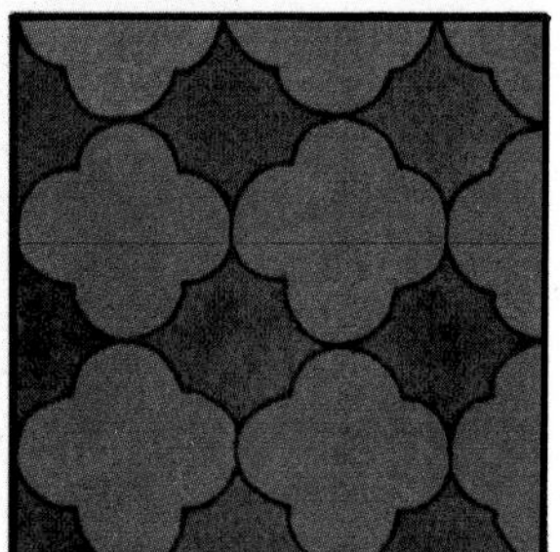

## Pattern and shape

The pattern or design should not be too complex or intricate because the detail will be lost on most rugmaking techniques. If there are small patterns, these need to be edged with a contrasting colour unless a muted effect is desired. Pattern need not necessarily be interpreted through colour, but can be shown in contrasting pile lengths, directional stitching, or creative use of material. Interesting angular shapes or curved outlines in the room can be recreated in a rug design to focus attention. Personal motifs can be used, especially for children's rugs. Repeat designs are very effective and can be alternated to make a variety of patterns within a single rug.

When designing, bear in mind the type of fabric to be used, particularly whether it frays and will have to have the edges turned under.

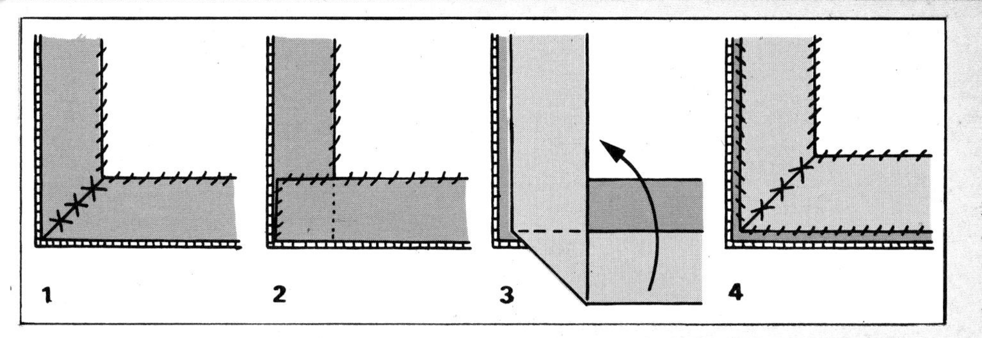


## Size

Consider the space available, and measure exactly where the rug is to fit if between walls or objects. A smaller rug may look a reasonable size when being made but it can be dwarfed if placed on a large empty floor space. Try not to squeeze a rug awkwardly between pieces of furniture which may be moved as it will always be in the way.

*Below* An oval braided rug, with matching circular seat pads.

*Above* Diagrams 1–4: turning under the edges of the backing. Allow for the turning when planning the design. (1): a mitred corner. (2): a double corner. (3 and 4): attaching binding to the turning, mitring the corner.

*Left* The same template was used for all 3 designs, but by different positioning and colouring 3 very different effects are achieved.

## Texture

This is what makes the rug soft, hard, coarse, smooth, tufted or stubbly. One can experiment with combinations of these or just use one texture to create an overall effect, perhaps in contrast to another floor or carpet surface. The other textures in the room on upholstery, walls or curtains may suggest a particular textural design.

## Colour

The choice of colours is extremely personal as we all respond differently to colour. Contrasting colours in a design emphasize the shapes and distinguish certain areas. Subtle colour changes in a design create a more mellow effect and a less prominent pattern. A very dark rug will look smaller than a lighter one the same size, so if you want to make a small room look larger, a lighter rug would be better. A room which gets little light can be brightened up with sunny colours such as yellows and whites, or made warmer with reds, oranges and rich browns. Blue and green can create a cooler more calming mood in a room. A bright mixture of colours can be cheerful and friendly. The choice of colours may be suggested by other things in the room. One small area of colour, such as a vase or a picture, can be pinpointed and developed.

## Designing rag rugs

Designs are more or less determined by the quantity and colours of the available rag strips. As one rarely has enough of a single colour to work a large, solid colour area, fabrics should be grouped in near-shades and tones for the best effects.

Short piles can be worked in geometric patterns, repeat motifs, alphabet letters, numbers and border patterns. A longer pile has a tousled surface which lends itself to designs with softer and less clearly defined outlines.

Draw the design directly onto the backing, using felt-tipped pens. If the design is complex, work it out on tracing paper first. Trace each area of the design onto thin card, then cut out the shapes and use these as templates. Lay templates on the backing fabric and draw round. Leave a 5 cm hem allowance around the edges of the design for all shapes of rug. Indicate the colours you intend to work on the backing.

If you are designing a textured rag rug, you can combine short and long piles and darning stitch. The rug can be made in one colour and a subtle pattern created by different textures.

*Left* Detail of a textured rag rug. String has been used for the long piles (dark brown stripes) and a number of different textured fabrics including loose-woven materials and towelling have been used for the areas worked in darning stitch.

*Above* A basic geometric pattern can be transformed into diagonal stripes, horizontal stripes or triangular motifs, as the use of colour emphasizes different aspects of the pattern. Compare this use of a basic pattern with the use of a template on page 126.

*Right* Pattern enlarging: mark off the pattern which is to be enlarged into small squares. Then, on a piece of paper the size of the required finished design, rule off the same number of squares as are marked on the original pattern. In each square of the large paper, draw the section of the pattern that is in the corresponding square of the original.

# Appliqué rugs

Appliqué means adding or laying on shapes to a base material. With this technique, pictorial, abstract, or geometric designs can be achieved successfully. Shapes of various sizes and textures create an interesting surface, and these can also be quilted (see Quilted Rugs).

Appliqué rugs can be made by hand or with a machine. Either way this technique offers plenty of freedom for your own creative ideas.

## Tools

Sewing machine (optional), dressmaking shears, pins, needles, sharp pointed embroidery scissors.

## Materials

Felt, blanket material, close weave wools, cottons, corduroy, velvet.

## Attaching shapes

The three methods of applying shapes to the background fabric are:

1. An ordinary line of machine or hand stitches worked around the outline (this is best used with non-fraying fabrics).
2. A close satin stitch worked on a sewing machine to neaten the raw edges.
3. A small hem turned and then sewn by hand.

Heavy fabrics are unsuitable for intricate patterns with small turnings. Keep heavier fabrics for designs with large masses of colour – cottons are easier to work with small shapes. Linen, and other naturally resilient fabrics, are also tricky for the beginner.

Choose a firm material for the foundation and the lining as appliqué rugs have no pile and are usually thin. Interesting borders can be appliquéd to give the rug a definite edge. Fringes, which are usually an extension of the foundation material, should be added instead of a hem allowance.

## Method

Working on a clear floor space or large table top, cut out the foundation material to the size of the finished rug plus 5 cm hem allowance all round.

Whether you choose to sketch your design on paper first or to work spontaneously with shapes, it is a good idea to cut coloured paper pieces before cutting out the fabric. Arrange these on the foundation material and mark on each the direction of the straight grain (parallel to the selvedge). If working from a sketch, make an actual-size drawing and use this as a plan. Take tracings of each part to use as pattern pieces.

Select fabrics and iron out creases. Pin each pattern piece onto the fabric aligning the straight grains of both the appliqué and the foundation material which you have marked on the pattern. Check the material is flat. Using dressmaking shears, cut around each shape, adding 5 mm turning allowance as you cut out. You will need less for machine-stitched pieces. Working from the centre outwards, pin and tack pieces in place. Stitch pieces one at a time, frequently stopping to lay the rug flat and check for pulling. If pulling does occur, reposition the unstitched pieces.

Stitching can be both functional and decorative. Contrasting threads, changes in technique and different stitches will all give added interest to a rug design.

Appliqué rugs offer scope for textural as well as pictorial design, but the fabrics used will affect the rug's durability and method of cleaning.

## Reverse appliqué

This technique involves cutting away shapes rather than adding them. Each colour in the design is represented by a complete layer of material. For a rug, it is better to organize the colours so that the greater area is covered by two or more layers. Thus, the base colour which is a single layer is only visible in small areas. The stitching techniques are the same as for ordinary appliqué. For this type of appliqué, precise designs are more successful with non-fraying fabric or satin-stitched edges. Finer fabrics suit the hand-stitched method.

*Above* Designing a child's appliqué rug. Top: the plan for the finished rug. Bottom: Tracing the pattern pieces.

*Right* A felt appliqué rug with inset detail of its design. The red base shows through at the centre and sides of each motif where the reverse appliqué technique has been used. The orange and yellow shapes have been appliquéed in the usual manner.

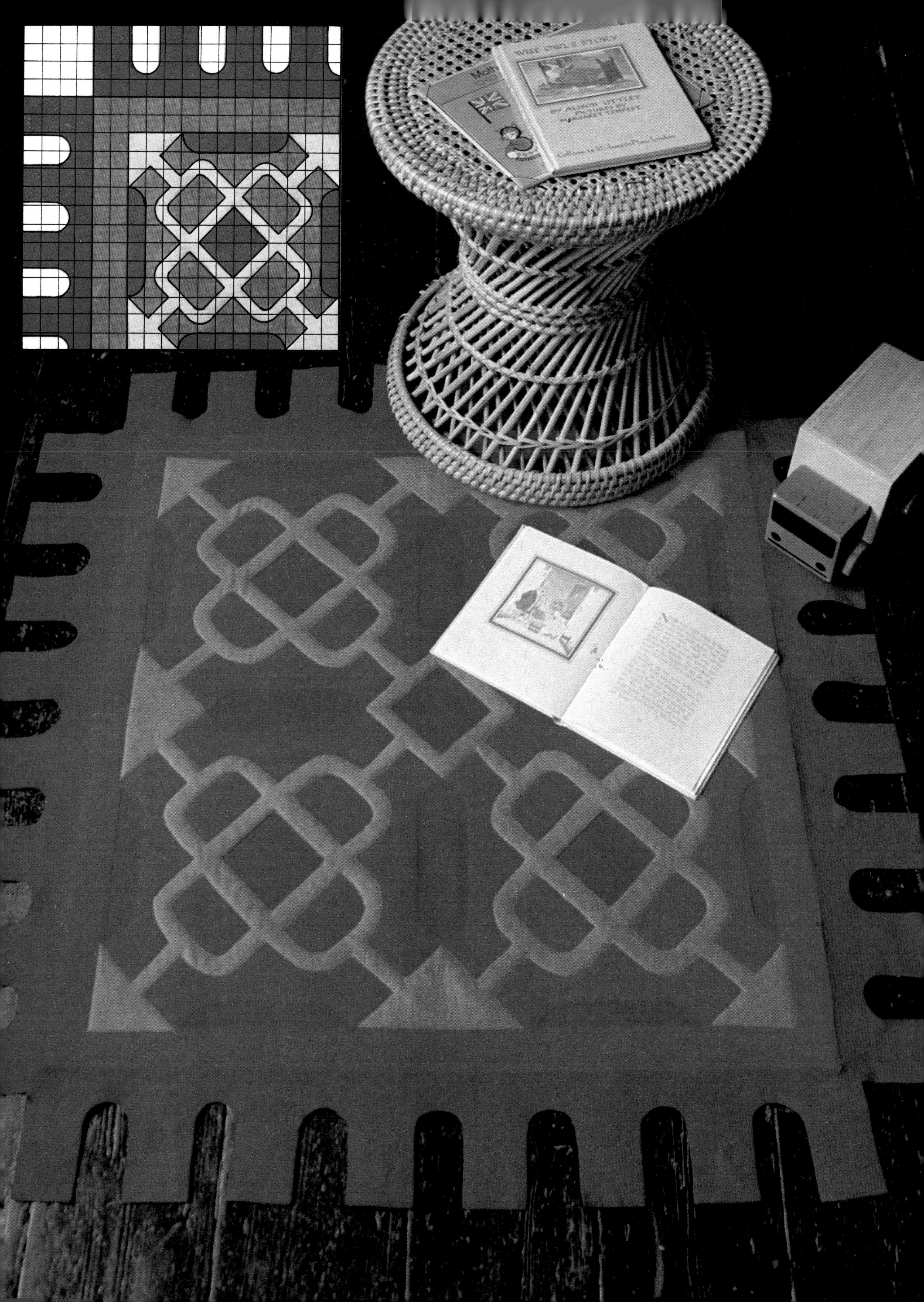
WISE OWL'S STORY
BY ALISON UTTLEY
PICTURES BY
MARGARET TEMPEST

# Quilted rugs

Quilted rugs are a rich and colourful addition to any room. The surface design is created by the quilting lines or the patchwork pattern, or both.

## Tools

Large pair of scissors, sewing machine, needle, pins, thread.

## Materials

Suitable materials are cotton, satin, corduroy, velvet and felt. You will also need batting for filling, and hessian or other backing.

A light-weight rug can be made as a single unit, but it is easier to sew a heavy-weight one in sections. The joins can be incorporated into the design. If using a variety of colours and textures lay them on the floor to see how they work together. Simple geometric shapes or bands of colour are a good starting point.

## Method

For a striped rug cut or tear the strips, allowing 1.5 cm each side for seams. Pin and tack these right sides together then machine. Press seams. Working on the floor cut out the batting and the backing to the same size as the top layer. Tack the three layers together starting from the centre and radiating to the corners (1). Then work in diagonals 5 cm apart, or less for smaller areas. It is essential that all three layers are firmly tacked as this makes the machining easier.

Machine close to the seam lines along the edges of the stripes with a large machine stitch (2). Panels can be individually quilted and shapes appliquéd once all three layers are secure.

## To make a border

Cut strips 5 cm wide for all sides. Pin one strip on each edge of the rug, right sides together with edges level. Machine the strip at least 1 cm from the edge. Fold border under the rug, turning under raw edges, mitre the corners and hem stitch round on the underside.

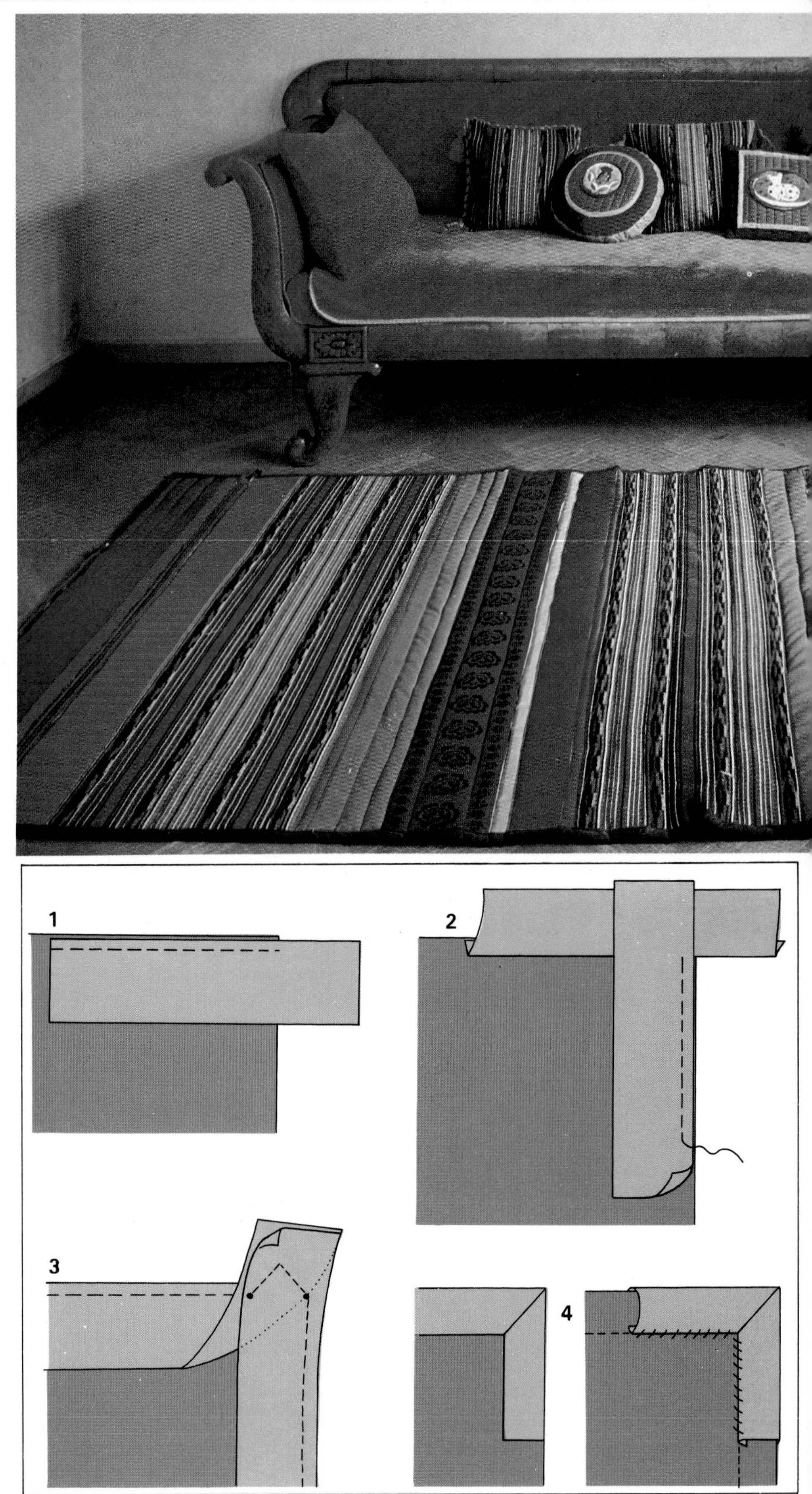


*Right* Making a border for a striped or sectioned rug. Top row left to right: stitching the border strips to the edge of the rug. Bottom row, left to right: folding the border under the rug, mitring the corners, and hem.

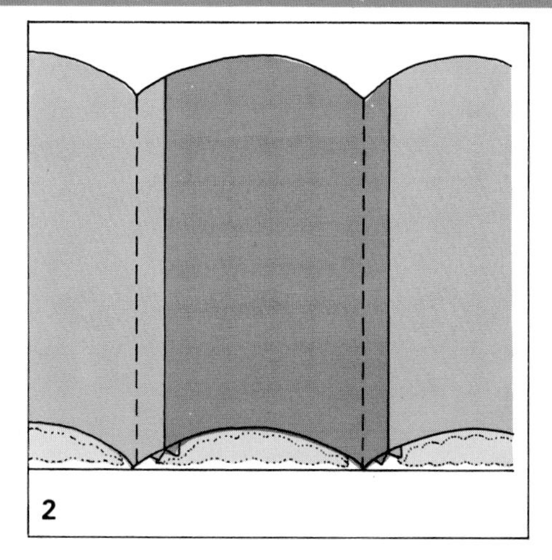

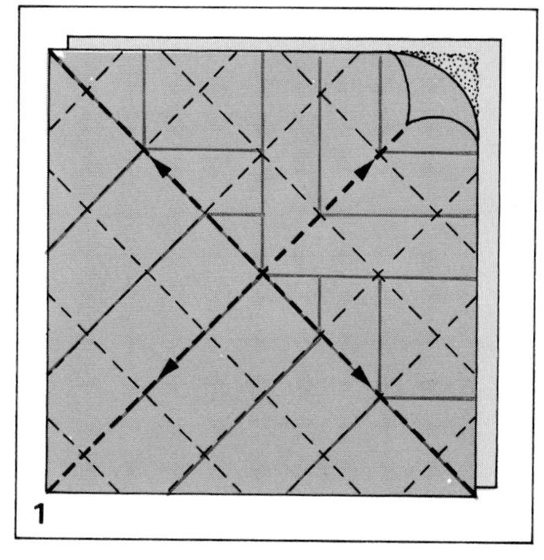

*Left* A quilted striped rug with a border. Some of the plain stripes have additional decorative quilting stitches running across them.
*Above* Diagram 2: Stitch quilting lines for a striped quilted rug, parallel to the seam lines.
*Below* Joining the sections for a quilted sectioned rug.

*Above* Diagram 1: Tacking lines for quilting start from the centre and radiate to the corners. Quilting lines are stitched and the tacking can then be removed. The decorative lines in this diagram are the same pattern as those used in the rug pictured below.

## A sectioned rug

A section can be made with an individual piece of material or with patches as for the striped rug. Each block is quilted before it is joined. Cut out the required number of pieces for the top layer and the backing. These should be the same size. Cut batting 2 cm smaller on all sides, you may need more than one layer for each section.

Using tailor's chalk, draw or trace a pattern onto the top layer of material. Place batting centrally on a piece of lining, then add the top layer. Pin in place then tack well as for striped rug. Repeat with all sections. Machine-stitch over chalk lines, according to your design.

Join the sections in rows. Pin, tack and machine the top layers only, right sides together with a 1.5 cm seam. Trim seams and press open lightly on wrong side. Join rows together in the same way, being careful not to stitch the lining. Place the rug face down, checking it is flat and fold in all edges of the lining and hem round each section.

# Braided rugs

Braided rugs are a creative way of recycling old material. Fabrics can be plain or printed and suitable textures include strong woollen fabrics, cottons, nylon stockings, sisals and heavy rug yarn. If you are using old clothes, undo any seams, remove fastenings, and wash and iron the material before use.

Cut or tear the fabrics into long strips. Cut knitted fabrics parallel to the selvedge and woven fabrics on the bias. A reasonable width for heavy to medium-weight fabric strips is 3 cm and for light-weight fabric 7.5 cm. The final braids will be 2 to 4 cm wide. Avoid making braids of different thicknesses or mixing light and heavy-weight fabrics or the rug will wear unevenly.

## Tools

Large pair of scissors, large needle, strong thread, bodkin, lacing cord, a peg, clamp, iron.

## Planning a design

Braided rugs can be worked in any size, in circles, stripes, squares or rectangles. It is best to start with a simple design. If you want to plan the colours for stripes, arrange your materials in colour groups, otherwise use the strips at random to get a speckled effect. A gradation from light to dark is achieved by changing the tones at intervals as the rug grows. Two dominant colours and one neutral one in the same braid create an arrowhead design.

## To join strips

Place two pieces right sides together at right angles to each other, sew across the corner on the bias (3). Trim the seam allowance and press open (4).

Fold under the raw edges of the strip, bring folds together and press well (5). As you become more experienced, you will be able to fold as.you braid. Roll up the strip and secure with a large pin or thread a piece of string through the centre of the roll and tie it. Unwind the roll as you work and join more strips to the end when needed.

## To start braids

Take three strips. Unfold two and join the ends on the bias. Trim and press open the seam. Lay the end of the third strip, still folded, on the two joined strips to make a 'T', wrong sides facing. Stitch together (6). Refold the first two strips and take third strip up and over to the front (7).

Clamp the end of the braid to a table top or tie with strong string to a chair. To make a straight braid, take right strip over centre, left strip over centre (8), right over centre and continue in this way. Give each strip a tug each time to make the braid firm.

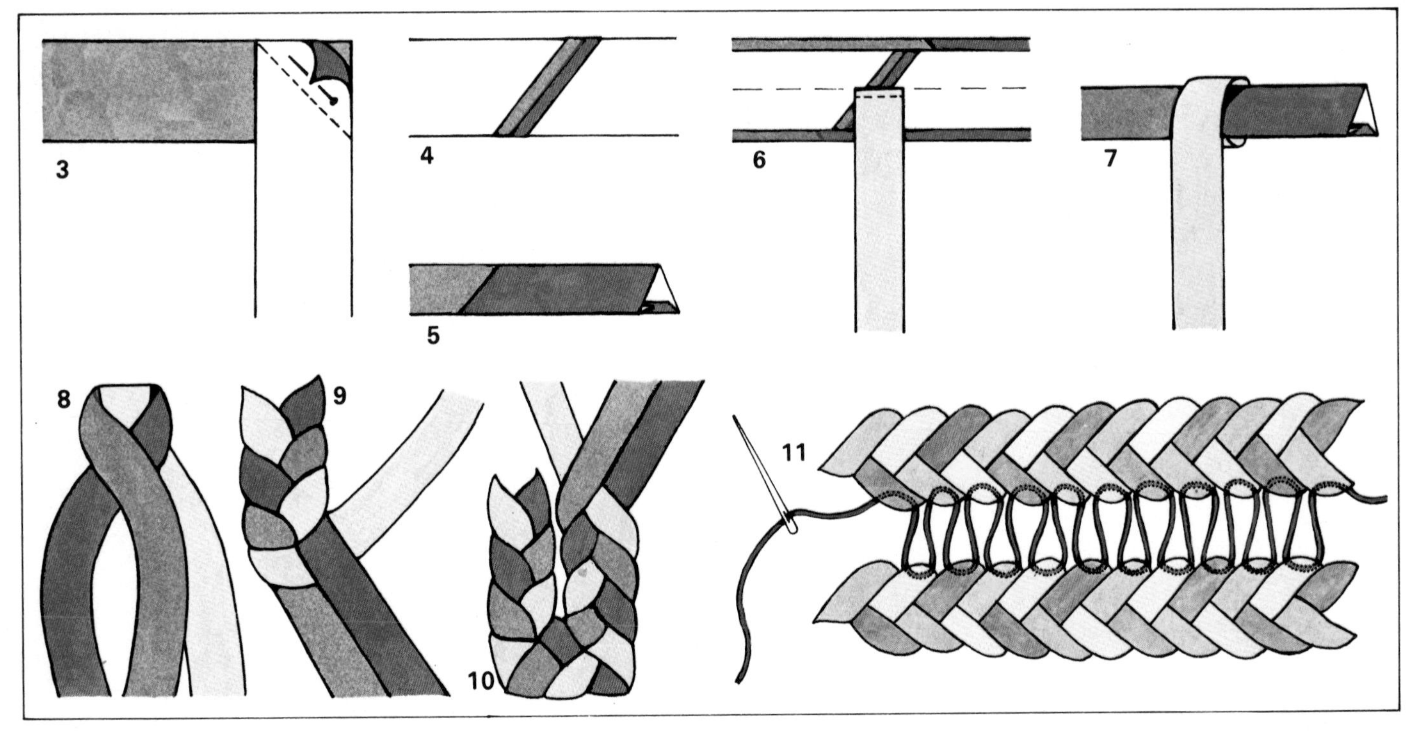

*Left below* Diagrams 3–5: joining strips; (6, 7, 8): starting braids; (9): a round turning; (10 and 11): 2 square corners; (12): lacing braids.
*Left* A rug made up of a number of small braided circles.

*Above* An oval braided rug. The colours have been carefully worked to give a very definite oval design.

## Round rugs

Round rugs have a tendency to turn up at the edges. To make sure that they lie flat, begin braiding by taking the left strand over centre, then left over centre again and then right tightly over centre. This is a round turning (9). After braiding about 15 cm, peg the braid with a clothes peg to stop it unwinding, and sew into a tight circle, working on the wrong side. Continue working in this way until the circle measures about 7.5 cm across (although this measurement will depend to some extent on the width of the braids), then work straight braids.

## Oval rugs

The length of the centre braid is the difference between the length and width of the finished rug so a 122 cm by 152 cm rug has a centre braid of 30 cm.

Braid a centre length, make a round turning, and then braid back. Lace together and begin straight braiding.

## Rectangular rug

A square-cornered rug needs a square-cornered centre to begin.

Braid a strip to the required length for the centre braid then make a square corner. To do this, take the left strip over centre, left over centre again, and left over centre a third time (10). Then bring the right strip over the centre and pull it tightly. Make a second square corner. Continue making straight braids until you have the same length as the first straight braid, make a third square corner, braid two more loops and make a fourth square corner.

Continue braiding and making square corners as necessary to shape the rug.

## Lacing

Braids are sewn together with lacing as the rug is being worked. When you have braided enough to make the centre of the rug, hold the working braid with a clothes peg to stop it unwinding. Thread a large-eyed needle with carpet thread. Tie a knot at the end. Take a stitch in a loop so that the knot is hidden. Draw loops together by passing the needle through them to make the central shape required (a circle for a round rug or a square-cornered double strip for a rectangular rug). Once you have sewn the centre shape, braids are laced together with lacing cord (or thin, strong twine). Cut the sewing thread short and tie the cord to the thread. To lace, the needle is passed through the loops of the braiding, not through the fabric (11). Pull the lacing cord tight so that the loops fit into each other.

## Finishing

For all braided rugs, taper off the braids by trimming each strand diagonally, fold in the raw edges. Continue braiding then pull the ends into the previous braid.

A braided rug does not need backing. If it is braided tightly it will be very hard wearing and can be turned over at intervals to avoid wear on one side.

## Rag rugs

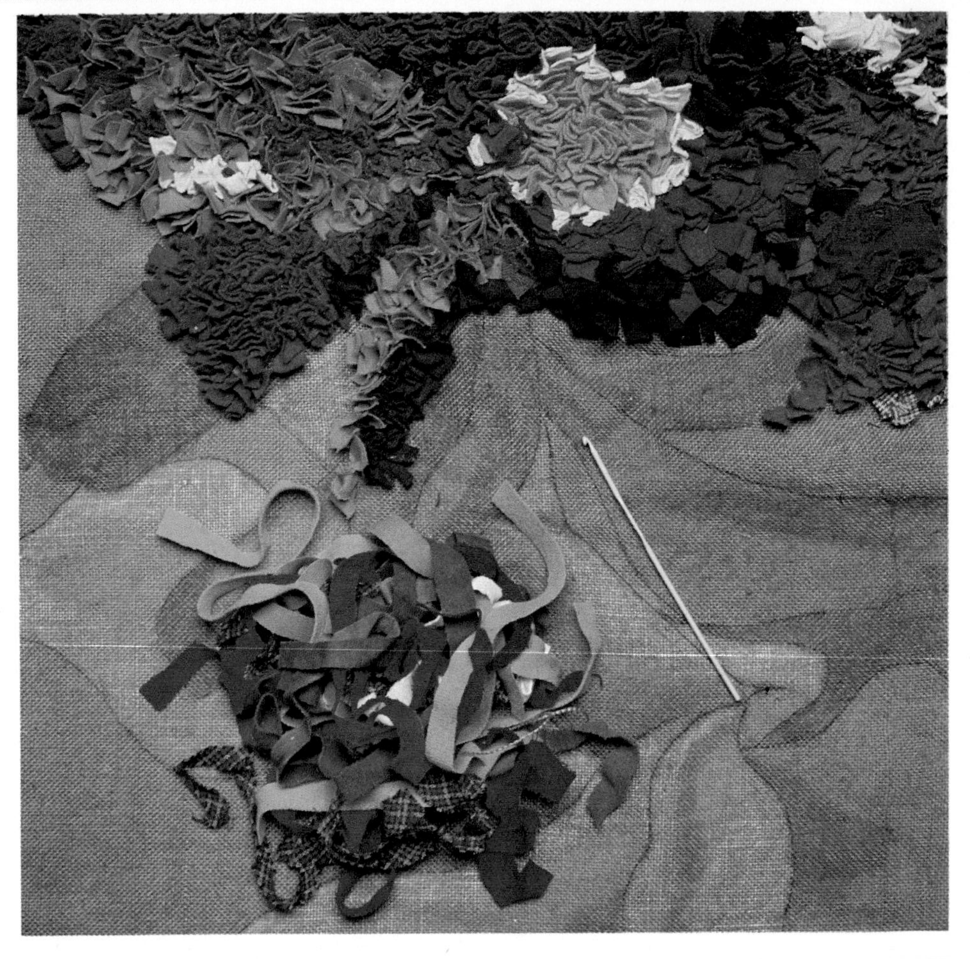

Traditionally, rag rugs are made from pieces of fabric which would otherwise have been thrown away – old clothes, worn-out furnishings, scraps left over from dressmaking, knitted garments, stockings and so on. The only fabrics which are unsuitable for making rag rugs are those which fray easily.

### Backings

Hessian is the best backing for rag rugs. For economy, sacks can be opened up, washed and ironed to make backings. Rug canvas can be used but it must be re-rolled to make it lie flat before using it.

If pieces of hessian have to be joined up to make widths or lengths, overlap the raw edges by about 5 cm. Pin, matching the weave of the hessian. Stitch the edges of the pieces with strong thread. Overlap rug canvas 2.5 cm and join in the same way.

**Binding the edges** Before work is started, prepare the edges of the rug with binding. Cut strips of binding to fit the rug sides plus 5 cm at each end. Binding for round or oval rugs must be cut on the bias. Hand sew or machine-stitch to the backing, right sides together, mitring any corners, and stitching 12 mm from the edge (13). The binding is now left until the rug is completed. When the rug is finished, trim the seam allowance of the rug edge to half and turn the binding to the wrong side and hem. On a round rug, the binding will have to be pleated a little for a neat fit (14).

To bind a canvas-backed rug, snip into the edges of the canvas (15) and turn under to the wrong side (16). Attach binding by hand, using a tapestry needle and strong thread (17 and 18).

If you prefer not to bind the edges of your rug, complete the work leaving 5 cm unworked all round the edge and then turn under close to the last row of stitches (19). Fold again and hem (20). On a round rug, make pleats as necessary for a neat fit.

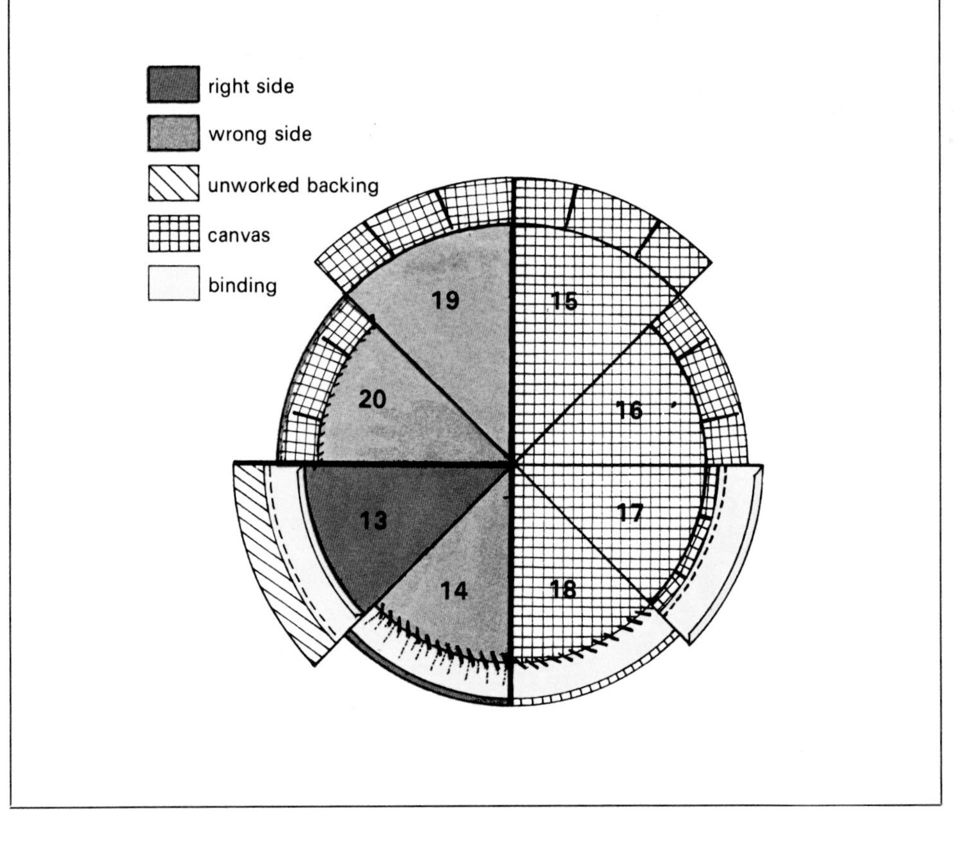


### Techniques for rag rugs

Two simple techniques for making rag rugs are looping and darning stitch. For both techniques, cut strips as you need them. Do not cut an enormous pile of any single colour because you may change your mind while you are working your design.

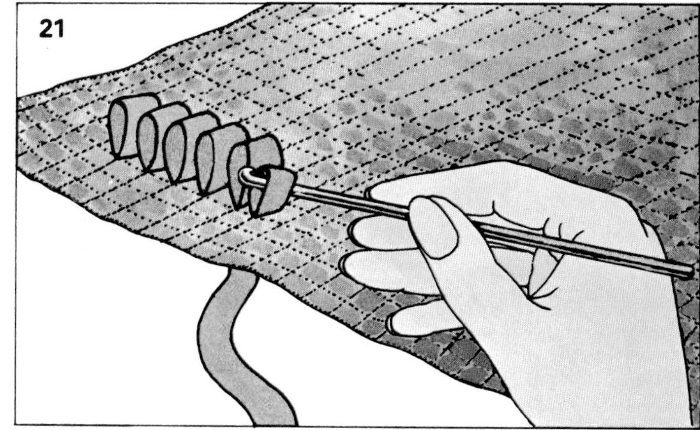


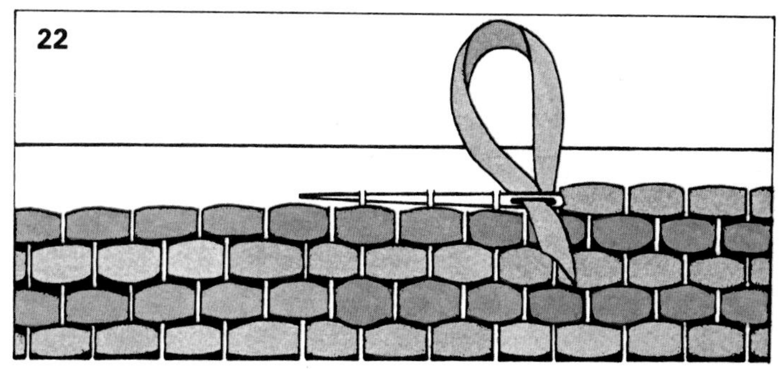


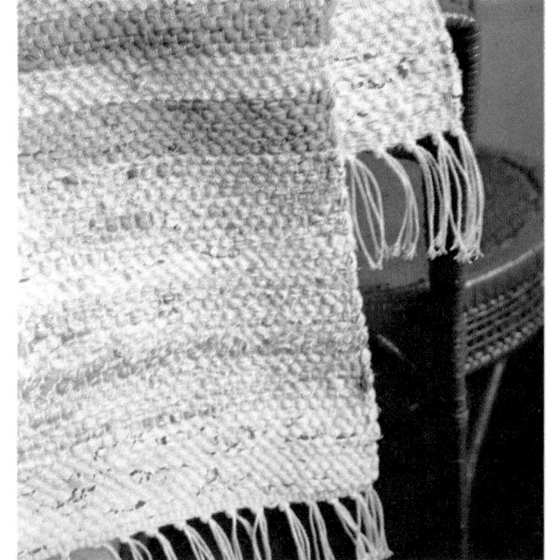

*Above left* Making a looped rag rug.
*Below left* Three methods of edging a rag rug. (13 and 14): hand-sewing binding to a hessian-backed rug. (15, 16, 17 and 18): binding a canvas-backed rug. (19 and 20): turning under the edges of a rug without binding.
*Above and right* A darning-stitch rag rug worked on canvas.
*Above right* Diagram 21: the looping technique. Diagram 22: the darning stitch technique.
*Far right* Method of joining two pieces of backing.

**Darning stitch** A loose-weave hessian is usual for rugs worked in this stitch. Use only thin or medium-weight fabrics. Cut strips to about 30–45 cm long. Do not cut them longer because the strips tend to fray as they are repeatedly pulled through the hessian.

Thread the end of a strip into a sacking or couching needle (these have large eyes). Start stitching 5 cm from one edge. Bring the needle through from the back and make the first stitch about 12 mm long. Pass the needle under two threads of the backing and make another 12 mm long stitch (22). Work a row of stitches and then start the next row immediately alongside the first row. The second row is started with a single 6 mm long stitch and then continues with 12 mm stitches. This 'staggers' the rows of stitches. The third row is worked as the first, the fourth as the second and so on. Leave the short ends of the strips on the wrong side of the rug.

**Looping** This technique produces a loop on the surface of the rug which can be as long or as short as you like. Loops can also be cut to make a tufted finish.

Cut the fabric into long strips, cutting on the cross or bias. Cut tights and stockings in a spiral, working round and round the leg. Thin knitted fabrics can be cut 2 cm wide. Thicker fabrics should be cut about 1.5 cm wide. Hold the end of the strip under the backing, insert a crochet hook or bodkin through from the front and pull a loop of the strip through the hessian (21). Decide what depth of pile you want and cut a piece of card as a guide to subsequent loops. Work loops close together in rows or round and round to fill motif. Work from the outside edges towards the centre of the rug. Leave the ends of the strips on the right side of the rug. Start the next strip from underneath as before. The looped finish can be left as it is, or cut to make tufts.

If you are working on rug canvas, the back of the finished rug should be coated lightly with latex adhesive to hold the stitches securely but this is not necessary for hessian.

Having the right tools will make all the difference to the standard of your work. It pays to invest in good tools and they will last for years. In the shops, use your eyes to judge tool quality: wood parts should be smooth with neatly-finished edges, metal parts should be virtually free from machining marks, screw heads should be evenly set and unmarked.

Keep your tools together in a large wooden box or a compartmented plastic tool holder. Protect your tools from damp, and lightly grease them from time to time to protect them against rust.

Here is a list of useful tools for a household kit that can cope with most furnishing crafts, plus jobs around the house. You may need to add specialist equipment for some jobs such as upholstery.

**Hammer** You will need two, one small and one large. The large hammer should have a 454g (16oz) head firmly fastened to the handle, with a claw end that can be used to lever out old or crooked nails. For light work use a small Warrington hammer which has a narrow tapered end for light nails such as panel pins.

> *Safety note*
> Remember that all tools can be dangerous, so put them away safely at all times, particularly when there are small children around. Keep cutting edges sharp but well-guarded. Tools and work should be kept tidy at all times: this helps to do a better job, and it is a safer method of working.

**General purpose hand-saw** This has a stiff blade and small cutting teeth (about 3 teeth per centimetre) for cutting wood.

**Hacksaw** Useful for many small cutting jobs, especially for sawing through metal pipes and rods. Keep a supply of spare blades as they need to be replaced frequently. The smallest type of junior hacksaw is quite adequate for most jobs.

**Screwdriver** You will need at least two. A medium-sized carpenter's screwdriver with a tapered tip will cope with most jobs. Although the ratchet kind is more expensive, it is easier to use because less strength is needed in the wrist. Ideally, the tip of your screwdriver should be slightly less than the width of your screw slot. Surfaces can be marked if the screwdriver tip extends beyond the screw slot. A small electrical screwdriver is useful for small fiddly screws.

**Bradawl** Before using a screwdriver to screw in a screw, you must make a small starting hole in the wood. Use a bradawl for this, twisting the spiked end round several times.

**Gimlet** This has a thread on its point and does much the same job as a bradawl, but is better for making holes for cup-hooks, etc., where the fitting is to be screwed straight into the wood without the use of a screwdriver.

**Drill** A hand drill is essential for many home furnishing crafts. The chuck jaws hold the drill bits in place; the bit is the part that actually bores the hole. You change the type and size of the bit according to the size of screw you are using, and the type of work you are doing.

| Screw size | Drill size in inches |
|---|---|
| No. 6 | $\frac{1}{8}$ |
| No. 8 | $\frac{5}{32}$ |
| No. 10 | $\frac{3}{16}$ |
| No. 12 | $\frac{7}{32}$ |
| No. 14 | $\frac{1}{4}$ |
| No. 16 | $\frac{9}{32}$ |
| No. 18 | $\frac{5}{16}$ |
| No. 20 | $\frac{11}{32}$ |

Twist drill bits are for making holes in brick or stone.

**Electric drill** If you are going to carry out a lot of heavier work, such as furniture making or fixing, you may want to invest in an electric drill. A two-speed or variable speed drill is a better buy as you will find you can use it for a wider range of surfaces. The slower speed is for making holes in hard masonry. Various attachments are available, including sanding and polishing discs.

**Rawldrill** An inexpensive alternative to a drill for making holes in masonry.

**Small portable vice** Invaluable for holding work steady while you cut, drill, etc. Can be fixed to any convenient surface, including the kitchen table, if you protect the surface you are attaching it to.

**Cramps or clamps** You will need two or three G cramps in various sizes to hold sections of wood together while glue sets.

**Pliers** A very useful cutting, levering and pulling tool; make sure you buy a good pair. The head tip will grip small objects such as nails protruding from wood. The cut-away circular section can grip small pipes etc. and the cutter blades will snip through wire. If you have a lot of wire cutting to do, consider buying a pair of Tinsnips.

**A steel straight edge** Useful for measuring and marking, and trimming. You will also need a steel measuring tape. Buy a long one that locks into an open position. The most useful kind has inches on one side and millimetres on the other.

**Trysquare** Invaluable for keeping edges and sides at right angles to each other.

**Spirit-level** Enables you to fix objects perfectly vertical or horizontal.

**Trimming knife** An essential tool for craft work. Buy the kind where the blade retracts into the handle for storage, because it is much safer. Blades can be changed for different kinds of work: there are special blades for cutting plastic laminates and hooked blades for cutting floor coverings. Always keep a selection of spare blades.

**A staplegun** Extremely useful for quick craft ideas – use it for upholstery, covering a bedhead, stapling carpet edges etc. Try out the gun in the shop to make sure that you have the necessary strength in your hand to work it.

1 Vice
2 G cramp
3 Small and large hammers
4 Drill and drill bits
5 Tenon saw
6 General purpose hand saw
7 Trysquare and steel rule
8 Hacksaw
9 Bradawl
10, 11, 14 Screwdrivers
12 Spirit level
13 Pliers
15 Staplegun
16 Trimming knife
17 Gimlet

# Hardware

## Using a hammer and nails

To knock in a nail, use one hand to hold the nail steady, and with the other hand, grasp the end of the hammer near its head. Placing the head of the hammer squarely on the nail, start off with a few light taps. Then remove your left hand, change your grip to the end of the hammer and strike firm blows with the hammer. Keep your eye on your work at all times.

Nails plus glue give a stronger joint, though screw and glue is stronger still.

Always join the thinner piece of timber to the thicker piece if possible.

Never fix nails in a line across a piece of wood, as the timber may split. Avoid this by staggering your line of nails. On thin timber, reduce the likelihood of splitting by starting nails off with a bradawl. Use a nail punch plus hammer for knocking nails below the surface of the wood.

## Nails

A wide range of nails is available and nails are now sold in metric lengths by weight.

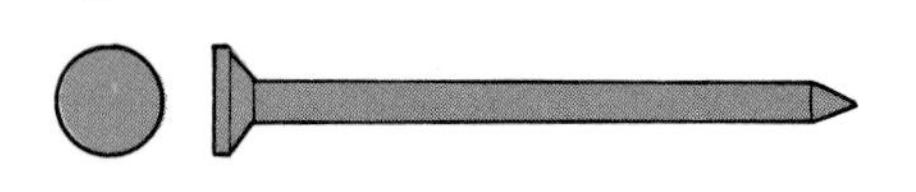

**Round wire nails** have a round head for general carpentry use.

**Oval nails** have a smaller head; smaller sizes are called brads. Ovals are less likely to split wood than round nails; drive them in with the longest side of the oval parallel to the grain. The heads can be driven down below the surface of the wood.

**Panel pins** are fine and are useful for very light work.

**Veneer pins** are very fine for veneer work and small mouldings.

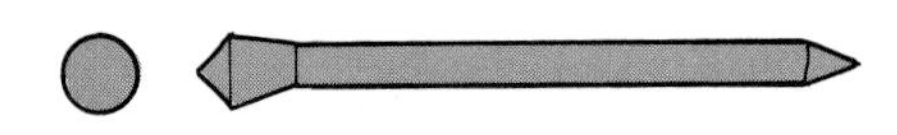

**Hardboard pins** have special diamond pointed heads which can be driven down below surface of board. The hole can then be filled and painted over.

**Screw nails** are for fixing sheet materials such as hardboard to wooden floors.

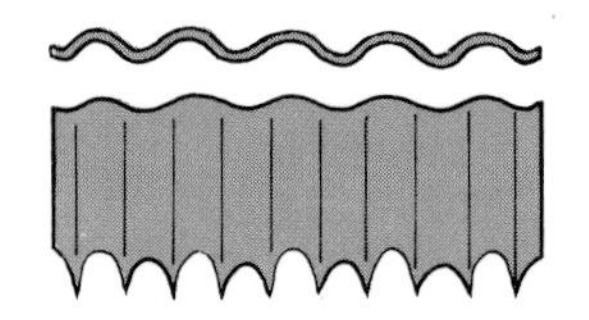

**Wiggle nails** (corrugated fasteners) are for pulling together a butt joint; use them for making simple frameworks.

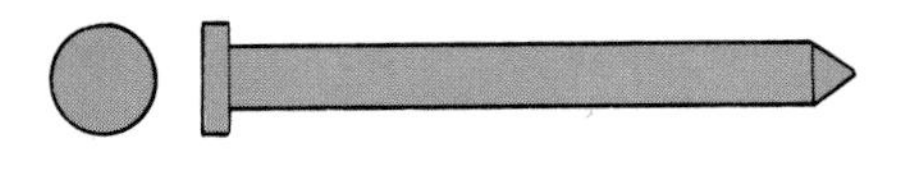

**Masonry nails** have hardened steel points to penetrate masonry and concrete. Protect eyes when using, as the wall surface is inclined to shatter.

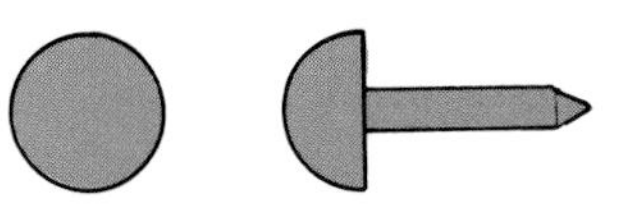

**Various decorative nails** are available for upholstery.

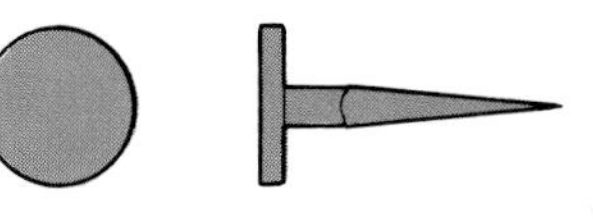

**Cut tacks** are for fixing heavy fabrics including carpets.

**Staples** can be used for fixing wire to wood.

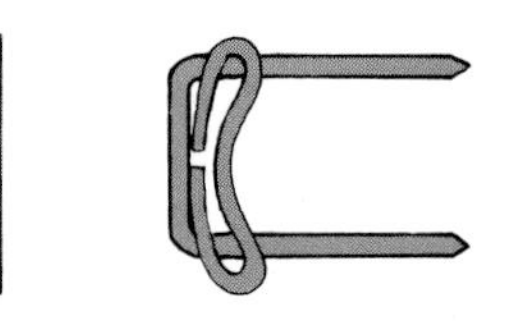

**Cable clips** in various sizes will hold down cable.

## Screws

These are firmer fixings than nails. Screws are still sold in imperial lengths. The thickness or gauge is expressed by a number; the larger the number, the larger the screw. Carpentry screws range from 4 to 20, with lengths from $\frac{1}{2}$ inch to 6 inches. Screws are usually made from steel but this will rust unless protected by primer and paint. Brass, zinc or chromium-plated screws will not rust. Normal wood screws have a countersunk or flat head which can be driven flush with the surface of the wood. Round head screws are used for attaching metal fitments to wood. Screws with a cross-shaped slotted head require a special Philips or Pozidriv screwdriver.

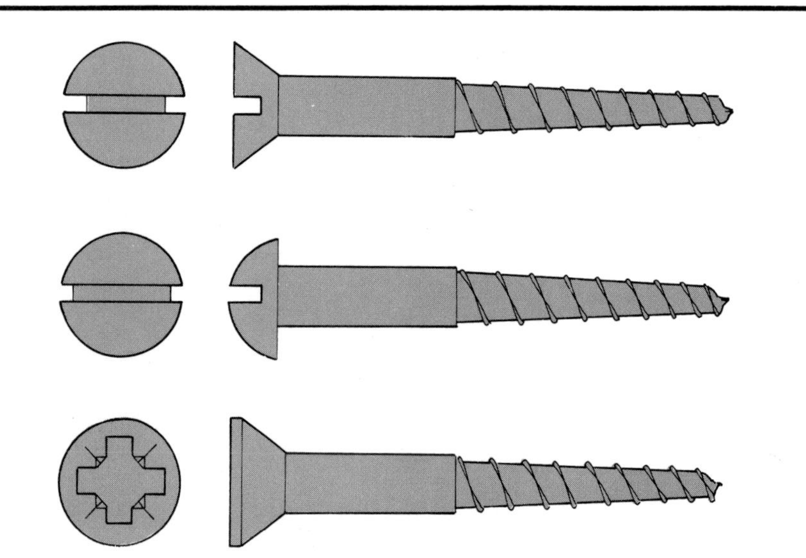

## Types of adhesive

**Clear household adhesive** Sold in tubes, useful for small quick jobs. Can be used to mend china, but will not withstand repeated washing. Expensive to use for large jobs. Will not stick polythene.

**Latex fabric glue** Sold in tubes or in handy small jars with brush. Sticks fabrics and paper to each other, and to wood. Useful for a wide range of craft work and can even be used for sticking fabric seams. Washable but will not stand up to dry cleaning. Stains must be removed by special solvent.

**PVA glues** Mostly used for woodworking, but can also be used for paper and card. Wood joints will need clamping together until set. Remove excess with damp cloth before it dries.

**Epoxy resins** Sold in two small tubes which have to be mixed together before using. Produces a very strong bond which is water- and heat-resistant and is therefore suitable for china, wood or metal. Takes a while to set, but there are new quick-setting varieties.

**Contact adhesives** For large scale jobs like sticking plastic laminates down onto a table top. Most types bond immediately though some newer types give a certain amount of slip. Contact adhesives are very inflammable.

**Polystyrene cements** Useful for model-making.

**Cellulose wallpaper glue** Sold in small packets for mixing with water; useful for making papier mâché.

**Cyanocrylate** A relatively new type of glue widely advertised for its instant powerful bond. Sold in small tubes, and suitable for most materials, but *keep away from hands as this glue will bond flesh to flesh!* As a precaution use a barrier cream on hands.

## Craft shop

In general, craft shops offer materials for a wide range of furnishing crafts including lampshade making, toy making, weaving, dyeing, printing, rug-making, and so on. A good department store will also offer a limited supply of materials for these crafts. Many sell illustrated catalogues which are well worth buying and studying in detail.

## Hardware store

This can be a useful source of handy odds and ends for furnishing projects. These include nails and screws of all types and sizes.

**Repair and corner plates** are available in various shapes and sizes and are useful for repairing old furniture, or for strengthening your own makes.

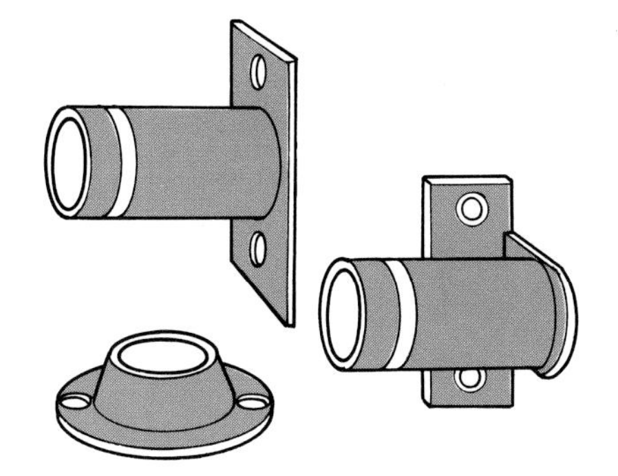

**Rod sockets** are handy for fitting heavy duty hanging rails, but for light loads, curtain rod brackets are adequate. They come straight, for fitting to a return wall or the side of a cupboard, or cranked for flush mounting.

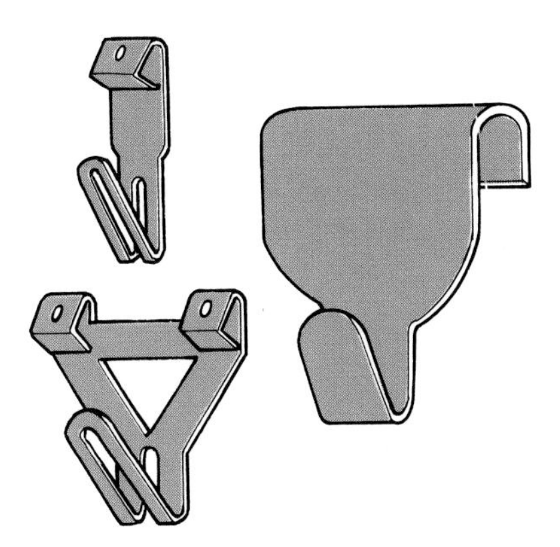

**Moulding hooks** can be used to hang pictures or wall hangings from picture rails.

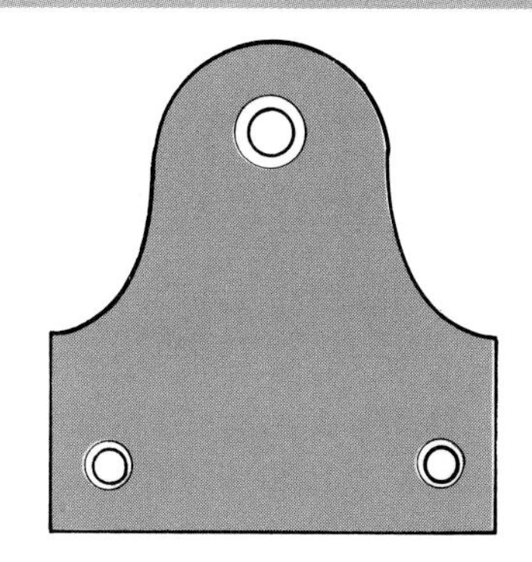

**Mirror plates** can be used for fixing small cupboards to the wall.

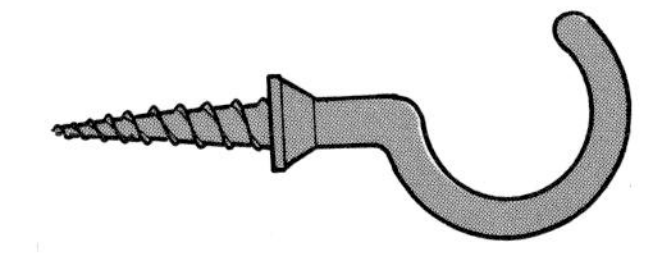

**Round cup hooks** in brass or coloured plastic can be screwed in vertically or horizontally. Besides holding all kinds of tools and utensils, two cup-hooks will hold a rod across a window for a light-weight curtain, or on a wall for a wall-hanging or macramé. You can also use them to secure curtain tie-backs.

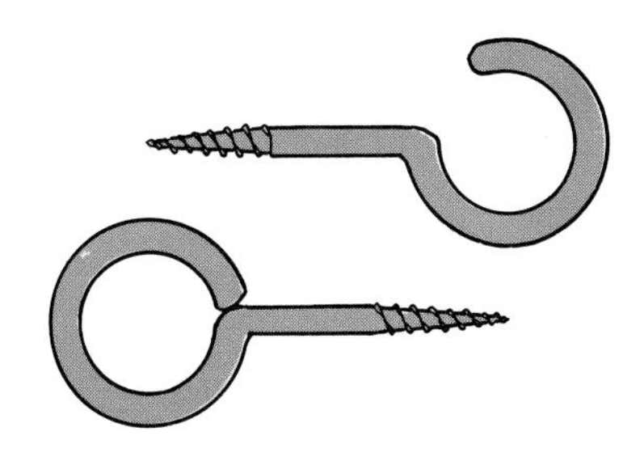

**Expanded curtain rod** is white plastic-coated wire which is easy to fix using small screws and hooks. Use it for fixing net curtains quickly. If you want to make up your curtains with a tape heading, the hooks in the back of the tape can simply be hooked over the wire.

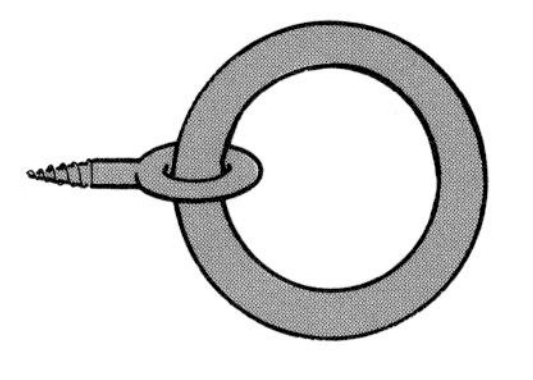

**Screw rings** are useful for hanging pictures; use with brass picture wire.

**Fuse wire** is easily bent and useful for many small projects.

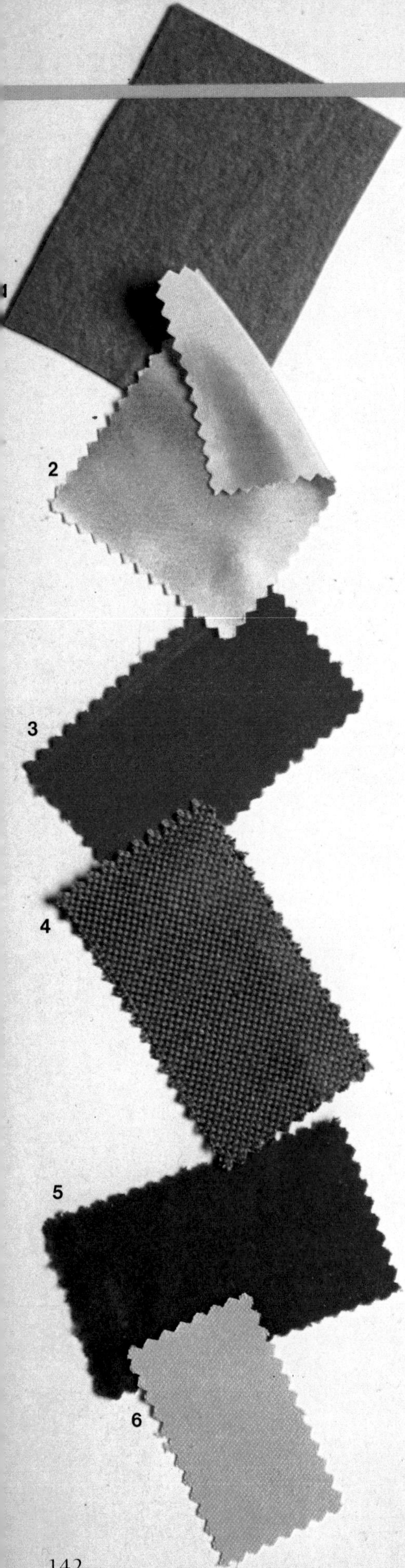

# Fabrics

Fibres from which fabrics can be made fall into two main groups: natural and man-made. Fibres from the two groups can be mixed in a fabric, such as polyester (man-made) and cotton (natural). By law, fabrics must be labelled with their fibre content, and labels for blends will list the fibres in order, according to how much of each fibre appears in the fabric.

## Natural fibres

**Wool** Warm, resilient, does not burn easily, takes cold dyes well, warm to the touch, hard-wearing. Can be obtained blended with viscose, nylon etc. All-wool fabrics may require dry-cleaning.

**Cotton** Used on its own for a wide range of furnishing fabrics but becoming increasingly expensive. Easy to wash and iron. Often blended with man-made fibres to stabilize costs and add easy-care properties.

**Linen** comes from flax and is very expensive, but can still be found for table linens. Very absorbent, and stronger when wet. Washable but tends to crease easily.

**Silk** Made from the natural products of the silk worm. Real silk is a luxury cloth but silky effects are widely imitated by man-made fibres, particularly viscose.

*Left* From top to bottom
1 Bonded (felt)
2 Satin weave
3 Pile weave (corduroy)
4 Plain weave
5 Pile weave (velvet)
6 Twill weave

## Man-made fibres

These can be divided into different families or generic groups; the name of the fibre group will appear on the label, plus (possibly) the brand name.

**Viscose (formerly known as rayon)** Used on its own, or in blends with other fibres. Widely found for curtaining, upholstery fabrics etc. Drapes well, but creases easily and some types may shrink. May be weak when wet. (Brands: *Evian, Sarille, Scandair*)

**Acetate** Found alone or blended with viscose for silky-looking fabrics. Not very strong, but drapes well and does not shrink. (Brand: *Dicel*)

**Triacetate** Often used for candlewick type fabrics. Similar to acetate, but has better resistance to heat, and can be given easy-care qualities, and can be permanently pleated. (Brand: *Tricel*)

**Modal** A newer fibre development with a high wet strength and good resistance to shrinkage. (Brand: *Vincel*)

**Acrylic** Often used for wool-like fabrics. May or may not require dry-cleaning, depending on fabric construction. Lightweight, strong, crease-resistant. (Brands: *Acrilan, Courtelle, Dralon*)

**Modacrylics** A new fibre development with inherent flame-resistant qualities.

**Nylon** Tough hard-wearing fibre used on its own or mixed with other fibres for a wide range of fabrics, many of which are washable. Quick drying, crease-resistant. Can be used for velvet effects, stretch fabrics etc. (Brands: *Bri-Nylon, Du-Pont, Antron*)

**Polyester** Will stay white and does not shrink. Also mixed extensively with cotton for curtainings and sheetings, and with linen for table linen. Takes colours well, does not fade. (Brands: *Terylene, Dacron, Lirell*)

**Polypropylene** Used for some upholstery fabrics, has good stain resistance and is reasonably hard wearing. (Brands: *Meraklon, Ulstron*)

## Woven fabrics

These are made from sets of interlacing threads. They will not stretch but may shrink, according to the fibre from which they are made. Every piece of woven fabric has two sets of threads running at right angles to each other, across and along the fabric, to form the *grain* of the fabric. Crosswise threads (the weft) end at the finished edge of the fabric which is called the selvedge, and in general will not fray. The selvedge may however shrink more than the rest of the fabric, and therefore should be snipped slightly at intervals in some projects, e.g. curtains. The lengthwise threads (the warp) run parallel to the selvedge. On the whole, straight lines in pattern pieces should always be aligned with the grain of the fabric.

For some projects (e.g. strips to cover piping) fabrics need to be cut on the bias, which means on the diagonal grain of the fabric. Fold the corner of the fabric over so that the cut ends run parallel to the selvedge. Crease along the diagonal fold, and then cut along the crease line.

Many of the names which you will come across in the fabric shop refer to basic weaves – woven fabrics are still by far the most common you will encounter.

**Plain weave** is the most common. It is non-directional and there is no right or wrong side. Includes calicos, ginghams, and many plain and printed cottons.

**Twill weaves** are woven to create a diagonal ridge running across the fabric. Used to produce such durable fabrics as denims, and gaberdine, and has a definite wrong and right side.

**Satin weave** has a similar diagonal weave to twill, but a special process creates a smooth lustrous texture.

**Pile weave** gives a soft and thick texture, with different variations such as terry, corduroy and velvet. Pile weaves have a *nap* which is a surface where the fibres stand up and can be directional. For some projects it may be important to ensure that the nap of the fabric is all running the same way. For a light shiny effect, cut fabrics with nap running down; for a darker richer look, cut pieces with nap running up.

**Slub effect** is woven from slub yarns which have pronounced variations in thickness at frequent intervals.

## Knitted fabrics

Machine-knitted fabrics are formed by interlocking loops of yarn. They will stretch, and may shrink according to the fibre from which they have been made. On many types, if one loop is cut, the fabric 'ladders'.

## Bonded fabrics

Made by bonding together a web or mass of man-made fibres, and then compressing them into a flat sheet, which will not fray when cut.

**Melded** fabrics (e.g. Cambrelle) are made by heat-bonding man-made fibres into strong fabrics which have a pleasant feel.

## Buying fabrics

The standard widths of fabrics are as follows: 90 cm/36 inches (usually sold as dress fabrics and therefore possibly unsuitable for some furnishing projects), and 120 cm/48 inches (usually sold for furnishing fabrics). New 'room high' fabrics are 270 cm wide so that you can make curtains without joining. The smallest amount a retailer in the U.K. will cut is 10 cm (4 inches).

When planning large furnishing projects, remember to take into account any pattern repeat on your fabric which may need matching. The make-up of a fabric will affect the way it should be cleaned. Some fabrics may only be dry-cleaned, others may only be washed. If working on a project which will be frequently washed, check whether the fabric is preshrunk. Fabrics that are likely to shrink should be rinsed in luke-warm water, folded in half lengthwise and allowed to dry flat. Press while still slightly damp, but do not press on the fold line.

Straighten fabrics before cutting by pulling a crosswise thread near the end of the fabric, and then cutting along the mark left by the drawn thread.

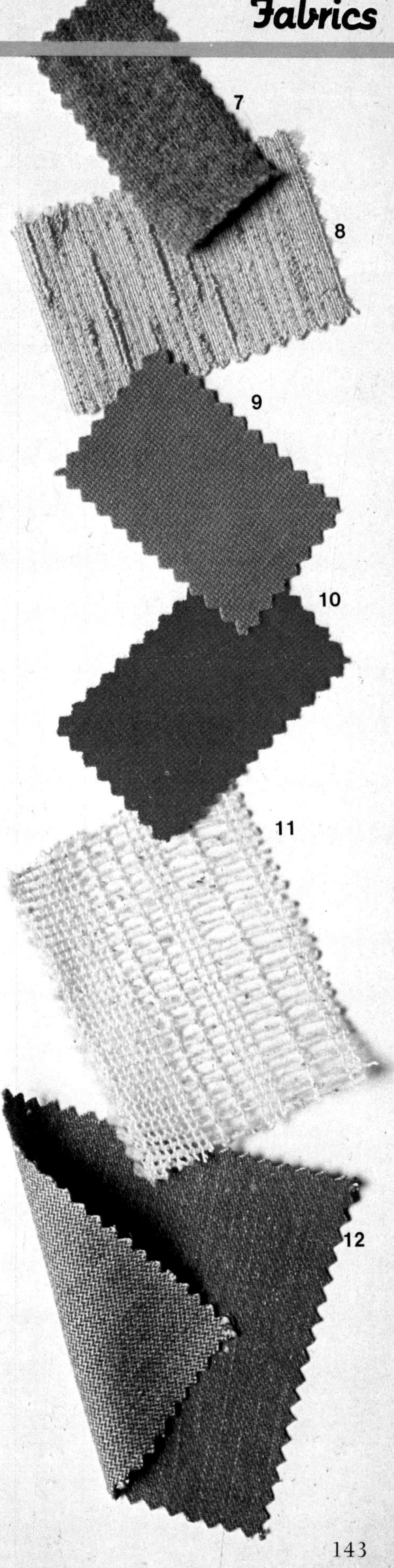

7

8

9

10

11

12

*Right* From top to bottom
7 Knitted
8 Slub effect
9 and 10 Knitted
11 Open weave
12 Twill weave (denim)

# Dyeing

1. Always choose correct dye for your fabric. Check with the manufacturer's instructions.
2. All fabric must be stain-free; most stains and existing colours can be stripped with special colour and stain remover.
3. Take into account existing colour of fabric, unless stripping colour (see chart).
4. With patterns, choose dye shade to blend with darkest shade in pattern, as this can never be completely obliterated.
5. Always use correct quantities of dye according to manufacturer's instructions, calculated on fabric weight.
6. Use sufficient water to cover fabric, but do not over-dilute dye.
7. Use a container which allows fabric freedom of movement. In a machine, only dye half maximum wash load.
8. Wash new fabrics before they are dyed to remove all dressings.
9. Wet all fabrics before dyeing and keep them well opened out as you immerse them and during the dyeing process if hand-dyeing.
10. Do not use bleaches or biological detergents on dyed fabrics. You can use soap powders or mild detergents.

## Unsuitable fabrics for dyeing

*Acrylics*
Acrilan
Cashmilon
Courtelle
Dralon
Leacril
Neo-spun
Orlon
Sayelle

Fibreglass
Drip-dry
Non-iron
Showerproof

Fabric is tied in different ways to prevent the dye from penetrating completely and this produces patterns such as stripes or circles.

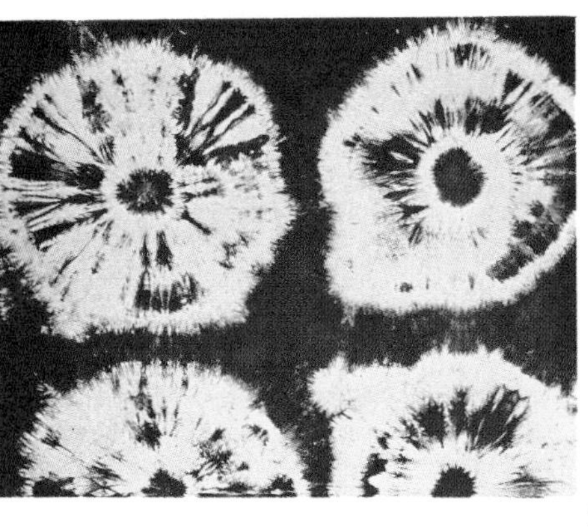

1

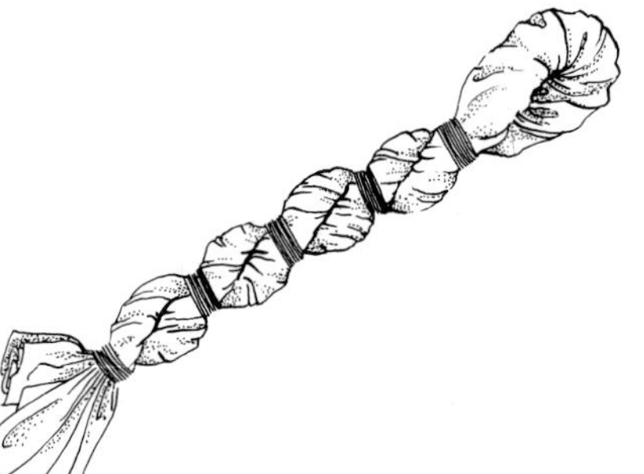

2

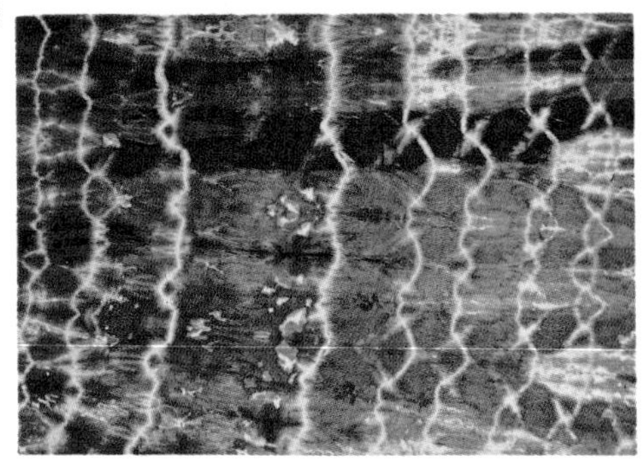

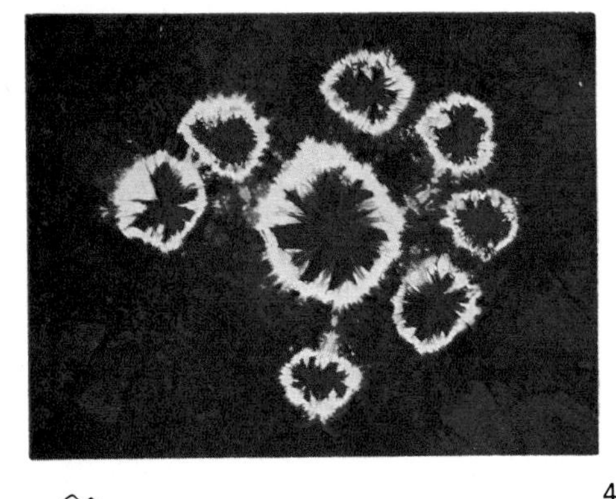

3

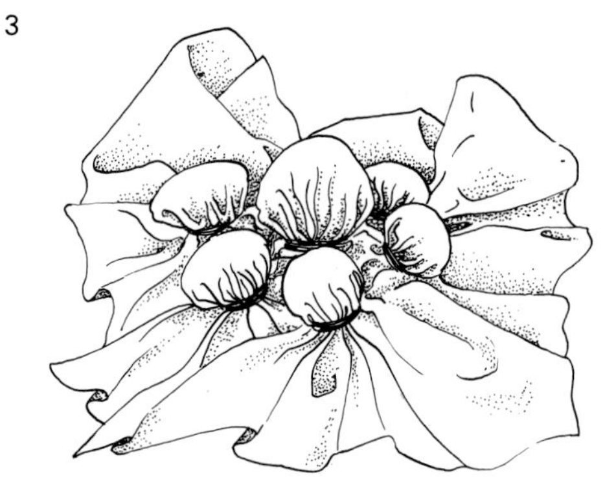

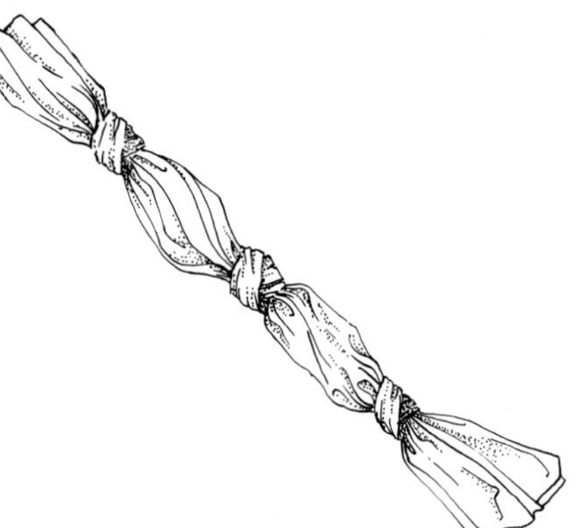

4

Fabric paints come ready-mixed in a range of colours, all of which are intermixable to produce different shades. They can be used on natural or synthetic fabrics without affecting the fabric's softness. Most fabric paints are non-toxic, washable and dry-cleanable. Paint them on with a brush.

If using the paints on a dark coloured fabric, apply a white base coat and allow to dry before putting on the colour. Brushes should be washed in warm water and dried between each colour change.

When the design is finished, 'fix' the paint by covering the fabric with a cotton cloth and ironing with a hot iron. Store left-over fabric paint in an air-tight jar for future use. If the paint thickens, add a few drops of cold water and shake well.

*Above* Methods of tying fabrics and their corresponding tie-dye effect.
1 Knotting
2 Twisting and coiling
3 Clump-tying, enclosing stones
4 Knotting
5 Sewing
6 Binding, enclosing a stone

5

6

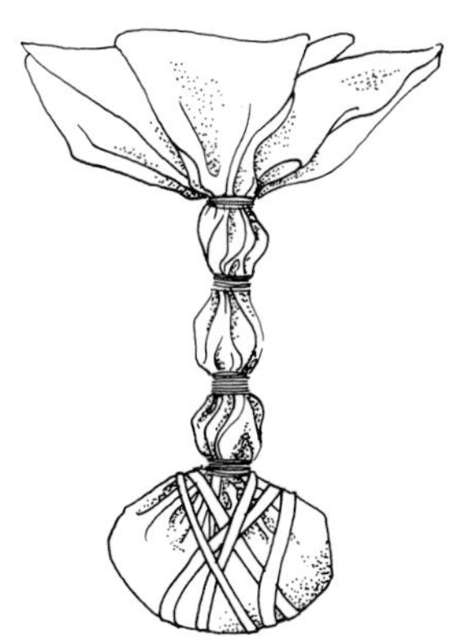

*Above* A variety of cushions which have been dyed and fabric painted.

## Fabric painting with cold dyes

By adding a thickener such as Paintex or Manutex, cold dyes can also be made into paints for fabrics. Use these only on white or light coloured fabrics. If they are used on fabric mixtures containing a high proportion of natural fibre, e.g. cotton/polyester, paler tones result. New fabrics should be washed and ironed before painting to remove any dressing. Brushes should be washed in warm water and dried between each colour change. No 'fixing' is required after painting with dye paints but when the design is dry, to regain the fabric's softness it is necessary to rinse the fabric in cold water to remove excess dye and thickener. Wash afterwards in hot soapy water.

Left-over cold dye fabric paint will not keep more than a day.

## Stencilling

Cut your own stencils from special stencil card available from art shops, or from cardboard. A limited range of ready-cut stencils is also available, including letter-stencils for personalized articles. Use a special stencil brush and take care not to get paint on the back of the stencil.

## Block printing

Make your own simple printing blocks from lino cuts, potato cuts, or string glued on a wooden block.

Lay the fabric on paper and secure with sticky tape to stop it slipping. With long lengths of fabric, move the fabric and paper together as you progress, making sure that the next area of fabric to be printed is always on a clean sheet of paper.

Tip a small quantity of fabric paint into a flat dish, press a flat sponge into this and lay on a flat surface paint-side up. Press the block on to the sponge so that it takes up the paint evenly and then press the block firmly on the fabric. Repeat as necessary. Use a clean, dry block and sponge for each colour change.

### Overdyeing guide

| Base Colour | | Dye Colour | | Result |
|---|---|---|---|---|
| Brown | + | Red | = | Rust |
| Blue | + | Yellow | = | Green |
| Green | + | Red | = | Brown |
| Green | + | Yellow | = | Lime |
| Pink | + | Light Blue | = | Lilac |

| Base Colour | | Dye Colour | | Result |
|---|---|---|---|---|
| Red | + | Blue | = | Purple |
| Red | + | Yellow | = | Orange |
| Yellow | + | Pink | = | Coral |
| Yellow | + | Purple | = | Brown |

# Sewing box

## Needles

Keep a plentiful supply of needles in a small flannel book. They are worth looking after carefully. Bent needles result in uneven work and a worn eye will fray your thread, so always discard damaged needles.

**Sharps needles** Medium length with a small eye, used for plain sewing, or for a single strand of stranded cotton. As sharps have small eyes, many people prefer to use crewel needles which have a larger eye, for general sewing.
**Crewel needles** Sometimes called embroidery needles. Common sizes range from 5 to 8; the higher the number, the smaller the needle and its eye. A crewel number 7, for example, is suitable for three strands of stranded cotton, but a number 5 is needed for tapestry wool.
**Chenille needles** Shorter than crewel needles but just as sharp and their longer eye makes them useful for wools and thicker threads.
**Tapestry needles** The same as chenille but with a blunt rounded point for canvas work. Common sizes are 20, 22 and 24.
**Darners** Very long needles with a long eye for mending work with wool or cottons.
**Glovers** These have triangular points to pierce leather, suede and other non-woven materials without tearing.
**Millinery** needles are long with round eyes for work on hats and are also suitable for pleating and decoration work.
**Betweens** or **quilting needles** Short, slim needles for quick even stitching.
**Carpet needles** These are a heavier size of sharps and used for sewing rugs and carpets.
**Bodkins** are flat or round and have large eyes for threading cords, tapes, and elastic through casings.
**Beading needles** are very fine and straight with long eyes.
**Mattress needle** Curved, this is useful for upholstery work and repairs.
**Sack needle** Useful for sewing hessian.

**Machine needles** Sizes are usually matched to the type and the thickness of the fabric being sewn although they may vary according to the make of the machine. Low numbers are for finer needles, higher numbers for thicker needles. Needles with special points are for sewing knitted fabrics and leather. A fine fabric demands a fine needle with a fine thread. If the needle eye is too big, friction will cause the thread to fray and if a fine needle is used on a thick material or through several layers of material, it will probably break. A thick needle on a fine fabric will make holes in the weave.

## Threads

Buy threads a tone darker than the fabric.
**Spun polyesters** (such as Drima) are all-purpose threads which do not split and have good strength.
**Chain cotton** is a matt soft thread for stitching all household cottons and plastic, in sizes 10 to 60 (the higher the number, the finer the thread).
**Machine embroidery** is for decorative machine stitching, common sizes are 30 and 50: 50 is the finer.
**Button thread** is very strong and is used for sewing on buttons and for making buttonholes.
**Stranded cotton** for embroidery divides into six strands according to fineness of the work.
**Soft embroidery cotton** has a thick matt finish and a good subtle colour range.
**Pearl** or **perle cotton** is a twisted corded shiny thread, used for embroidery. Number 5 is thick, number 8 is thinner.
**Tapestry wool** is a firm well-twisted woollen yarn with a matt surface used as a single thread.
**Crewel wool** is a finer, twisted matt-surfaced wool with separable strands.
**Silk** is soft and lustrous but very expensive nowadays.

## Pins

Always choose dressmaker's pins which are long and slim. Glass headed pins are made from broken needles and are very sharp, and they are good to use because they are easily seen. Pin at right angles to the seam. Twist pins are useful for holding loose or stretch covers in place on a chair. You will need a pin cushion.

## Thimble

Metal ones are best as plastic can split; use the thimble to protect your middle finger, particularly when working with coarser materials.

## Scissors

One large pair of dressmaker's shears for cutting out – never use this pair for paper as this will blunt them. One small sharp pair for trimming threads. A special stitch-ripper is also handy for undoing seams.

## A tape measure

Essential, choose one with both metric and imperial measurements and made of fibreglass so that it will not stretch. A metre-stick and a set-square are useful for soft furnishing work.

*Above right* The important functional parts of a sewing machine.

*Right* Correct and incorrect stitch tensions.

*Below* Contents of a sewing box.

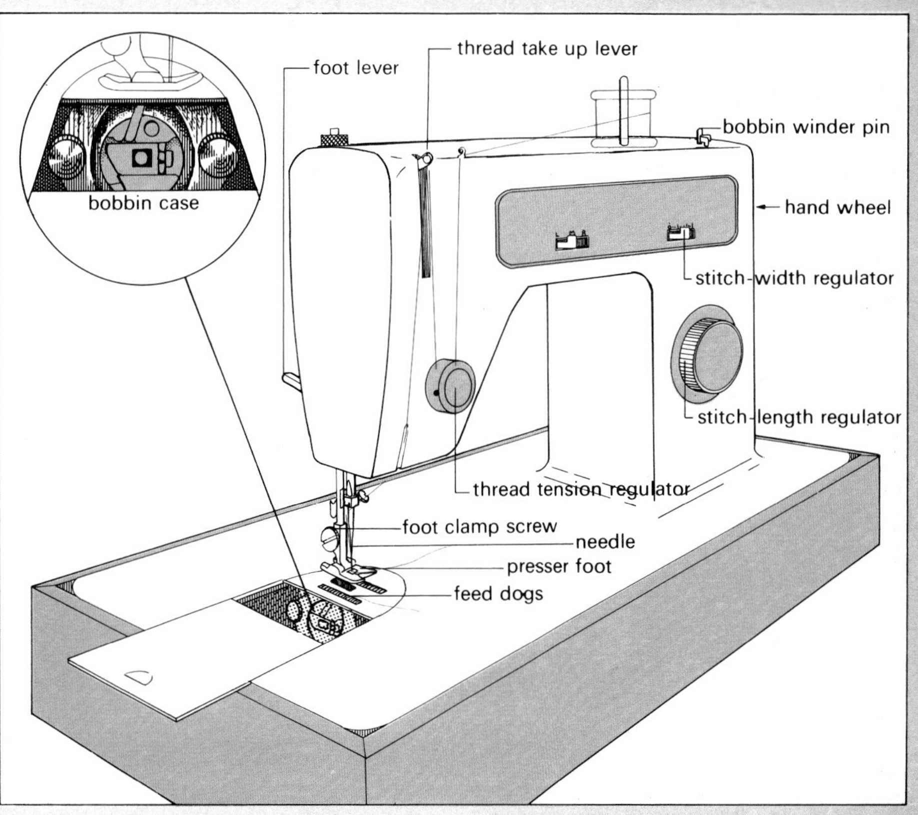


## Routine maintenance

To ensure trouble-free running of your sewing machine, clean and oil it regularly and have it serviced every 6 months. Using a small brush from the accessory box, remove all the dust and lint that collects around the bobbin case and the feed dogs. Oil your machine by putting one or two drops of fine-grade sewing machine oil into the oiling holes indicated in the instruction book. Store your machine in its carrying case away from direct heat. Never leave a machine with the electric plug connected. Even if the light is switched off, the power can burn the motor.

## Tension adjustments

For a seam to be strong and look perfect, the upper and lower thread tensions must be balanced so that the stitch locks in the middle of the layers of material. The majority of machines have a 'normal' thread tension which means that you can do most sewing jobs without changing the tension. But if you do need to alter it, because the stitching is unsatisfactory or because you are doing a special job, experiment on a scrap of the same fabric, changing the tension controls until you achieve a perfect stitch. If the upper thread of the stitches appears in loops below the material then the upper tension is probably too loose so tighten it by turning the control to a higher number. If the lower thread of the stitches appears above the material then the upper tension is probably too tight, so loosen it by turning the control to a lower number. In most cases it is sufficient to adjust the upper thread tension only. If however the stitches are still unsatisfactory and you do have to change the lower tension, take out the bobbin case and, using a small screwdriver, make slight turning adjustments, testing the stitch on a scrap of material after each turn until you are satisfied.

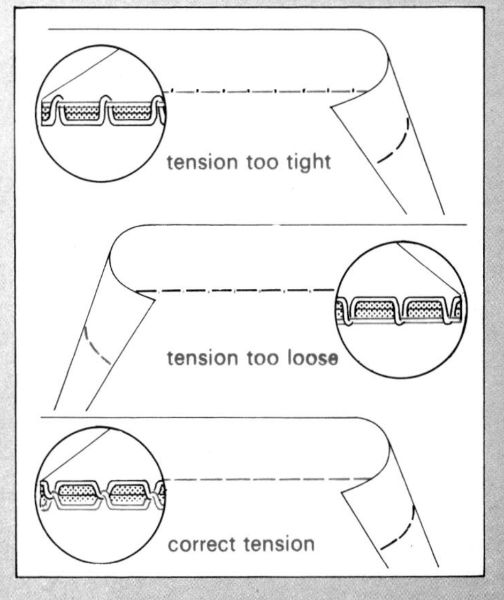

# Basic stitches

Listed below are the fundamental stitches, seams and sewing methods which you are likely to need for home furnishing projects.

**Tacking**
This stitch can also be called basting. It is a temporary stitch, used to hold pieces of fabric in place while permanent stitching is worked. It is more satisfactory than pinning because it does not pull the fabric, or get in the way of the needle.

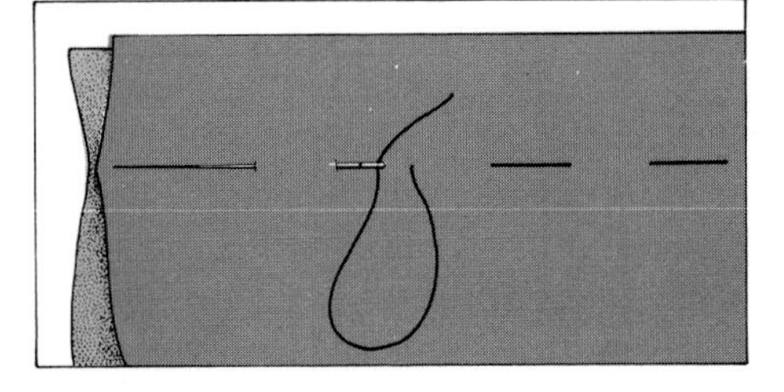

**Hem stitch**
The hem is folded under so that the stitch is worked on the fold of the turning, and only one or two threads are picked up from the single thickness so they do not show on the right side of the material.

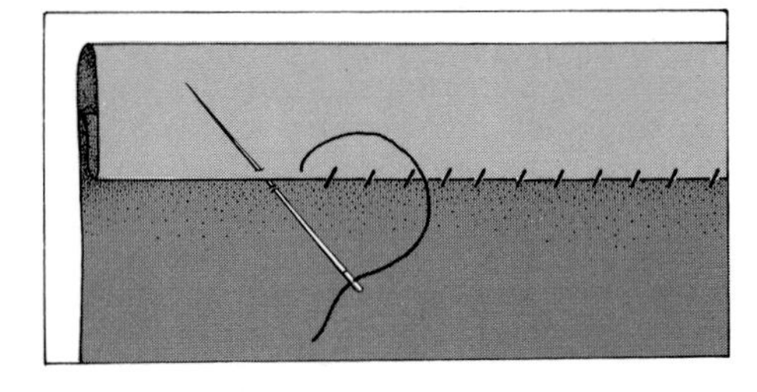

**French seam**
Tack along the seam line on each of the pieces of fabric to be joined. Place the pieces wrong sides together and stitch along the length of the seam, halfway between the seam line and the raw edges of the fabric. Press the seam open. Fold back the fabric so right sides are together and sew along tacking line, enclosing the first seam.

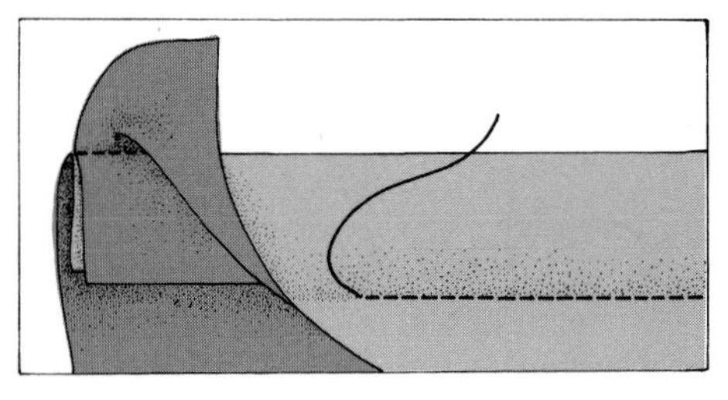

**Back stitch**
This is a very strong stitch and it is particularly useful when sewing without a machine. Prick stitch is very similar but only a minute back stitch is taken and it is therefore more suitable for areas where the stitching might show, such as zips.

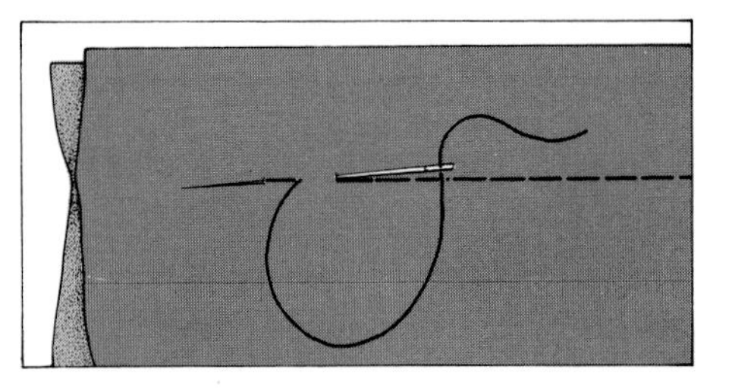

**Herringbone stitch**
This stitch is particularly useful for hemming when only a single turning is required as it protects the raw edge. Since it is also a decorative stitch it is widely used for appliqué.

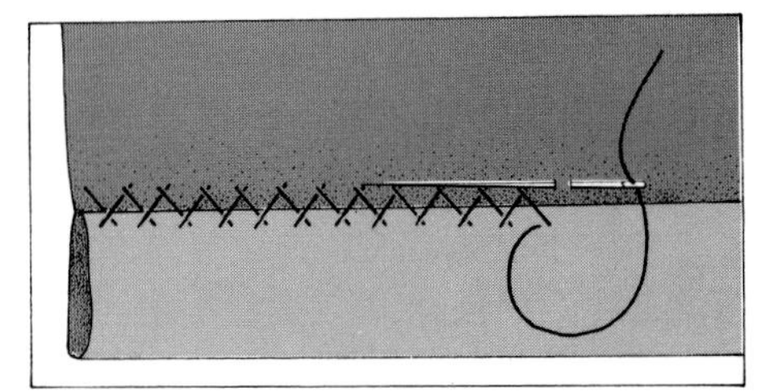

**Machining a square corner**
Keep the needle in the down position at the corner, while you lift the presser foot and turn the fabric 90°.

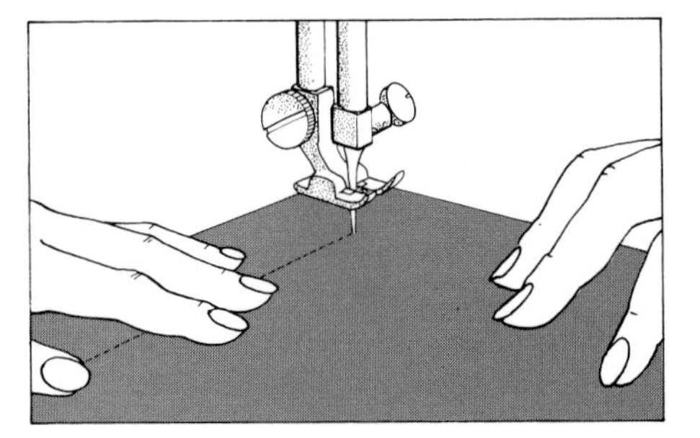

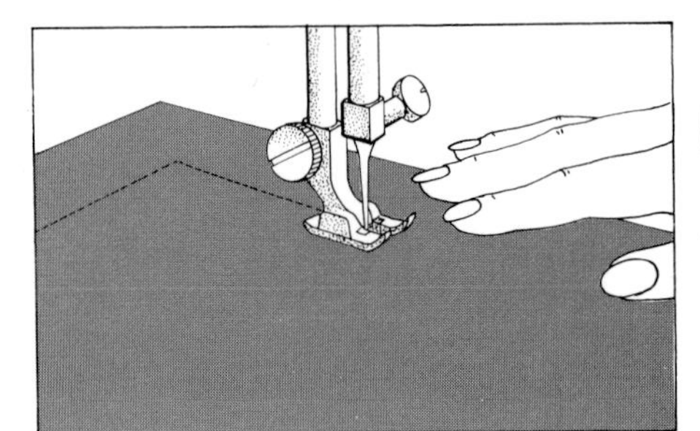

**Blanket stitch**
Like herringbone stitch, this is a useful stitch for finishing raw edges and it is often used for decoratively attaching appliqué pieces.

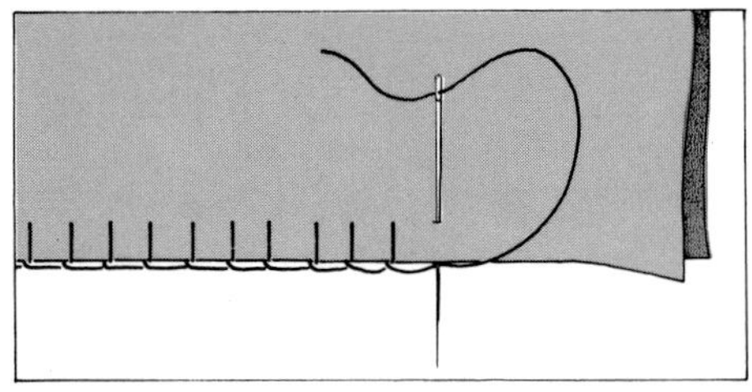

**Putting in a zip**
Fold in the seam allowance on both edges of the seam. With the zip closed, pin one seam fold to the zip so that the fold line just overlaps the centre of the zip. Pin the opposite fold in the same way. (The slight overlap will disappear once the stitching pulls the seams back.) Tack both folds to the zip and remove pins.

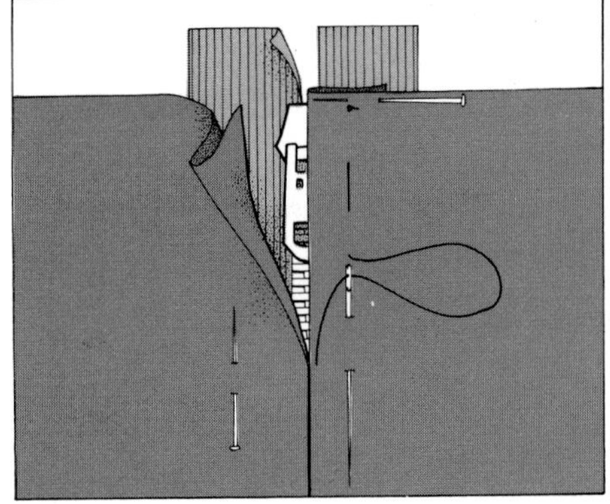

Machine stitch or prick stitch parallel to the tacking line, making square corners at the base of the zip. Take care to check that the needle has gone past the teeth before making the square corner or the needle will break.

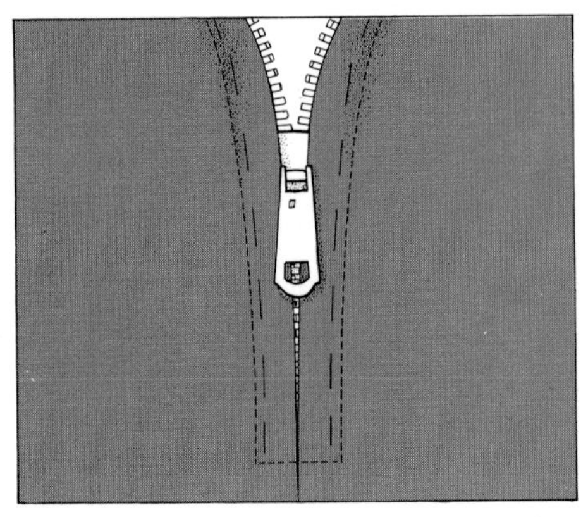

# Glossary

**Appliqué** A design or ornament applied to another surface; used for cushions, bedspreads etc. Motifs can be sewn or stuck into place, and further decorated with embroidery.
**Art Deco** A distinctive design style of the period 1925–1935. Typical motifs were rainbows, lightning flashes and sunrays. Popular colours were pale greens and pinks. Sometimes referred to as 'Odeon' style.
**Art Nouveau** Popular at the end of the 19th century, a style of pattern which based itself on the curving lines of flowers and stems arranged as repeating motifs.

**Batik** Method of fabric painting. Some areas of fabric are coated with wax and then the fabric is dipped in dye. Dye penetrates only the waxed parts. Finally, wax is removed.
**Batten** A thin strip of timber.
**Beading** A small strip of semi-circular moulding used to finish off work, either to conceal a joint, or simply for decoration.

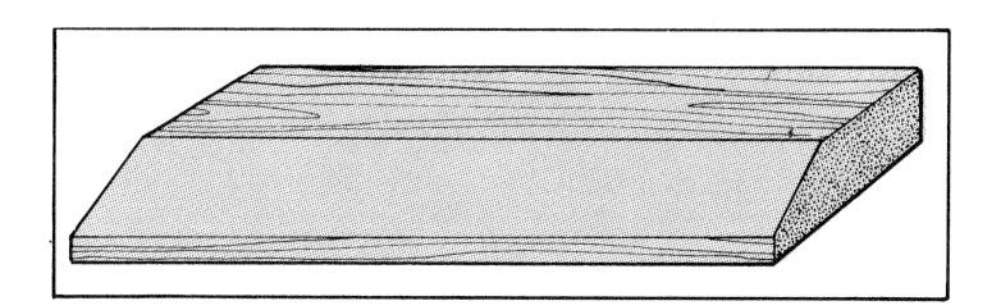

**Bevel** An angled or sloping edge.
**Bias** The diagonal grain of a fabric.
**Bleeding** When colouring from one substance (e.g. an undercoat of paint) passes through into another to discolour it.

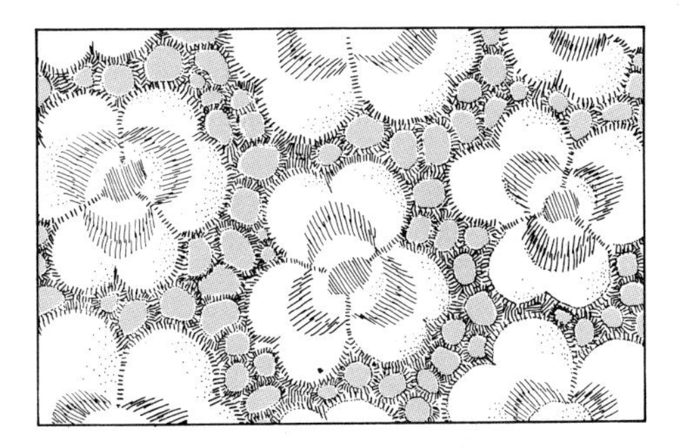

**Broderie anglaise** Cotton or cotton/polyester fabric, with embroidered cut-out designs.
**Buckram** Coarse fabric made from cotton, linen or jute, and used for stiffening pelmets. Some types can be iron-on.
**Bump** Used for curtain interlining, and made from cotton waste. Must be dry-cleaned.
**Butt-jointing** Joining two materials together without any overlap.

**Cabriole leg** Curves outwards at the knee, which is rounded, and then tapers into a concave curve below. Can be finished off with club, hoof, bun, paw, claw-and-ball or scroll feet.
**Calendering** A finishing treatment for some fabrics to give a polished, glazed or embossed effect. Fabric is pressed through heavy rollers.
**Calico** A generic term for plain cotton fabrics.
**Canvas** Plain, coarse-woven, and heavy-weight cloth. Soft hemp canvas is used for furnishing work, close-weave is for other jobs. Linen, open-mesh canvas is for embroidery. Canvas for needle-point can be double or single thread. The density of double-thread canvas is determined by the number of holes to the inch, and number 10 is suitable for most kinds of furnishing work.
**Casement** A lightweight, plain woven, all-cotton fabric, with an unribbed texture, piece-dyed, and suitable for curtains or curtain linings.

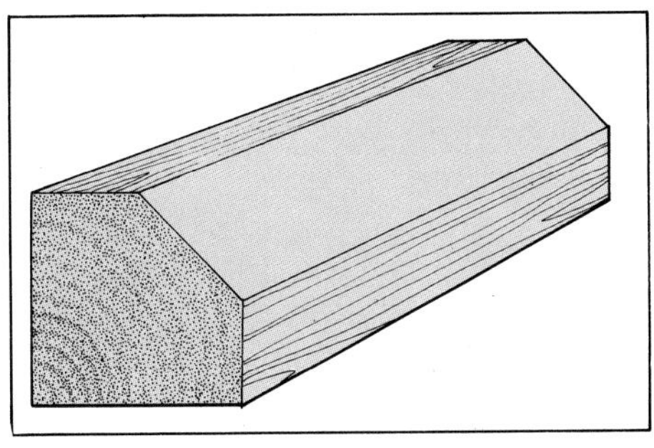

**Chamfer** The surface produced by bevelling a square corner equally on both sides.
**Chevron** A pattern made up from zig-zags.
**Chinoiserie** A term used to describe patterns with Chinese influence based on dragons, lotus flowers etc.
**Chintz** is a highly glazed printed calico with a stiff finish. The term 'fully glazed' may be applied only to a chintz which has been stiffened by resin or starch with heat and pressure applied.
**Coated** Knitted and woven upholstery cloths can be coated for protection, normally with PVC (polyvinyl chloride) or with polyurethane.
**Colourway** The particular combination of colours in which a design is printed for fabrics or wallpaper. For example, a fabric design may appear in four or five colourways.
**Concave** Rounded like the inside of a sphere (the opposite of convex).
**Console table** A wall table supported by two brackets.
**Convex** Rounded like the outside of a sphere (the opposite of concave).
**Co-ordinated ranges** Fabrics and wallpapers in designs intended to be used together. Their patterns 'relate' in various ways; for example, one pattern can be a smaller or simplified version of another.
**Cornice** An ornamental moulding running around the wall at ceiling level.
**Cornice pole** Wooden or metal pole from which curtains are hung by large rings. Usually used for curtains, but can also be used for bedheads.
**Countersink** To enlarge the upper part of a hole to receive the head of a screw.

**Denier** Term used to express gauge of silk and man-made filament yarns – the lower the denier, the finer the yarn.

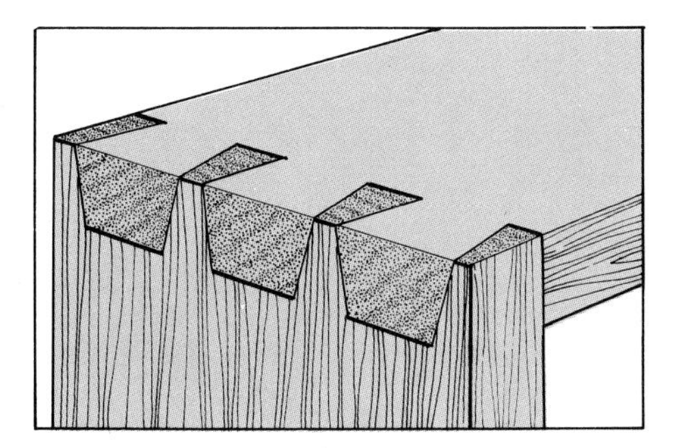

**Dovetail** Used to describe a timber joint in which two pieces of timber to be joined at right angles are cut into a series of fan-shapes which fit into each other.
**Dowel** Cylindrical length of wood. *Dowelling* is available from timber merchants in diameters up to 5 cm, and is useful for curtain rods etc.

# Glossary

**Drop pattern** A term used for wallcoverings where the pattern does not repeat in a horizontal line from edge to edge.

**Eggshell** Paint finish with a slight sheen, usually oil-based.
**Emulsion** Water-based paint. Quick-drying modern emulsions usually contain vinyl, and have a matt, silk or gloss finish. Brushes wash out in cold water.

**Facing** A veneer or thin layer of one material over a core or base of another. Can also be used to describe the backing for a material.
**Felt** Non-woven bonded fabric made from wool fibres. Available in a good range of muted and bright colours, and can be cut without fraying. Must be dry cleaned.
**Festoon** A motif of hanging clusters of fruit, tied with leaves, flowers and ribbons. Also a draped style for lightweight curtains.
**Filament fibres** Continuous fibres which are twisted and made into yarns.
**Filet net** Woven in such a way that each square is locked. The term 'filet' is not applied to non-lockstitch net.
**Fillers** Wide range of preparations available for filling holes, cracks, dents and chips in such materials as metal, wood, plaster.
**Flush** To finish flush is to make (a joint) level with the surface.
**Fluting** Channels or grooves carved vertically.
**Fretwork** Work carved in a decorative pattern – for example a screen.

**Gauge** A standard of measure for the thickness of such items as wire or screws.
**Gilding** Originally the application of gold or silver leaf to timber surfaces. Nowadays often means applying gold-coloured products.
**Gingham** Cotton cloth, yarn-dyed and woven into stripes, checks, plaids, usually in two colours.
**Glasspaper** The correct term for sandpaper.
**Glazing** Covering or filling an area with glass.
**Gloss** Term used for oil-based, hard-wearing, slow-drying paints which dry to a shiny finish. Brushes must be cleaned with white spirit.
**Grain** This describes the direction in which the fibres of a piece of wood or fabric run.
**Grosgrain** Fabric with pronounced narrow ribs.
**Ground** The background colour of a fabric or wallpaper.

**Gusset** Triangular piece let into garment to strengthen or enlarge some part.

**Handle** A fabric term to describe the 'feel' of a cloth – e.g. a 'soft' handle.
**Hardwood** Timber from a deciduous tree.
**Hessian** Inexpensive, coarse, loosely woven fabric made from jute. In its natural state, it is light brown but can be dyed to various shades.

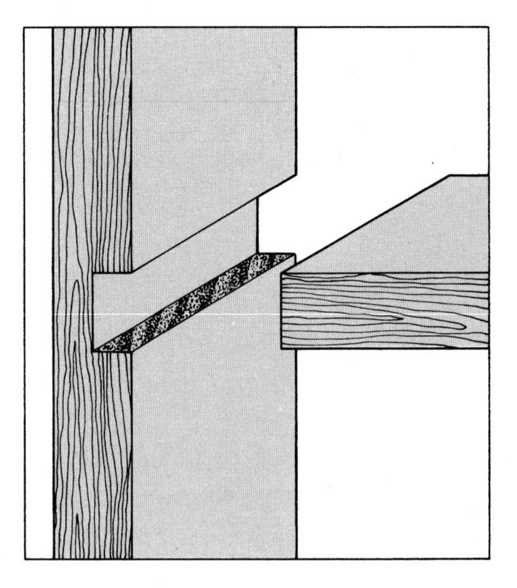

**Housing** A channel (or groove) usually cut across the grain to 'house' or hold fittings.

**Jelly paint** – see **Thixotropic**.
**Japanned** A black lacquered finish.
**Jersey** Single jersey is a fabric made from one layer of knitted loops; double jersey is made from two inter-knitted layers of loops. Used for stretch covers.

**Laminated** Material built up in strips or layers.
**Laying-off** A term used in painting for the final brush strokes, which should leave the surface absolutely smooth. As a general rule, you should 'lay off' on wood in the direction of the grain.

**Macramé** Decorative art of knotting string.
**Making good** Getting rid of surface defects before painting or papering.
**Marbled** Describes swirly marble-like patterns, originally created by hand on paper and fabrics. Once used for book endpapers.
**Masking out** Covering up a surface (e.g. with adhesive tape) to prevent paint from adhering.
**Mercerization** Treatment of cotton yarns to give increased strength and lustre.

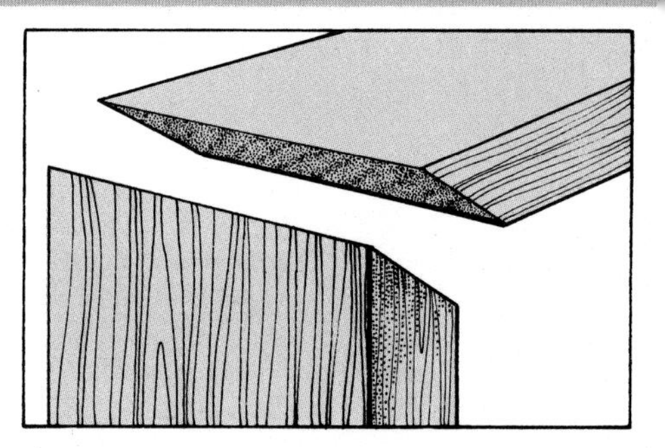

**Mitre** A 90 degree join between two surfaces, each cut at 45 degrees. In timber, usually cut with the aid of a mitre block. Corners of hems and the join between trimmings such as ribbon are usually mitred.
**Moquette** A heavy upholstery velvet, usually having a wool or cotton pile and cotton ground. It may be figured or plain, cut or uncut.

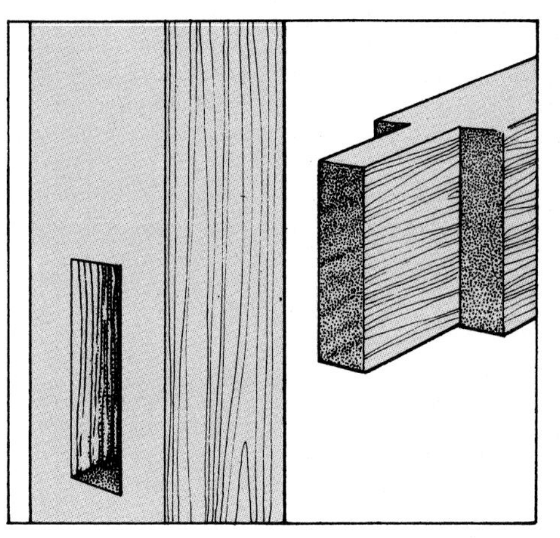

**Mortise** A hole, usually rectangular in shape, which has been cut out of a piece of wood to take a fitting. In the case of joints, the mortise is cut to take the tenon, which is the shaped end of the piece of wood to be joined, cut exactly to fit the mortise hole.

**Net** Woven or knitted open fabric with knotted or twisted threads to form pattern. Commonly made from polyesters, but also made from traditional cotton. Tulle is fine net, fishnet is coarse.

**Offering up** Fixing instructions will sometimes tell you to 'offer up' the fixture to the wall; this means hold it in the right position, so that you can mark the correct position for the fixings.

**Petit Point** A term for fine tapestry work where there are eighteen or more stitches to the inch usually worked in tent stitch

**Pilot hole** A hole drilled to make passage easier for the subsequent screw.
**Piping** Fabric-covered cord sewn into seam to add trimming and to strengthen. Used for cushions, upholstery, etc.
**Placket** A slit or opening on a skirt for convenience in putting on or off.
**Plinth** The base of a pillar or pedestal, or piece of furniture. Can be used to describe a simple block base for a piece of sculpture.
**Plug** To plug a wall is to fill a pre-drilled hole with a material (e.g. wood, fibre, or nylon) which will take a screw.
**Ply** Yarns can be made from one strand (single-ply) or from several strands twisted together (e.g. four-ply).
**Portière** A draught-excluding curtain hung over a door.
**Primary colours** Red, yellow and blue which cannot be mixed from any other colours.
**Primers** There are many different types suitable for different surfaces. They are a vital part of many painting processes, ensuring that the paint can adhere to the surface. On some surfaces, primers prevent staining; on metals they guard against corrosion. Primers are also used to seal porous surfaces.

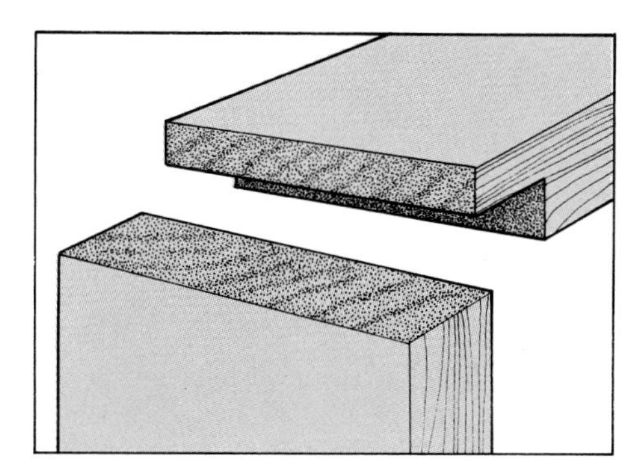

**Rebate** A rectangular recess or step cut along an edge of a piece of wood.
**Repeat** The lengthways distance between the beginning and end of a pattern before it 'repeats' again. It is important to take the repeat into account when estimating fabrics for curtains.
**Repp** A heavy ribbed furnishing fabric, of which the ribs may run in either direction.
**Reveal** The side surface of a window or door opening.
**Right angle** Perpendicular, an angle of 90 degrees.
**Rubbing down** The process of making a surface level by using an abrasive such as glasspaper.

**Sailcloth** Stiff cotton cloth in plain colours.
**Satin** A fabric woven in such a way that one set of yarns (usually the warp) forms the surface, while the other set of yarns forms the back of the fabric. The result is a fabric with a lustrous, smooth and unbroken surface. Originally, satin was made only from silk.
**Scallop** Curved decoration for edges, based on the shape of a scallop shell. Used effectively for pelmets. Embroidered scalloped edges can be worked automatically on some sewing machines.
**Seconds** Pieces of fabric with small faults usually offered at reduced prices – useful for cushions, patchwork etc.
**Section** The shape of an object (e.g. a moulding) as you would see it if the whole thing was cut through at right angles to its face.
**Selvedge** The non-fray edges to a fabric, running parallel with the warp.
**Serge** A heavy, coarse, woollen fabric, woven in twill weave and piece-dyed. Poorer qualities are sometimes made from a mixture of wool and cotton.
**Skirt** Piece of straight, gathered or pleated fabric around the bottom of a chair which hides the legs. Sometimes used on dressing tables.
**Softwood** Timber from evergreen trees.
**Solvent** Liquid which will dissolve or soften other substances.
**Spindles** Turned wooden pieces sold in various lengths, for use as stair balusters, screens etc. Larger versions can be used for four poster bed effects, and smaller sizes for lamp bases.
**Spreading capacity** The average area covered by paint, varnish etc., expressed in square metres per litre to help estimate quantity. Will vary according to porosity of surface.

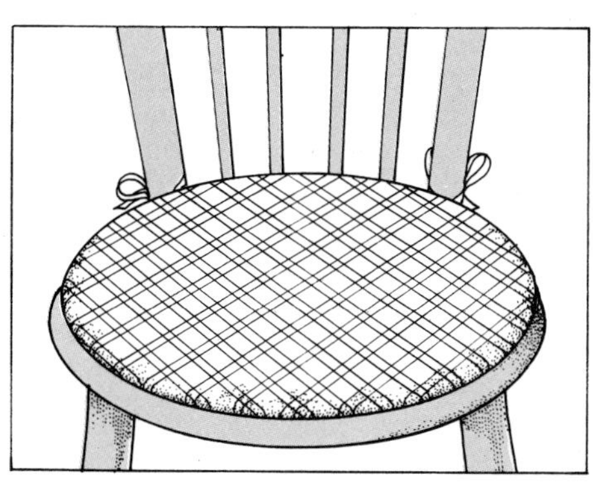

**Squab** A loose cushion, usually made from a slab of foam, and tied to a chair or stool seat.
**Staple fibres** Short lengths of fibre drawn or twisted into strands.
**Stopping** Term for filling gaps and cracks before painting.
**Stretch yarns** Fully synthetic yarns which have been given stretch and elasticity by crimping or twisting and heat-setting.
**Strippers** Various proprietary mixtures of chemical solvents which are applied to remove old paintwork or varnish.
**Sugar soap** A caustic substance which is dissolved in water and used for washing down dirty paintwork before repainting.
**Swags and tails** Traditional way of arranging fabric for a pelmet. The swags are a series of large folded loops across the top of the pelmet which hang down in shaped tails at each end.

**Taffeta** A fine fabric in a plain weave, originally of real silk. Taffetas may be self coloured or shot (warp and weft threads of different colours).
**Template** A pattern used as a guide for marking out a shape before cutting. For some projects you can use a simple household object for a template, e.g. a saucer for scallops. Patchwork templates are available ready-made.
**Thinners** Liquids which are mixed with oil-based or cellulose paint to make it more workable.
**Thixotropic** Describes specially-constituted jelly paints which cover in one coat, will not run, and do not need stirring.
**Tie back** Cord or loop made to loop curtain back from window. Creates pleasant decorative effect, and allows more light into a room.
**Tolerance** Agreed amounts by which sizes may differ from standard sizes, to allow for imperfections in cutting etc.
**Trompe l'oeil** A French term meaning 'deceiving the eye'. This is a decoration painted flat but which, by careful use of proportion, light and shade, looks like a three-dimensional feature or scene.

**Veneer** Very thin sheets of decorative timber, used as a surfacing material.
**Valance** Soft fabric top for a curtain, pleated or gathered, as opposed to a pelmet which is stiff and flat. Can also be used to describe pleated or gathered fabric around a bed base to conceal the legs.

**Warp** Parallel yarns running along length of fabric.
**Weft** Yarn which runs from side to side across the width of a fabric interlacing with the warp.

**Yarns** The long strands of fibres used for weaving or knitting a fabric.

# Suppliers Index

Most of the materials required for the crafts in this book can be found easily at craft shops, department stores or hardware shops throughout the country. However, the list below has been compiled to help readers who may have difficulty in obtaining any particular materials to locate a supplier. Most of the suppliers listed provide a mail order service, but if not they can usually give advice on where their products may be obtained. The list is not comprehensive.

Whilst every effort has been made to ensure that the information given below is correct, suppliers do sometimes move premises or alter their stock. Always check with the supplier before sending an order.

**Blind kits**

John Lewis,
Oxford Street,
London W1.
T: 01-629 7711

J. Barker & Co. Ltd.,
63 Kensington High Street,
London W8.
T: 01-937 5432

**Cane**

Deben Craftsmen,
9 St. Peter Street,
Ipswich.
T: Ipswich 215042

Dryad Handicrafts,
P.O. Box 38,
Northgates,
Leicester.
T: Leicester 50405

Eaton Bag Co., The,
16 Manette Street,
London W1.
T: 01-437 9391

Jacobs, Young & Westbury,
Bridge Road,
Haywards Heath,
Sussex.
T: Haywards Heath 412411

**Frame mouldings**

Knightsbridge Frames & Prints,
5 High Street,
Potters Bar,
Hertfordshire.
T: Potters Bar 43989

**Furniture restoration**

brass fittings

Beardmore's,
3 Percy Street,
London W1.
T:01-637 7041

découpage

Paperchase,
216 Tottenham Court Road,
London W1.
T: 01-637 1121

finishes

Woodfit,
Whittle Low Mill,
Chorley,
Lancs.
T: Chorley 79521

graining comb

Dryad Handicrafts,
P.O. Box 38,
Northgates,
Leicester.
T: Leicester 50405

graining roller

Ridgeley Trimmer Co.,
117–119 Clerkenwell Road,
London EC1.
T: 01-837 9171

scumble

J.H. Ratcliffe & Co.,
135a Linaker Street,
Southport,
Lancs.
T: Southport 37999

shellac, woodfiller etc.

Gedge & Co.,
88 St. John Street,
Clerkenwell,
London EC1.
T: 01-253 6057

Rustins Ltd.,
Drayton Wks.,
Waterloo Road,
London NW2.
T: 01-450 4666

stencils

Packerson Design,
P.O. Box 191,
London SW10.
T: 01-223 2459

**Rushes**

Deben Craftsmen,
9 St. Peter Street,
Ipswich.
T: Ipswich 215042

Jacobs, Young & Westbury,
Bridge Road,
Haywards Heath,
Sussex.
T: Haywards Heath 412411

**Sewing materials**

John Lewis,
Oxford Street,
London W1.
T: 01-629 7711

The Needlewoman Shop,
146 Regent Street,
London W1.
T: 01-734 1727

**Specialist fabrics**

Felt & Hessian Shop,
34 Greville Street,
London EC1.
T: 01-405 6215

Russell Trading Co.,
75 Paradise Street,
Liverpool.
T: 051-709 5752

**Upholstery**

Baxell Grant,
195a Upper Richmond Road,
London SW15.
T: 01-788 7423

Buck & Ryan,
Tottenham Court Road,
London W1.
T: 01-636 7475

Russell Trading Co.,
75 Paradise Street,
Liverpool.
T: 051-709 5752

**Craft shops**

Dryad Handicrafts,
P.O. Box 38,
Northgates,
Leicester.
T: Leicester 50405

Hobby Horse,
15–17 Langton Street,
London SW10.
T: 01-351 1913

Northern Handicrafts Ltd.,
Cheapside,
Burnley,
Lancs.
T: Burnley 33713

# Index

## A

## C

# Index

## E



## F



## G



## H



## I



## J



## K



## L

# Index



## T



## U



## V



## W

# Contributors

Curtains & blinds
Loose covers
**Lynette-Merlin Syme**

Cushions
Upholstery
**Lindsay Graham**

Caning
Rushing
**Barbara Maynard**

Picture framing
**Mick Paul**

Furniture restoration
**Kitty Grime**

Woodwork
**Trevor Ray**

Lampshades
**Angela Fishburn**

Rugs
**Christine Pilsworth**

Appendix information
**Barbara Chandler**

# Acknowledgments

The publishers would like to thank the following organisations and individuals for their kind permission to reproduce the photographs in this book:

Camera Press Limited 8, 18–19, 86 below left, 86 below right, 89, 132–133, 134–135; The Designer's Guild 28, 44–45, 118; Dylon Press Office 110–111, 111, 115 below, 144 above left, 144 centre right, 144 centre left, 144 below right, 145 above left, 145 above right, 145 below left; International Magazine Service (Bjorn Sjoden) 51, (Carl Nordin) 84 below right, 84 below left; Val Jackson 105 above; Bill McLaughlin 14–15, 17, 20, 20–21, 25 below, 29, 37, 56, 61, 96–97, 114–115 above, 119; National Magazine Company Limited Back & Front Endpapers, 16, 23, 48, 49, 83 above left, 83 above right, 113, 114 below, 120, 125, 128; PAF International Press Services Limited 45, 50; Rentokil Limited 91 above right 91 below right; Jessica Strang 26, 82 below; Transworld Feature Syndicate (UK) Limited 9, 10–11, 46, 47, 52–53 above, 82 above, 100 above, 104, 135; Elizabeth Whiting 22, 83 below, 97, (S. Powell) 25 above; Zefa Picture Library Limited 84–85, 107;

Special Photography: Bryce Attwell 4–5, 6–7, 30–31, 42–43, 65, 73, 152–153; Rob Matheson 64–65, 67, 70–71, 75, 88 above and below, 90 above, centre and below, 91 above left, 92, 93, 94, 95, 98, 106, 109 above left and right, 109 below right, 126–127, 136, 138–139, 142–143, 146–147; Bill McLaughlin 12, 18, 24, 32, 34, 38–39, 52–53 below, 54–55, 58, 63, 69 above and below, 74–75, 77, 79 below, 81, 95, 100 below, 102, 103 above left and right, 103 below, 105 below, 116–117, 122–123, 123, 124, 131, 133, 137 above and below; David Prout 40–41 above, 41, 79 above, 86–87 below; 87, 99.

The publishers would also like to thank the following organisations for the loan of items used in photography:

Title page: The Conran Shop (rug, fabric); The Designer's Guild (cushions); 'Mr. Light' (lamp); Richard Morris (table); Tulley's (Chelsea) Ltd. (armchair).
Contents page: Richard Morris (cabinet).
pages 30–31: John Lewis (armchair, lampshade and table); Browns of South Molton Street (rug, pictures, decorative boxes and plant holder).
pages 42–43: CVP Designs Ltd. (cushions).
page 75: Magnolia Mouldings Ltd. (mouldings).
page 77: K. Scharf Ltd. (oil paintings).
page 88: Camping Gaz (blowlamp): Black and Decker (electric sander).
page 92: J.D. Beardmore & Co. Ltd. (handles and castors).
page 100: Dylon Ltd. (staining).
pages 100, 103: Liden Whitewood (whitewood furniture).
page 106: Trada (wood samples).
page 109: Barkers of Kensington (saw and plane).
pages 122–123: The Designer's Guild (pleated lampshade).
pages 126–127: Browns of South Molton Street (braided rug and seat pads).
page 137: The Designer's Guild (rag rug).
pages 138–139: Barkers of Kensington (hacksaw, bradawl, trysquare, toolbox).
pages 142–143: John Lewis (fabric samples).